T0339491

Rethinking Work

This collection of brief essays by thought-leaders, scholars, activists, psychologists, and social scientists imagines new workplace structures and policies that promote decent and fair work for all members of society, especially those who are most vulnerable.

The world of work has been deteriorating for decades and the very institution of work needs to be systematically understood, critiqued, reimagined, and rebuilt. This book offers thoughtful suggestions for new work arrangements, individual strategies for enhancing one's work life, and recommendations for innovative systemic and institutional reforms. The collection offers critical analyses in conjunction with constructive solutions for rebuilding work, providing direction and context for ongoing debates and policy discussions about work.

The book will be of interest to activists, policy makers, management and leaders, scholars, professionals, students, and general readers interested in work-based reform efforts and social change.

David L. Blustein is Professor and Golden Eagle Faculty Fellow in the Department of Counseling, Developmental, and Educational Psychology at Boston College, Chestnut Hill, MA, USA. David is the author of *The Psychology of Working: A New Perspective for Career Development, Counseling, and Public Policy* and *The Importance of Work in an Age of Uncertainty* and has been instrumental in developing the psychology of working theory.

Lisa Y. Flores is Professor in the Department of Psychological Sciences at the University of Missouri, Columbia, MO, USA. She has published extensively on the career development of Latinx and women.

"David Blustein and Lisa Flores have curated a remarkable collection of essays in which some of the world's finest minds tackle one of the world's most urgent questions: How can we make the modern workplace more humane and just? The voices and perspectives in this timely book will spark you to think bigger and will equip you with the ideas and practices to transform both workforce policies and your own work life."

—**Daniel H. Pink**, #1 New York Times bestselling author
of *Drive*; *When*, and *The Power of Regret*

"Blustein and Flores have given us an amazing gift in their edited book, *Rethinking Work*; the gift of reimagination. This book intricately weaves together a tapestry of essays that reimagine our relationship to work, and introduce provocative possibilities about humanity at the center of work. The authors call readers to the metaphorical dinner table to speak to us from their hearts as they discuss implications of the current inflection point in the world of work and then invite us to step outside to have a fireside chat and wrestle with the questions raised at the table. If you are ready for out-of-the-box thinking to build a better workplace, this it!"

—**Angela Byars-Winston**, Professor in the Department
of Medicine, *University of Wisconsin-Madison, USA*, and senior author
of the National Academies of Sciences, Engineering, and Medicine
report entitled *The Science of Effective Mentorship in STEMM*

"This rich and compelling series of essays describes, prescribes, and proscribes policies and practices in the world of work. The authors portray the importance of work for a wide variety of populations, paying particular attention to the plight of oppressed and marginalized communities. But the contributors go far beyond describing the current state of affairs; they offer persuasive and practical recommendations for imagining thriving workplaces around the world. This magnificent book will enlighten the mind and empower the spirit to do better, to work better, and to live better. I highly recommend it to leaders, workers, students, and policy makers."

—**Isaac Prilleltensky**, the Mautner Endowed Chair in
Community Well-Being at the *University of Miami, USA*,
and co-author, with Ora Prilleltensky, of *How People Matter:
Why it Affects Health, Happiness, Love, Work, and Society*

"The answer to the common question "What do you do?" is usually one's occupation, because work is so fundamental to one's identity. Much deeper questions follow this basic one: "Can decent work be accessible and equitable for all?," "How are technology and globalization affecting the nature of jobs, education, and the labor market?," and "Who all are really benefiting from our work?" *Rethinking Work: Essays on Building a Better Workplace* provides refreshing expert insights to questions such as these. Moreover, discovering how chapters are usefully related in addressing workplace issues is, to me, as rewarding as the chapters in their own right."

—**Fred Oswald**, Ph.D., Professor and Herbert S. Autrey Chair in Social
Science, Department of Psychological Sciences, *Rice University, USA*

"In light of the clear evidence that the institution of work is not working for individuals or society, this thoughtful and thought-provoking volume brings together voices from across the globe to reimagine a people-focused future of work. It is through imaginative exercises such as these that one sees a pathway to a more hopeful future of work—one that is built around the ideas of decency, dignity, equity, social justice, well-being, agency, and sustainability. This book is a must-read for students, scholars, workers, organizational leaders, policy-makers, and anyone looking to understand and positively impact the institution of work."

—**Mindy Shoss**, Professor of Psychology, *University of Central Florida, USA*; Honorary Professor, *Australian Catholic University, Australia*

"By providing a sustained critique of the 'language', form and practice of work that includes a rich plethora of approaches and positions, Blustein and Flores do every policymaker, researcher, employer and employee an invaluable service.

Rethinking Work: Essays on Building a Better Workplace introduces new, thought-provoking and challenging perspectives that resonate with the challenges the world currently faces. At a time of unemployment/underemployment, precarity, the Great Resignation, automation and marginalization, this book provides a much-needed antidote, mapping paths to a more just and honest world of work that serves the interests of all members of society."

—**Rie Thomsen**, Professor of Career Guidance, *Aarhus University, Denmark*

"This very timely book presents a highly informative collection of chapters that explore the various topics that should be considered as we face the many changes, challenges, and opportunities of working in the present and future. Written by some of the leading scholars in the field, the chapters provide much-needed reflections to understand better key work and career development issues on how work can be meaningful, inclusive, and sustainable for all."

—**Andreas Hirschi**, Chair of Work and Organizational Psychology, *University of Bern, Switzerland*

"This book represents a major contribution to the understanding of the evolution of work and the labor market in the post-COVID period. This contribution brings to light the profound transformations of work and the function of work in the lives of the most disadvantaged people across the globe. The book constitutes an important step in helping us to develop a global view on the nature of working in the 21st century. The contributors, who represents many regions of the world, provide insights about various aspects of work, including racism and culture, inequalities, precarity, unemployment and underemployment, and technology. This must-have book provides readers with an in-depth knowledge of the major challenges that people face in our changing contemporary world."

—**Valérie Cohen-Scali**, *INETOP-Conservatoire National des Arts et Métiers, Paris, France*

"What lies ahead in the future of work, how will it change? How can we express ourselves and find value in being someone that works? Will the challenges of a strained work/life balance, race, ethnicity and gender forever weigh us down? What can be done so work can be decent and meaningful for all—is there a roadmap we can follow?

I invite you to join me in learning from the experience and knowledge that permeates this book, from seasoned researchers and writers that study work and how it affects our lives. As I read, I learned about the challenges, we face but also about what can give hope.

Can we be optimists? I think the answer from this book is an unequivocal yes!

—Ingrid Bakke, Faculty of Social and Health Sciences, *Innland Norway University of Applied Sciences, Lillehammer, Norway*

"In *Rethinking Work: Essays on Building a Better Workplace*, Blustein and Flores provide the perfect venue to reflect on the interrelated factors impacting the current state of work, while simultaneously providing a space to begin reimagining a world of work that is more just, equitable, and fulfilling for all. Indeed, the innovation strategies, ideas, models, and tools delineated in this volume offer a starting point for transforming a system that has created differential classes of workers—those who work for survival and those who work for self-determination—to a system that lifts up ALL workers as they survive and thrive in healthier workspaces. There is no doubt that this volume of work will guide future research, training, organizational structures, management strategies, and public policy that will transform the world of work for the better."

—Rachel L. Navarro, Ph.D., Professor, College of Education and Human Development, *University of North Dakota, USA*

Rethinking Work

Essays on Building a Better Workplace

Edited by David L. Blustein and Lisa Y. Flores

Routledge
Taylor & Francis Group

NEW YORK AND LONDON

Designed cover image: Getty Images/Nikada

First published 2023
by Routledge
605 Third Avenue, New York, NY 10158

and by Routledge
4 Park Square, Milton Park, Abingdon, Oxon, OX14 4RN

Routledge is an imprint of the Taylor & Francis Group, an informa business

© 2023 selection and editorial matter, David L. Blustein and Lisa Y. Flores; individual chapters, the contributors

The right of David L. Blustein and Lisa Y. Flores to be identified as the authors of the editorial material, and of the authors for their individual chapters, has been asserted in accordance with sections 77 and 78 of the Copyright, Designs and Patents Act 1988.

Library of Congress Cataloging-in-Publication Data
A catalog record for this title has been requested

ISBN: 9781032223902 (hbk)
ISBN: 9781032161365 (pbk)
ISBN: 9781003272397 (ebk)

DOI: 10.4324/9781003272397

Typeset in Bembo
by Apex CoVantage, LLC

Contents

Contributors

Aron Ain serves as executive chair of the UKG Board of Directors. Before transitioning into this role, Aron served as the longtime CEO of UKG (Ultimate Kronos Group), a $3.3 billion technology company with more than 15,000 employees around the world. Aron is the author of *WorkInspired: How to Build an Organization Where Everyone Loves to Work*.

Saba Rasheed Ali is a professor of counseling psychology and associate dean for research at the University of Iowa within the College of Education. Her research interests include work psychology, economic justice, and career development.

Blake A. Allan is an associate professor of counseling psychology at the University of Houston. His primary focus is on the quality of work, encompassing constructs such as underemployment, precarious work, decent work, and meaningful work.

Nancy Arthur is a professor and dean of research, UniSA Business, University of South Australia and Professor Emeritus, University of Calgary. Nancy's research focuses on diversity and social justice in professional practice, international students, and work transitions.

Gideon Arulmani is a clinical psychologist with an interest in the interface between culture and mental health. He is the founder director of the Promise Foundation and visiting professor at a number of universities. His approaches to intervention have been implemented in more than 30 countries through collaborations with various multilateral agencies.

Kelsey L. Autin is an assistant professor of counseling psychology at the University of Wisconsin-Milwaukee. Her research focuses on how people access decent work and processes by which work satisfies basic human needs and supports overall well-being.

Tara S. Behrend is an associate professor of industrial-organizational psychology at Purdue University. Her research concerns the ways that technology can be used to support human flourishing in the context of work.

Stephanie G. Burrows is a doctoral candidate in counseling psychology at the University of Wisconsin-Milwaukee. Her research interests emphasize the role of contextual barriers and sociocultural identities in college students' career decision-making and the impact of career shocks on career development across the lifespan.

Allison R. Bywater is a doctoral student in counseling psychology at the University of Iowa. Her research focuses on how reproductive access and parenthood influence well-being and career-related decisions.

Germán A. Cadenas (he/his/el) is an assistant professor of counseling psychology at Lehigh University and an action researcher who has been involved in the movement for immigrant rights for over a decade. His work focuses on the psychology of immigration, including immigrants' psychological health, educational/career outcomes, activism to transform policy, and effective strategies to support their overall well-being.

Fiorella L. Carlos Chavez is an assistant professor in community health at Arizona State University. Her work focuses on the health and development of unaccompanied Latinx migrant adolescents in US agriculture.

Stuart C. Carr is the UNESCO Chair on Sustainable Livelihoods and a co-founder of Project GLOW (Global Living Organisational Wage).

Sundiata K. Cha-Jua is a Black/Africana studies scholar-activist who uses historical methodologies. He teaches in the Department of African American Studies and the Department of History at the University of Illinois.

Rachel Gali Cinamon is a full professor of career counseling at Tel Aviv University; her research focuses on work-family relationships through the lifespan, career interventions, and career development of at-risk populations. Her research group develops theory-driven and evidence-based practice to enhance the career development of vulnerable groups. She currently serves as the Dean of the Faculty of Humanities at Tel Aviv University.

Rosie Phillips Davis is a professor of counseling psychology at the University of Memphis, where she focuses on career counseling, poverty, advocacy, ethics, and consultation. She is a past President of the American Psychological Association.

Ryan D. Duffy is a professor of psychology in the University of Florida's Counseling Psychology program. His research focuses mainly on the connection between work and well-being.

Keona K. Ervin is an associate professor and program director of Gender, Sexuality, and Women's Studies at Bowdoin College. Her research interests include Black women's history in the United States, gender and sexuality studies, and the US labor and working-class history.

Gabriel N. Ezema is a doctoral student in counseling psychology at the Department of Educational Psychology, University of Wisconsin, Milwaukee. His research interests include how privilege and oppression impact people's career development journey and access to decent jobs, youth mentoring, positive youth development, and how the family and social contexts affect youth psychosocial development.

Aisha Farra is a counseling psychology doctoral student at the University of Massachusetts, Boston. Her research broadly focuses on the academic and vocational development, outcome, persistence, and experiences of minoritized individuals.

Caroline S. Fawcett is a labor economist with 35 years of research, teaching, and policy-making experience on labor markets, youth employment, and education projects. Most recently, Dr. Fawcett has served as a senior advisor in the design and development of its new policy arm, the Labor Market Observatory.

Nadya A. Fouad is the Mary and Ted Kellner Endowed Chair of Educational Psychology and a Distinguished Professor at the University of Wisconsin-Milwaukee. Her research focuses on gender and race in vocational behavior.

Patton O. Garriott is an associate professor of counseling psychology at the University of Denver. His work examines access and equity in higher education and STEM fields.

Alexander Glosenberg is an assistant professor in entrepreneurship at Loyola Marymount University and is a co-founder of the not-for-profit Foster Workforce Development Institute (FWDi). Alex studies how to assist entrepreneurs from marginalized backgrounds and has worked with initiatives supported by the United Nations Development Programme, the White House Office of Science and Technology Policy, and the United Nations Educational, Social, and Cultural Organization.

Paige Guarino is a counseling psychology doctoral student at Fordham University. Her research focuses on the relationship between work, mental health, and intersectional identity, as well as implicit bias mitigation from a strengths-based perspective.

Donna Hicks is an associate at the Weatherhead Center for International Affairs at Harvard University. She has conducted dignity leadership training for governments, the corporate world, education, non-governmental organizations, and the military.

Nancy Hoffman is a senior advisor at Jobs for the Future (JFF). Prior to joining JFF in 2002, she taught at Brown University and elsewhere.

Tristram Hooley is a professor of career education. His research focuses on the interaction between careers, technology, and politics, and he is particularly interested in what kind of interventions we can deliver that can help people to have better careers (career guidance). His work is informed by critical theory, and he hopes that it can make a positive impact on social justice. Ultimately, he believes that in order for people to have better careers, we will need to rethink the nature of work and learning in profound ways.

Margo A. Jackson is a professor at Fordham University, Counseling Psychology Program. Her research focuses on constructively addressing hidden biases and strengths, career development across the lifespan, and ethical training.

Stephanie Malia Krauss is the Founder + Principal of First Quarter Strategies; a staff consultant with the Youth Transition Funders Group; and a senior fellow with the CERES (Community-Engaged Research and Evaluation Sciences) Institute for Children & Youth at Boston University, Education Northwest, and the Children's Funding Project. He is the author of *Making It: What Today's Kids Need for Tomorrow's World and Whole Child, Whole Life: 10 Ways to Help Kids Live, Learn, and Thrive.*

Sachin Kumar is an associate professor at a Government College in Himachal Pradesh, India. Dr. Sachin Kumar is the President of the Indian Association of Career and Livelihood Planning (IACLP), and the National Correspondent to the International Association for Educational and Vocational Guidance (IAEVG).

Betty S. Lai is an associate professor at the Lynch School of Education and Human Development at Boston College and the author of *The Grant Writing Guide* (Princeton University Press).

Robert W. Lent is a distinguished university professor, Counseling Psychology Program, University of Maryland.

Seung-Ming Alvin Leung is a professor in the Department of Educational Psychology at the Chinese University of Hong Kong. His latest research work focuses on career adaptability, career assessment, and international issues. This essay was written while the author served as Visiting Professor, Center for Asian American Studies, College of Education, University of Houston, during the 2021–22 academic year.

Belle Liang is a professor in the Lynch School of Education and Human Development at Boston College and the coauthor of the bestselling book, *How to Navigate Life: The New Science of Finding Your Way in School, Career, & Beyond* (St. Martin's Press).

Brenna Lincoln is a counseling psychology doctoral student in the Lynch School of Education and Human Development at Boston College. Her scholarship focuses on purpose development among adolescents and emerging adults.

Anthony Mann is a senior policy analyst (career readiness) at the Organization for Economic Co-operation and Development, where he leads work on how schools can better prepare students for working life. He has published extensively on subjects related to career guidance, employer engagement in education, and vocational education and training.

Jonas Masdonati is an associate professor at the Institute of Psychology of the University of Lausanne, Switzerland, and the director of the Research Center in Vocational Psychology and Career Counseling (CePCO). His research mainly focuses on career transitions, decent work, the meaning of work, and vocational education and training.

Gloria G. McGillen is a doctoral candidate in counseling psychology at the University of Missouri—Columbia and a fellow at Temple University's Tuttleman Counseling Services.

Mary McMahon is an honorary associate professor at the University of Queensland, School of Education. She researches and publishes career development across the lifespan, narrative, and systems approaches to career counseling and qualitative career assessment.

Ishbel McWha-Hermann is an associate professor in the International Human Resource Management at the University of Edinburgh Business School. She studies social justice at work, particularly for workers who are historically marginalized and focuses on pay fairness and decent work.

Ellen Hawley McWhirter is the Ann Swindells Professor in Counseling Psychology and directs the Spanish Language Psychological Services and Research Specialization in the Counseling Psychology & Human Services Department at the University of Oregon. Her scholarship includes a focus on Latinx adolescents and factors that influence their postsecondary plans and school engagement, including critical consciousness, experiences of discrimination, and documentation status.

Uma Chandrika Millner is an associate professor in the Division of Psychology and Applied Therapies at Lesley University and the Principal Investigator of the Mental Health Identity and Adaptability (MHIA) Research Lab. Her overall professional approach is grounded in social justice, spirituality, and multiculturalism.

Helen A. Neville is a professor in the Department of Educational Psychology and the Department of African American Studies at the University of Illinois at Urbana-Champaign. She is a scholar-activist whose research focuses on racial ideologies and healing among People of Color.

Kristen Jiin Park is a doctoral student at the University of Denver. Her scholarship focuses on the mental health and academic outcomes of marginalized students in higher education, including first-generation, low-income, and/or students of color.

Shékina Rochat is a substitute senior lecturer at the Institute of Psychology of the University of Lausanne. Her research interests focus mainly on motivation, career decision-making difficulties, and interventions in career counseling.

Jérôme Rossier is vice-rector for Human Resources and Lifelong Learning and full professor of vocational and counseling psychology at the University of Lausanne. His teaching areas and research interests include counseling, personality, psychological assessment, and cross-cultural psychology.

Jerry Rubin is currently a visiting fellow at the Harvard Kennedy School Project on the Workforce and a foundation fellow at the Eastern Bank Foundation. He was previously the President and CEO of Jewish Vocational Service, a Boston-based workforce development organization.

Donna E. Schultheiss is a Professor Emerita at Cleveland State University, where she previously served as Interim Dean and Associate Dean of the College of Graduate Studies, and a professor of counseling psychology. Her research interests concern women's work, leadership, work-life integration, and international contexts of career development.

Barry Schwartz is a Professor Emeritus of psychology at Swarthmore College and a visiting professor at the Haas School of Business at Berkeley. He has written *The Battle for Human Nature, The Costs of Living, The Paradox of Choice, Practical Wisdom* and most recently, *Why We Work*. Schwartz has spoken four times at the TED conference, and his TED talks have been viewed by more than 25 million people.

Ofer Sharone is an associate professor of sociology at the University of Massachusetts, Amherst. His research focuses on career transitions, unemployment, and the sociology of aspirations.

Sandra Bertram Grant Solis is a doctoral candidate at the University of Denver. Her scholarship is focused on increasing diverse representation in leadership and reducing inequities in mental healthcare.

Ronald G. Sultana is a professor of sociology and comparative education and founding director of the Euro-Mediterranean Centre for Educational Research (EMCER) at the University of Malta, Msida, Malta.

Hsiu-Lan Shelley Tien is currently the dean of the College of Education at the National Taiwan Normal University. She earned her doctorate at the University of Iowa and was a Fulbright scholar at the University of Maryland. From the National Career Development Association, she earned the award of International Career Practitioner in 2016 and received the Fellow award in 2020.

Femina P. Varghese is a professor in the Department of Psychology and Counseling at the University of Central Arkansas. Her research focuses on the work issues of the justice-involved and the risk factors for recidivism.

Brandon L. Velez is an associate professor in the Counseling Psychology Program at Teachers College, Columbia University. His research focuses on the associations of marginalization with mental health and career outcomes among women, racial/ethnic minoritized people, and sexual and gender minority people. He is also interested in exploring ways to enhance the social justice training of psychologists and other mental health professionals.

Jerod C. White is a PhD candidate in Industrial-Organizational Psychology at Purdue University. His research focuses on the psychological effects of workplace technologies, particularly in the contexts of employee selection, training, and performance management.

Kerrie Wilkins-Yel is an assistant professor of counseling psychology at the University of Massachusetts, Boston. Her research broadly focuses on equity, justice, and access both at work and in pursuit of work. Specifically, she takes an intersectional approach to understand the influence of oppression and marginalization on the academic and career development of women from diverse racial/ethnic backgrounds.

Tracy S. Woods is a peer consultant, Massachusetts Certified Peer Specialist, a COAPS (certified older adult peer specialist), and a recovery coach. She has contributed as both a student and an instructor at the Boston University Center for Psychiatric Rehabilitation's Recovery Education Program since 2007.

Introduction

1 Rethinking Work

An Introduction

David L. Blustein and Lisa Y. Flores

The institution of work is one of the most important contexts of people's lives; however, like so many other institutions, work has changed in complex and unexpected ways in the past few decades. Prior to the COVID-19 pandemic, working had increasingly become more precarious, with losses in stability, dignity, and decent work for many people (Blustein, 2019; Hoffman et al., 2020; Kalleberg, 2018). Since the advent of the pandemic, work disruptions have become ubiquitous. Massive fluctuations in unemployment, increasing unsafe and unstable work conditions, growing inequality, and The Great Resignation have all embroiled people across the globe in a whirlwind of unexpected changes that have been hard to follow, understand, and navigate. Amidst the anguishing disruptions evoked by COVID-19, underlying shifts in work have continued unabated as reflected by automation, robotics, inequality, inadequate safety nets, and long-needed questioning about the purpose of work.

This book serves as a necessary and broad-reaching reflection on the institution of work. The pace of change in the workplace and in people's relationships with work has been relentless, seemingly taking place without much systemic or institutional planning. We envision this book of invited essays as a critical opportunity to deeply consider how societies may optimally organize and support humane conditions and structures for all of those who work, whether by necessity or desire. As societies consider if and how work should be reformed, we argue that people first need to dream of a different future that reflects humane values of decency and dignity at work.

To meet this challenge, we have organized this book of brief essays from scholars, activists, psychologists, workforce development professionals, corporate leaders, and others who are engaged in understanding, critiquing, and improving the nature of work. We have challenged the invited authors to imagine new workplace structures, policies, and support systems that promote decent and fair work for all members of society, especially those who are most vulnerable to the adverse impacts of contemporary work. We have asked the authors to address reform in structural vulnerabilities in the workplace that can support people in their striving to survive and experience some degree of meaning and purpose in their work lives. Each of these

DOI:10.4324/9781003272397-2

essays provides a specific set of perspectives and recommendation(s) on how to reimagine work as an institution that ideally nourishes people and communities. We then integrate themes from these essays in the conclusion to provide direction and context for ongoing debates and policy discussions about work.

This edited collection consists of compelling, non-academic, and non-technical essays with a focus on the psychological and social aspects of working, which have often been in the background in public debates that typically have emphasized economic and policy issues. While the psychological and social perspectives form a central theme of the contribution, the essays will include authors across academic fields, such as psychology, sociology, management, organizational studies, and other leaders from workforce development, racial and social justice movements, business, and public policy.

This book fills a needed gap in the literature on the current status and future of work. In contrast to the general focus on books on the future of work, we hope that this book inspires a concerted conversation and debate that *focuses on people as opposed to technology and profits. In short, we are hopeful that this book serves as a transformational contribution that will inform work-based reform efforts and social change.*

The Landscape of Contemporary Work

To set the stage for the essays, we provide a brief overview of some of the most notable changes in working at the present time. Each of these issues has been exacerbated by the global COVID-19 pandemic but is not unique to this particular challenge. The pandemic has revealed fault lines and fissures in work that have been evident for many decades. However, deliberations about the nature of working have clearly preceded the pandemic and will continue well beyond this very difficult period. In the following sections, we review some of the more prominent sources of changes in work that set the stage for the essays that follow.

Unemployment and Underemployment

Unemployment (the inability to secure a job for those seeking employment) and underemployment (working below one's experience, skills, or training or working less than full-time but wanting a full-time position) can have profound psychological effects on individuals who are out of the workforce. Multiple structural and environmental factors can contribute to unemployment and underemployment, including the demands of the labor force, the economy, and technological advances.

Unemployment and underemployment rates vary across countries. In general, many countries are struggling with high rates of unemployment and underemployment, and some countries and jobs are expected to make slow recoveries to employment rates prior to the start of the pandemic. The Organization for Economic Cooperation and Development (OECD), an international organization that works with governments across 38 countries to shape policies that enhance people's lives, tracks a number of outcomes in social, economic, and environmental spheres to inform policy recommendations. In February 2020, near the start of the global pandemic, the overall unemployment rate in OECD countries was 5.3% (OECD, 2022); this rate peaked in April 2020 at 8.79%. The average unemployment rates across OECD countries ranged from 3.2% or lower in Czech Republic, Japan, and Poland to 15.5% or higher in Spain, Columbia, Greece, and Costa Rica. The overall unemployment rate in the United States has gradually decreased since 2020, eventually falling below the pre-pandemic rates in February 2022. Still, several countries continue to experience relatively high rates of unemployment (over 10%) and some countries have experienced slow rates of recovery from the high levels of unemployment experienced during the initial months of the pandemic. Economic and labor policies can anticipate labor force downturns that result in high unemployment, and government programs and labor policies are needed to provide a safety net for people who want to be employed but are experiencing difficulty securing employment.

Precarious Work

Precarious work has become increasingly common in the past few decades. Precarious work refers to "work that is unstable and insecure in the continuity and quantity of work, restricts the power of workers to advocate for change, and does not provide protections from workplace abuses and unsafe working conditions" (Allan et al., 2021, p. 2). The pervasive lack of stability that defines precarious work became even more pronounced in recent decades as the consequences of neoliberal economic and political policy became embedded in the workplace (Blustein et al., 2022). Since the advent of market-based reforms that sought to liberalize (or reduce) regulations for the private sector, the rights of workers diminished and the notion of a lifelong career became increasingly the province of relatively privileged people (Brewster & Molina, 2021; McWhirter & McWha-Hermann, 2021).

Into this unhealthy mix, the pandemic emerged with the force of a tsunami, creating further ruptures in an already insecure work context. The erosion of enforceable policies and consensually agreed-upon norms within the workplace and within the broader institution of work over the past few decades has included significant losses of worker protections, diminishing stability at work, growing inequality, loss of workers' voice, and reduced power for workers to negotiate decent and dignified work lives (Allan et al., 2021; Kalleberg, 2018). Moreover, precarious work has become increasingly widespread across most occupational groups, although long-standing vulnerable groups (such as women, Black, Indigenous, People of Color, and older workers) have suffered the most from growing precarity in the workplace (Kalleberg, 2018).

The Great Resignation

More people are voluntarily leaving their jobs today than at any time before. Dubbed *The Great Resignation*, there has been a gradual increase in the number of people leaving their positions over the past decade, but the global pandemic is believed to have spurred more people to quit their jobs. In 2021, over 47.8 million people in the United States quit their jobs (U.S. Bureau of Labor Statistics, n.d.), averaging over 4 million a month. Young adults (those under 30 years of age) represent 37% of those who quit their jobs in 2020, and 24% are individuals with lower incomes (Parker & Horowitz, 2022).

The motivations for choosing to leave a job are numerous. According to a survey by the Pew Research Center, people who quit their jobs in 2021 cited low pay, lack of opportunities for advancement, and feeling disrespected at work as the major reasons for their resignation (Parker & Horowitz). Other important factors related to work–life balance and benefits, including childcare issues, little flexibility with the work schedule, poor benefits, or putting in too many hours at work (Parker & Horowitz). Whereas the high demands and risks during the pandemic drove some people out of jobs in healthcare and teaching, this global crisis provided others the opportunity to reset and consider their quality of life and caretaking responsibilities. Some workers wanted to continue remote work opportunities that were common during the early stages of the pandemic. Many workers today expect to be treated humanely by their employers and are seeking employment that aligns with values and supports them in living fulfilling lives outside of work. When these conditions are not met at work, recent trends suggest that today's workers are more willing to give up their jobs and seek other work opportunities that do so.

Automation and Robotics

Since the advent of the Industrial Revolution, people have been concerned that technology will take away jobs and leave many people without work and a means for sustainability. Currently, advances in automation and robotics are reshaping some work environments, particularly in manufacturing and in tasks that do not require emotional labor (National Academies of Sciences, Engineering, and Medicine, 2017). A widely cited report by Frey and Osborne (2013) along with other books and articles (e.g., Ford, 2015) raised concerns that automation and robotics could potentially replace a considerable number of jobs, resulting in growing unemployment and underemployment. Recently, debates about the current wave of technological innovation has served to highlight the deep worries of working people and the broader public about the future of work. However, serious scholars from across the social sciences and technology have pushed back against the doomsday scenarios by noting that new jobs and occupations are being developed which are not easily replaceable (see Hoffman et al., 2020; Oswald et al., 2019, for reviews of these positions).

In this book, we expand concerns about the future of work beyond the prevailing questions about technology and automation. We believe that debates about the institution of work need to embrace long-standing concerns about equity, opportunity, and decency (Hooley et al., 2018). At the same time, concerns about technology would also benefit from a systematic integration with the broad array of challenges that exist in contemporary work.

Marginalization at Work

The exploitation and marginalization of workers from vulnerable groups (i.e., based on race, gender, nationality, gender identity, sexual orientation, education, social class) have long been a mainstay of the global labor force. Although workplace equity issues are not new, the recent global pandemic along with the racial awakening in the United States following the killing of George Floyd in the summer of 2020 brought to light the disparities experienced by marginalized and vulnerable workers in the labor force. These disparities can take many forms, such as unequal pay for equal work, limited opportunities for advancement, limited representation in specific occupational fields, and experiences with harassment and discrimination.

These disparities were exposed during the pandemic when marginalized members of the workforce were more likely to be employed in "frontline" positions that required workers to show up for work in-person when many of the workers across the globe were shifting to remote work. Despite the risks of exposure and putting themselves and their family members at risk of COVID-19, many workers from marginalized groups went to work throughout the pandemic to provide healthcare services and to prevent disruptions in food and manufacturing. The pandemic exacerbated these inequities for marginalized workers, who were more likely to experience negative economic consequences and precarious work conditions (Blustein et al., 2020).

Why Rethinking Work?

The brief summary of some of the most troubling trends in the institution of work certainly raises important questions about the current and future role of work in people's lives. These changes coupled with the COVID-19 pandemic have coalesced to produce both major challenges and opportunities. The advent of The Great Resignation speaks to the fact that people are relating to work in different ways and making statements about it, as reflected in their actions (Sull et al., 2022). In our view, this time period reflects an inflection point that will require significant thought and deliberation.

This book provides fresh perspectives about work that can inform deliberations about how to create more inclusive and empowered work. The essays also tackle issues that intersect with work, such as racial justice, inequality, training and education, and the structure of organizations and the economy. In short, this book is framed around presenting new ideas and sparking the imagination of readers.

Statement of Aims

This book project is guided by interrelated goals that cluster around the following themes:

Explore and identify values to guide an engaged rethinking of work:

A key theme in this book project is to explicitly discuss the role of values in considerations about working. The changes that are taking place in the workplace represent the manifestation of identifiable values about economic structures, government policies, lifestyles, distribution of resources, and racial and social justice. The essays, individually and collectively, explore diverse values about work, providing critical perspectives that can inform a systemic rethinking of work.

Support and inform reforms in policies and norms about work:

We envision the process of rethinking work as an initial step in advocating for reforms that will serve to create more equitable and humane working conditions and policies. The authors of the essays discuss values about work, which are often implied, but not stated clearly in deliberations about the current status and future of work. In addition, many of the authors provide specific recommendations for reforms to transform specific challenges and policies about work.

Inform individual and organizational interventions to enhance the quality of work:

In addition to the focus on the macro-level perspective, the essays examine how individual and organizational interventions can be designed to overcome existing structural barriers in the contemporary workplace.

Identify and discuss social and racial justice challenges within the workplace:

The workplace represents an institution that places people into social and economic contexts that they often have not chosen. Each of society's ongoing struggles is replicated in the workplace, often exacerbated by the hierarchical attributes of work. As such, many of the essays discuss the challenges of injustice in social structures, interpersonal relationships, and gendered and racialized interactions in the workplace.

Inspire further reflections and research about work:

A major objective of this book is to inspire readers. By providing accessible and compelling essays on a wide array of issues pertaining to the rapid and radical shifts in work, we hope to attract a broad-based community of citizens who will advocate for a new and more humane workplace.

The Structure of the Book

The Functions of Work in People's Lives: These essays address the major functions of work in society today, such as personal and social economic benefits, community and societal benefits, social interactions, and personal fulfillment.

Changing Nature of Work: The next set of essays focuses on significant ways in which the world of work has changed in the 21st century and in turn, how these changes have altered available work and how work is performed (e.g., remote work and gig work).

Inequality and Work: Inequities have long persisted in work institutions. These essays address work inequality in the treatment, experiences, and opportunities of people based on gender, social class, sexuality, nationality, and other groups.

Precarious Work, Unemployment, and Underemployment: Essays that address the rise of temporary work in the gig economy or work that provides low pay and benefits and little security and protection to workers are grouped in this theme. In addition, essays that address ways to lessen unemployment and underemployment are included in this section.

Race, Culture, and Work: These essays address the role of race and culture in work and the role of work for diverse racial and cultural groups. Some essays may cover the experiences of specific racial groups in the world of work or how cultures have shaped work.

Practice, Systemic, and Policy Perspectives on Work: These essays review innovations in individual practice, organizational/institutional, and public policies that can support and protect workers and strengthen work as an institution.

Technology and Work: Technology affects all aspects of work and the work environment today. Technology has improved working conditions and increased productivity, but it also introduced considerable challenges in the workplace. These essays address how technology will reshape the work world, including work itself and interactions within work environments (among coworkers, with supervisors, etc.).

Conclusion: The concluding chapter consists of an analysis of the essays. We highlight common threads within each theme, areas of debate, key recommendations, and barriers to transformation and policy change. We conclude with a summary of the major takeaways with a focus on public policy, individual and psychological well-being, and community impacts.

Readership

We have invited accessible and compelling essays from a diverse array of contributors to capture the public imagination about work. We therefore hope that this book is relevant to anyone who is concerned about or interested in how work functions in life and how work can be improved for all. In addition to a broad, lay audience, we envision that the book will serve as a foundational contribution within the literature in organizational studies, labor relations, public policy, vocational and organizational psychology, occupational sociology, and related fields. In addition, we envision this book serving as a resource for work-based reform efforts by local, state, regional, and national organizations and governments. By collecting and integrating essays from a broad swath of perspectives, we hope that the book will be useful to policymakers as they grapple with the emerging demands of a radically changing work context. In addition, the book will be useful for psychologists, career counselors and coaches, organizational consultants, mental health providers, and other professionals who provide direct services to people facing career and work-based challenges. Furthermore, we anticipate that the book will be used by students in undergraduate classes on work and careers as well as in graduate classes in career development, organizational psychology, occupational sociology, management, industrial relations, labor studies, and related fields.

Final Thoughts for Readers

The contributors of these essays devoted considerable effort and time to crafting their essays. In our view, the results of their work are impressive and inspiring. We encourage readers to approach these essays with an open and curious mind, allowing them to connect to the informative musings of people who have been immersed in thinking and reflecting about work in some context for much of their lives. Moreover, the essays also reflect the contributors' lived experiences as workers, which have encompassed many of the challenges noted at the outset of this Introduction. While it is difficult to shape a book's impact, we do hope that the readers of this book will continue the deliberations, conversations, and debates that are evident on these pages. If we can capture the imagination of readers who share their enthusiasm for this work, we can ignite a systematic process of rethinking work that can improve the lives of people across the globe.

References

Allan, B. A., Autin, K. L., & Wilkins-Yel, K. G. (2021). Precarious work in the 21st century: A psychological perspective. *Journal of Vocational Behavior, 126*, 103491. https://doi.org/10.1016/j.jvb.2020.103491.

Blustein, D. L. (2019). *The importance of work in an age of uncertainty: The eroding work experience in America.* Oxford University Press.

Blustein, D. L., Duffy, R., Ferreira, J. A., Cohen-Scali, V., Cinamon, R. G., & Allan, B. A. (2020). Unemployment in the time of COVID-19: A research agenda. *Journal of Vocational Behavior, 119*, 103436.

Blustein, D. L., Smith, C. M., Wu, X., Guarino, P. A., Joyner, E., Milo, L., & Bilodeau, D. C. (2022). "Like a tsunami coming in fast": A critical qualitative study of precarity and resistance during the pandemic. *Journal of Counseling Psychology, 69*(5), 565–577. https://doi.org/10.1037/cou0000615.

Brewster, M. E., & Molina, D. A. L. (2021). Centering matrices of domination: Steps toward a more intersectional vocational psychology. *Journal of Career Assessment, 29*(4), 547–569. https://doi.org/10.1177/10690727211029182.

Ford, M. (2015). *The rise of the robots: Technology and the threat of a jobless future.* Basic Books.

Frey, C. B., & Osborne, M. A. (2013). The future of employment: How susceptible are jobs to computerisation. Working paper, *Oxford Martin Programme on the Impacts of Future Technology.* www.oxfordmartin.ox.ac.uk/downloads/academic/The_Future_of_Employment.pdf.

Hoffman, B. J., Shoss, M. K., & Wegman, L. A. (Eds.). (2020). *The Cambridge handbook of the changing nature of work.* Cambridge University Press.

Hooley, T., Sultana, R. G., & Thomsen, R. (2018). *Career guidance for emancipation.* Routledge.

Kalleberg, A. L. (2018). *Precarious lives: Job insecurity and well-being in rich democracies.* John Wiley & Sons.

McWhirter, E. H., & McWha-Hermann, I. (2021). Social justice and career development: Progress, problems, and possibilities. *Journal of Vocational Behavior, 126*, 103492. https://doi.org/10.1016/j.jvb.2020.103492.

National Academies of Sciences, Engineering, and Medicine. (2017). *Information technology and the US Workforce: Where are we and where do we go from here?* National Academies Press.

Organization for Economic Cooperation and Development. (2022). *Short-term labour market statistics.* https://stats.oecd.org/index.aspx?queryid=36324#.

Oswald, F. L., Behrend, T. S., & Foster, L. L. (Eds.). (2019). *Workforce readiness and the future of work.* Routledge.

Parker, K., & Horowitz, J. M. (2022). *Majority of workers who quit job in 2021 cite low pay, no opportunities for advancement, feeling disrespected.* www.pewresearch.org/fact-tank/2022/03/09/majority-of-workers-who-quit-a-job-in-2021-cite-low-pay-no-opportunities-for-advancement-feeling-disrespected/.

Sull, D., Sull, C., & Zweig, B. (2022). Toxic culture is driving the great resignation. *MIT Sloan Management Review, 63*(2), 1–9.

U.S. Bureau of Labor Statistics. (n.d.). *2021 home.* U.S. Bureau of Labor Statistics. Retrieved July 23, 2022, from www.bls.gov/opub/mlr/2021/.

The Function of Work
in People's Lives

2 Livelihood Thinking for Career Development

Rethinking Work From Alternative Perspectives

Gideon Arulmani and Sachin Kumar

Work as a Manifestation of Culture

The propensity to work has been an integral and continual aspect of human existence ever since the hands of our ancient ancestors, grasped a chunk of stone and transformed it into a tool. It is the human being's highly developed capability to intentionally and intelligently direct effort and energy toward reaching a goal and achieving a target that lies at the heart of not just our survival but of our evolution and progress as a species. Across millennia, human work gradually transformed from being a primordial fight against the elements for survival to an act of cognition, characterized by consideration, forethought, and planning. Formed and forged in the crucible of exigency, human ability began to manifest as skill. Over time, skills agglomerated and clustered into sets and types. And this gave birth to a foundational human institution: the occupation. Gradually, the manner in which an occupation was practiced developed cultural overtones and began to vary across societies and economies. Thus, for example, while carpentry might exist as an occupation in multiple cultures, how it is practiced, the manner in which the skills of this occupation are transmitted, and the social status of its practitioner are likely to vary greatly.

The Divergence of Career From Livelihood

The Protestant Reformation of the 1500s gave a new direction to the practice of occupations in Western societies. The spirit of enterprise and materialistic individualism promoted by Protestantism freed workers to work for personal profit and wholeheartedly focus on accumulating wealth (Weber, 2002). By the middle of the 18th century, primarily in England and Europe, the first Industrial Revolution created numerous new areas of occupation that called for new sets of skills and expertise. Undergirded by the Protestant work ethic, the practice of occupations developed individualistic overtones. These circumstances engendered a new form of work: the career. This new

DOI:10.4324/9781003272397-4

form of practicing an occupation called for fitting into predefined institutional structures and following prescribed rules while competing constantly to excel against others. Put differently, an individual consciously chooses to engage with the tasks and responsibilities of a career and willingly meets its demands because this investment of effort is expected to yield substantial personal gain. But since the last century of its existence, has the career approach to the practice of occupation lived up to these expectations?

The Great Rethink

At the time of this writing, the COVID-19 crisis is waxing and waning around us. Among the widespread outcomes of this global event are economic and labor market shocks leading to the derailment of careers and loss of jobs of unprecedented magnitude in all economies. Paradoxically, an opposite trend has also emerged. An increasingly large number of people who have successfully engaged with their careers are beginning to express the desire to exit the "careerist" path. People are saying that they feel trapped and exploited by their jobs, that modern work is exhausting and stressful, that jobs are abusive and unrewarding, and that workplaces are toxic. Millions of workers are reassessing their connections with their careers. Coining the phrase "The Great Resignation," Anthony Klotz predicted that a large number of people would quit their jobs in the wake of the pandemic (Jorgenson, 2021). In what Klotz refers to as pandemic epiphanies, being under lockdown has given workers the time and space to reflect upon their lives and the meaning and sense of purpose they derive from their work lives. In fact, we could say that The Great Resignation has been brought about by the opportunity for a great rethink.

Dissonant Equilibrium

The obvious question here is whether this phenomenon has been caused by the pandemic. Will these deep frustrations with work abate as the pandemic declines? A closer look indicates that while the pandemic might have been a trigger, unhappiness with work, not just the conditions of work, runs deeper. Arulmani (2014) points out that reciprocal workings between cultural learning, enculturation, and acculturation bring the individual/group to a unique state of equilibrium that influences engagement with work. When the equilibrium is characterized by contentment and feelings of fulfillment, it is consonant with the person's well-being. In contrast, persistent and unresolved adversity in people's lives induced by cultural, social, structural, or legislative environments accumulating over a period of time could bring about a dissonant equilibrium. Rethinking work could imply reckoning with the possibility that the pandemic has unmasked not just an immediate but also a chronic unhappiness with work leaving the careerist worker in a state of dissonant equilibrium.

Bidirectional Collaborations Between Career and Livelihood

Weary and tired, people are leaving their careers. While what they are abandoning is of significance, of greater import is what they are shifting toward. Many are preparing for new careers. But would fatigue and frustration be reexperienced, once the honeymoon with their new career has passed? Is a more fundamental, attitudinal shift required of the careerist? This essay proposes that livelihood thinking could be an aspect of this attitudinal shift. In the following, we present four themes that emerged from our interviews with workers practicing livelihoods and those pursuing careers who shifted away from the careerist approach.

"Integrates me with my community": The Collectivistic Perspective

Career has its being in the dynamic interaction between the garnering of personal gain and the services the person renders to society. As we have seen, career progress suffers or even grinds to a halt when this delicate balance is disturbed. From the livelihood perspective, the practice of occupations tends to be an extension of family and community relationships. The livelihood approach seems to foster a sense of belonging and of being enfolded by the community. This excerpt from our interview with an accountant who quit a high-profile city career and returned to his ancestral village provides an illustration, "I'm doing more or less the same thing I did in my career . . . adding up numbers, but now it's without the overwhelming need to beat the competition . . . now I feel my work integrates me with my community." An important point to be noted here is that this person continues to use the same knowledge and skills that he did as a careerist. It is in the practice of these skills that his way of living changes. Arulmani (2014) points to competition versus collaboration, individual progress versus group success, independence versus interdependence, and duty to the in-group versus personal rights as examples of attitudes to work and occupation that lie along the individualism-collectivism continuum. *Examining these differences and their impact on the practice of occupation could be a guideline for rethinking work.*

"I'm happily sewing buttons now . . . not tapping them": Rediscovering Craft and Manual Work

The industrial revolutions of the last two centuries have taken us from direct, human effort-based engagement with work, through mechanization, automation, and digitalization. Today, the hallmark of the fourth industrial revolution is the autonomization of work tools and processes (e.g., robots and driverless cars). These innovations perhaps improve the ease and quantum of production. But they lead to an almost forced abdication of human cognitive and cultural engagement with work (Arulmani, 2018).

Conversely, manual work is a core feature of livelihood thinking. A clear theme emerging from our interviews was a greater feeling of connectedness with work tasks. A computer scientist who shifted to a much more manual engagement with work said:

> It was all very exciting at first . . . pushing buttons to get machines to do things. But over time, I felt mentally tired . . . I was not using any actual skills. The algorithm was doing it. I've left all that now . . . some friends and I have gotten together to start a haberdashery. I'm happily sewing and selling buttons now . . . not tapping them! I'm a craftsperson now . . . !

Indeed, there are sound work principles to be learned from the craftsperson and artisan who even before the industrial revolution, working by hand, used simple tools with highly developed skill, to weave cloth, construct furniture, and build pyramids, temples, and cathedrals and ships! *Efforts at rethinking work could explore what manual work could mean in an increasingly digitalized and virtualized world.*

"Observing and working with my elders": Alternate Epistemologies

Knowledge pertaining to modern careers is encoded in the written form. It is only when the individual, through a prescribed curriculum, formally acquires this knowledge that he/she is allowed entry to a career. On the other hand, indigenous knowledge pertaining to livelihoods is usually not coded and accumulated in the same way. Songs, proverbs, rhymes, dances, music, art, and folklore can all carry information pertaining to the practice of an occupation. Learning is facilitated through observation, continuous conversation, and supervised practice in a master–apprenticeship relationship. Having lost employment, one of our interviewees returned to his family occupation of farming and poultry keeping. He says, "My people know about our traditional livelihood. There are no textbooks! I learn by observing and working with elders." Indigenous knowledge systems lie outside formal schooling systems. They are intangible repositories of the community's experience over centuries encompassing a wide range of human concerns including food security, human and animal health, education, biodiversity, and natural resource management. Since very few of these knowledge systems fall within the purview of positivist epistemologies, these age-old, time-tested repositories of knowledge are often viewed as primitive, unscientific, and not relevant to the exigencies of modern times. Increasingly, however, these knowledge systems are being accepted as alternate epistemologies that can guide the generation of hypotheses, the formulation of research designs, and the creation of methods and systems for contemporary practice (e.g., United Nations Interagency Support Group, 2014). *Rethinking work could involve engaging with such alternative paradigms to gain broader insights into human engagement with work.*

"Going to bring the cows home": Work as Education

Within the contemporary, career-oriented family, typically, the adults go off to work and the children go to school until they are ready to work. Livelihood orientations seldom separate work from education. The practice of an occupation is a family enterprise. Mahatma Gandhi (a champion of livelihoods) based his educational philosophy (*Nai Talim*—New Education) upon the principle that learning would be located around work. One of our adolescent interviewees, from a farming family, said, "I've just returned from school and I'm going to bring our cows home. So, hurry up with this interview!" Within livelihood orientations, children are a part of the fabric of the family's ethos of work. Educating children such that they begin to ponder over the meaning and purpose of work for themselves is a crucial requirement if future generations are to engage with work with perspicacity and discernment. *Rethinking work could consider how modern pedagogical systems might use livelihood thinking as an instrument for education.*

Conclusion

The intention of this essay is not to extol the virtues of one form of work over the other. Instead, the intention is to deliberately blur the lines between artificial dichotomies. An interplay can exist between the preindustrial, the industrial, and postindustrial, the personal and the shared, and the hand-crafted and the machine-made. Rethinking work would scaffold a continuous, ever-renewing dialogue between career and livelihood.

References

Arulmani, G. (2014). The cultural preparation process model and career development. In G. Arulmani, A. J. Bakshi, F. T. L. Leong, & A. G. Watts (Eds.), *Handbook of career development: International perspectives* (pp. 81–104). Springer International.

Arulmani, G. (2018). Cultural preparedness: Equilibrium and its alteration. In M. McMahon & N. Arthur (Eds.), *Contemporary theories of career development: International perspectives* (pp. 195–207). Routledge.

Jorgenson, D. (2021). The great resignation. *Washington Post*. www.washingtonpost.com/washington-post-live/2021/09/24/transcript-great-resination-with-molly-m-anderson-anthony-c-klotz-phd-elaine-welteroth/.

United Nations Interagency Support Group. (2014). *The knowledge of indigenous peoples and policies for sustainable development: Updates and trends*. IASG.

Weber, M. (2002). *The protestant ethic and the spirit of capitalism* (P. Baehr & G. C. Wells, Trans.). Penguin Books (Original work published 1905).

3 Working to Survive, Thrive, or Something More?

Rosie Phillips Davis

Some ask the question: do you work to live or live to work? The answer is both and even more. Work is often thought of as something that is done for which one gets paid in wages and/or other benefits. Merriam-Webster (n.d.) defines work as

> **activity in which one exerts strength or faculties to do or perform something**: a: activity that a person engages in regularly to earn a livelihood . . . b: a specific task, duty, function, or assignment often being a part or phase of some larger activity.

The work of the career counselor involves helping individuals decide about the type of work they want to do; if they want to continue climbing the career ladder in a particular area; or even if they want to work outside of their homes. In my many years teaching courses on career development and working with clients, I generally focused on work as part of a pathway that leads to earning a salary, including developing investments that would enable individuals to care for themselves and eventually lead to a retirement that would allow them to continue providing for themselves and for those for whom they were responsible. Yet as I talked with people about what work means to them, their answers revealed a more complicated and nuanced process; a process that will influence the workplace at home, in the office, and on the road.

While the dictionary definition of work embraces all such concepts and more, including paid and unpaid work no matter the physical location, some researchers have drafted additional definitions of work. Mary Sue Richardson (2013) categorized work as market work (i.e., work for financial compensation) and personal care work (i.e., unpaid caretaking for a loved one). Her description placed unpaid work into conversations in a more defined manner. Unpaid work can include keeping one's home clean, mowing the lawn, or any activity that produces a good or service. Perhaps, work has always been that way, and certainly, the definition of work embraces all such concepts, that is, work is both paid work and unpaid work no matter the physical location.

DOI:10.4324/9781003272397-5

Work seems to have been a part of the human experience since the beginning of time. Work appears to have begun so that humankind survived. Over time the need for work and the meaning of work have changed. When I engage people with the question about why they work, responses vary little by race/ethnicity and more by developmental age status. For example, when I ask people who are more at the beginning stages of starting jobs and careers, they are more likely to say they work to earn a living, whereas those closer to the end of their paid work lives are more likely to mention that work gives them purpose. Sometimes the answers to questions about the meaning of work in their lives vary by the economic condition of the individuals. Those who must work to put food on their table are more likely to say they work to earn a living and to meet basic needs, while those for whom money is not a concern are likely to say that work provides them with purpose, a sense of accomplishment, fun, and joy.

Most people with whom I spoke indicated a need to **work to survive**. Many individuals said they work to take care of themselves and the people who depend on them. They must find ways to provide food, drink, and shelter. That notion is consistent with what animals and early humans did. People said they needed to keep a roof over their heads. Certainly, one critical issue facing society is homelessness. When people cannot obtain decent work, shelter often is one of the vital things they sacrifice. Blustein (2019) talked about the need for decent work to enhance survival. In the wake of homelessness, two reasons for work intersect: the need for survival and the need for purpose. Those individuals without homes might say they need work to survive. Those individuals who do the work to end homelessness might say that such work gives them purpose.

So, **purpose** is another reason to work. That kind of purpose-based work, like eradicating homelessness, creates important interventions or counters to calamities that might threaten existence. For example, it is important to design interventions that are labeled work when there are natural disasters such as hurricanes or major wildfires. Those workers may say that such work gives them purpose. Almost every individual with whom I spoke talked about work as giving them purpose. I wonder why most humans express a need for purpose in their lives? Some writers say that purpose gives us our reasons to live or just to be. Indeed, some studies have shown that those individuals who have purpose live longer, keep their independence and functioning longer into life, and even make more money (Cohen et al., 2016). Others described work purpose as answering a call so deep within, or living within them, that it demands to be manifested. Their only choice is to do that work (M. A. Davis, 2022, personal communication). These individuals must have jobs or other means of income so that there is enough money to answer their (often underpaid) calling. They must do survival work to create or make manifest the work purpose. Such individuals are most easily understood as the artist who works at a fast-food restaurant to pay their bills so that they can paint, act, or sing. These individuals often feel as though they must do their art just to feel alive. Their conception of work goes far beyond the notion of survival. When such individuals answer or respond to their purpose, they appear to grow into the next category of work, which individuals name *thrive*.

Some people need to be in touch with other human beings to feel alive; **to thrive**. Work provides that outlet. During the COVID-19 global pandemic, communities around the world were shut down. In the United States, schools, businesses, medical spaces, and so on were closed for extensive periods. People were required or encouraged to remain inside their homes. Before the pandemic, 1 in 10 people reported symptoms of depression and anxiety. During the pandemic, that number rose to 4 in 10. People reported more interruptions in sleeping, eating, and drinking patterns. Those changes appeared to have been caused by isolation and job loss. Numerous individuals said that work provided spaces for them to have contact with others and live richer lives and thrive. Sometimes the word thrive can mean gaining more wealth. The sense that I got from people when they talked about work as helping them to thrive seemed to encompass internal growth, joy, and happiness. They spoke of feeling more alive. They talked about flourishing. These individuals felt healthy mentally, spiritually, emotionally, and psychologically when they worked. Some had no monetary need to work, but they reported being happy and fulfilled at work. Interestingly, the work could be paid or unpaid.

Finally, there were individuals who said they needed to have a sense of *accomplishment.* They said it was in their paid work environment that they could achieve that sense of accomplishment. Setting and meeting goals appear to be a part of the definition of accomplishment. One individual described it as an exercise for the brain. Work provided numerous ideas and challenges before them. Their brain was stimulated by those challenges at work in a way that was different from when they were home or when they were doing unpaid work. Perhaps, accomplishment is linked with what some term ego enhancement. Work provides some individuals with a sense of worth. That worth appears to come from being judged very favorably for the work that they do. One individual mentioned that it was especially fulfilling to be a Black man and to be praised, honored, and lauded for his work. His accomplishments made him feel like "skipping to work." The rewards and recognition for individuals in these paid environments are sometimes more fulfilling than similar rewards they obtain in their volunteer work. In the United States, great emphasis is placed on paid work. Perhaps in those paid work environments, it is easier to be recognized for one's accomplishments.

Survive, purpose, thrive, and accomplishment seem to be interlocking concepts, yet they may be separate for workers. Some individuals spend their work lives in jobs that they may never love, but the job "pays the rent" and allows them to survive. Their jobs may never be linked with a purpose. Others might work for their purpose and never need to get paid to meet survival needs. Survival could appear to be the first and a precondition for purpose. Or these two could be separate because of circumstances of wealth or others who take care of them. The third step could be to thrive. These individuals are working for more than survival needs or purpose. They are flourishing on the job. Finally, are the people who need to accomplish something at work and be recognized for those accomplishments. Of course, accomplishment might be present through every reason for work. Individuals who are working to survive, to serve a purpose, or to flourish or thrive may want and need to feel as if they have accomplished something. However, it may not be as important to them as it is for those individuals who work to accomplish it. It may even be that the better word for them is recognition. My conversations revealed that these individuals must do the work, feel very successful, and be recognized for those accomplishments. The more they accomplish and the more they are recognized, the more satisfied they are.

Employers might improve work environments if they know more about which of these four reasons for work is most important to their workers. For example, if the employer knows that the worker is there for survival, the work reinforcement might only need to be regular increases in pay or hours worked. If the worker is there to fulfill their purpose, then the employer could match that employee with duties and responsibilities that align with that individual's purpose. If that purpose is creating, then a job that allows creative expression might keep that worker better engaged. Employers might need to inquire more or observe more to determine how to help fulfill those individuals who thrive at work. It is useful to ask employees what about their job makes them feel most alive and satisfied. The answers may reveal ways that work could be structured to prompt thriving. Employers can measure the impact of accomplishment in a similar way. If promotions and awards improve employee performance, then it is wise to ensure promotion opportunities and recognition programs.

There are people like me who need all four elements. My first need was to earn enough money to take care of myself. That need may have arisen from growing up in poverty, but I found that I needed to take care of family members and I needed to help other people in need. It was not enough to earn money for me; I needed to fulfill a purpose. The thriving part of my job is the place where I could be the wind beneath the wings of others, that is, when I saw that I had an impact on the growth of other people, I felt satisfied. I do like to be recognized for my work. That recognition helps me to work even harder. Unlike the colleague who said such accomplishments made him want to skip to work, recognition communicated that my work was visible and appreciated.

It is important for workers to know what work means to them and why they work. Such self-knowledge can guide the trajectory of work life. If employers want to have the most productive workforce, they must continue to understand what is important to workers and provide those elements as effectively as possible. The nature of work may change: the reasons for working remain the same.

References

Blustein, D. L. (2019). *The importance of work in an age of uncertainty: The eroding work experience in America.* Oxford University Press.

Cohen, R., Bavishi, C., & Rozanski, A. (2016). Purpose in life and its relationship to all-cause mortality and cardiovascular events: A meta-analysis. *Psychosomatic Medicine, 78*(2), 122–133. https://doi.org/10.1097/PSY.0000000000000274.

Merriam-Webster. (n.d.). Work. *Merriam-Webster.com.* Retrieved January 16, 2022, from www.merriam-webster.com/dictionary/work.

Richardson, M. S. (2013). Counseling for work and relationship. *The Counseling Psychologist, 40*, 190–242.

4 Rethinking Work and Building Better Workplaces

Who Gets a Say and Who Needs a Say?

Mary McMahon

Introduction

When I read the proposal for this book, I was struck by who was being invited to "have a say" about building better workplaces for vulnerable workers by contributing chapters to this book, specifically, "thought leaders, scholars, activists, psychologists, and related social scientists." I then reflected on the current media debate about work, growing inequality, and the need for labor market reform which seems dominated by the privileged voices of politicians, business and industry leaders, and also, but less often, by trade union officials and social advocates. It is not surprising that these voices are heard; they have an intrinsic stake in these work–related issues. Work, however, is a deeply systemic issue that impacts individuals, families, business, industry, and societies. I wondered about the current debate and where the voices of the less privileged, the workers themselves, are and why they are seldom heard despite the issues under discussion also being of intrinsic interest to them, their families and their futures. Do they not have real-life experience with the issues? Do they not have ideas about improving workplaces and work conditions? Have their ideas also been marginalized? I come to my essay with questions, concern that continuing to do more of the same and hearing the same voices may not progress rethinking work and building better workplaces, and curiosity about ideas that could bring news of difference to the vexed issue of workplace reform. I do not propose solutions. Rather, in light of this book's aims, my intention is to reflect on dominant discourses and briefly engage with four constructs that may introduce new ideas to the discourse, specifically intersectionality, kyriarchy, co-design, and social innovation.

Systems of Discrimination and Oppression

Systems of discrimination and oppression are not new. They have been evident throughout history. For example, the feudal system resulted in a stratified pyramidal society with the majority of people being oppressed by a wealthy and privileged few. More recently, neo-liberal policies have seen a

DOI:10.4324/9781003272397-6

growing divide between the rich and the poor that perpetuates a stratified, pyramidal society, diminished job quality, a decline in real wages, declining job security, and an increase in non-standard employment. Gender discrimination, with its origins in patriarchal systems, has been and remains evident in many cultures and countries and is reflected internationally, for example, with fewer women than men holding positions of power in businesses and governments. Discrimination on the basis of race has been rife throughout history and remains to the present time as does inequality between and within countries. The effects of western colonization of many countries continue to be experienced by indigenous people. These examples of complex systems influence work, workers, workplaces, and in turn society and manifest in privilege, power, oppression, and discrimination.

What now seems to be emerging are the green shoots of a new consciousness that society can do better. For example, the grassroots "Me Too" and "Black Lives Matter" movements are signs that many people now want to and are committing to bringing about change. In addition, at a policy level, the four pillars of the International Labour Organization's (ILO, 1999) long-standing decent work agenda—employment creation, social protection, rights at work, and social dialogue—are aimed at fair globalization and poverty reduction and have subsequently been incorporated into the United Nations (2015) 2030 Agenda for Sustainable Development. Despite these grassroots and policy initiatives, the complex systems (e.g., political, educational, geographic, socioeconomic, and patriarchal) that sustain oppression remain (Brewster & Molina, 2021). These systems influence social identity development and opportunity.

Intersectionality

Social identity is constructed by individuals on the basis of their experiences in the groups and communities to which they belong and social categories such as gender, sexual orientation, geographic location, socioeconomic status, educational background, race, and class. Identity thus is multifaceted; individuals have multiple identities which interconnect, and their cumulation results in an experience greater than the total of the parts. A singular focus on, for example, gender, may not accurately represent levels of oppression, privilege, power, disadvantage, or access to resources. Intersectionality, a term first coined by the Black feminist Kimberlé Williams Crenshaw in 1989, recognizes that these social categories are not independent of each other but rather intersect and create systems that advantage or disadvantage individuals or groups. Crenshaw (1989), for example, considered how the intersection of gender and race influenced the experiences of black women in political and social systems. The multi-leveled intersection and interaction of systems and structures can oppress, discriminate, stigmatize, and create barriers and power imbalances (The State of Victoria, 2018). Policy and practice foci on only one category may go some way to addressing disadvantage but ignores other forms of oppression and therefore may not be comprehensive enough to benefit all. For example, vocational psychology and career counseling have been criticized for their focus on individuals and less on the intersectionality of a broad range of dominant systemic influences that continue to oppress (Brewster & Molina, 2021). Recognizing intersectionality is critical to inclusion and equity (The State of Victoria, 2018) in policy and practice. Systems and structures, such as social services and labor market reform, are frequently determined by privileged dominant groups that fail to understand and take into account the needs of all individuals and groups.

Kyriarchy

Kyriarchy considers the power structures that intersectionality produces (Osborne, 2015). Kyriarchy concerns structural power and refers to social systems that dominate and oppress. More expansive than patriarchy, the neologic term kyriarchy was proposed by Elisabeth Schüssler Fiorenza (1992) to recognize the complex intersection of systems of oppression and privilege that influence individuals' experiences. Historically, kyriarchy was "the rule of the lord, slave master, husband, elite freeborn, propertied, educated gentleman to whom disenfranchised men and all wo/men were subordinate" (Schüssler Fiorenza, 2005, p. 130). A feature of kyriarchy is a "complex pyramidal system of intersecting multiplicative social structures of superordination and subordination, of ruling and oppression" (Schüssler Fiorenza, 2005, p. 130). Kyriarchal pyramidal political and social systems are evident in modern society and are stratified by social categories such as gender, class, age, race, and socioeconomic status and result in dominance and superiority and subordination and inferiority (Schüssler Fiorenza, 2005). Simultaneously, however, individuals may benefit from and be oppressed by the system. Kyriarchy has implications for decision-making, policy formulation, and practice in relation to rethinking work and building better workplaces. Kyriarchy tends to privilege the voices of the already privileged at the top of the stratified sociopolitical system.

Internationally, there is evidence that when previously marginalized voices (e.g., Martin Luther King, Emily Pankhurst, and Nelson Mandela) are heard, change is possible that impacts the lives and work of millions of people. Unfortunately, despite the efforts of past and present reformers, policy and practice that build better workplaces, improve workers' conditions, and reduce inequality remain a work in progress. Historical and deeply entrenched oppression is systemically multileveled (e.g., in communities, organizations, society, and institutions) and suggests a need for "systemic changes through collective action and coalition building" (Brewster & Molina, 2021, p. 548). It is time that looking for solutions to the complex system problems related to work is approached differently and involves different voices, specifically those with lived experience of the problem, and different approaches. Co-design is one such approach.

Co-Design

Co-design is an inclusive, respectful, participatory process that involves stakeholders in "an approach to designing with, not for, people" (McKercher, 2020, p. 14) and is increasingly being used by governments, business, and community groups to develop new products, services, and policies. In co-design, the voices of those with lived experience of a problem are elevated and heard along with those of professionals and other community members; the expertise of all is recognized and valued. Co-design challenges imbalances of power by involving those who are most likely to be impacted by decisions (McKercher, 2020) in the process as well as the solution. Key principles of co-design include power sharing, relationship building and prioritization, participatory processes, and building capability. Essentially co-design involves understanding and defining an issue or a problem, developing potential solutions, testing the ideas with stakeholders, and producing an outcome that addresses the issue or problem and meets the identified needs. Co-design can be viewed as a paradigm through which some key elements of social innovation may be understood (Britton, 2017).

Social Innovation

Similar to co-design, openness and participation by all stakeholders are central to social innovation (Hillgren et al., 2011) which "deals with improving the welfare of individuals and community through employment, consumption or participation, its expressed purpose being therefore to provide solutions for individual and community problems" (OECD, 2018). Social innovation offers the possibility of meaningful improvement for complex problems (Britton, 2017). The concept of networking (i.e., connecting as peers working together) is preferred over top-down hierarchies, and problems and solutions are viewed systemically rather than through linear, causal thinking (Britton, 2017).

It is becoming increasingly clear that old approaches to finding solutions for complex and challenging social and economic problems are no longer fit for purpose; new approaches involving all stakeholders, including end-users, such as social innovation are gaining traction (Britton, 2017; Hillgren et al., 2011). Social innovation focuses on finding solutions to individual and community problems by:

- Identifying and delivering new services that improve the quality of life of individuals and communities

- Identifying and implementing new labor market integration processes, new competencies, new jobs, and new forms of participation, as diverse elements that each contribute to improving the position of individuals in the workforce

(OECD, 2018).

At the heart of participatory approaches such as social innovation are power relations and therefore voices that traditionally have been less heard, marginalized, and often socially excluded are included and take an active part in all stages of the process (Hillgren et al., 2011). Co-design can be used to shape social innovation; social innovation can reflect features of co-design although tensions exist in the field about the relationship between the two (Britton, 2017). Rethinking work and building better workplaces is a social problem impacting the welfare of individuals, their families, and communities; social innovation could have a role to play in finding solutions.

Conclusion

The four constructs of intersectionality, kyriarchy, co-design, and social innovation introduced in this essay are by no means proposed as a panacea to the deeply entrenched issues related to work and workplace reform. Rather, I hope that they offer news of difference to the discourse. The green shoots of a new consciousness that society can do better cannot be achieved if we continue to hear from the same voices and engage in the same approaches. News of difference is needed in our current systems to change the discourse and stimulate thinking about new approaches and who else could contribute toward the construction of solutions to the deeply entrenched and worsening issues related to rethinking work and building better workplaces.

References

Brewster, M. E., & Molina, D. A. L. (2021). Centering matrices of domination: Steps toward a more intersectional vocational psychology. *Journal of Career Assessment, 29*(4), 547–569. https://doi.org/10.1177/10690727211029182.

Britton, G. (2017). *Co-design and social innovation: Connections, tensions, and opportunities.* Routledge.

Crenshaw, K. (1989). Demarginalizing the intersection of race and sex: A black feminist critique of antidiscrimination doctrine, feminist theory and antiracist politics. *University of Chicago Legal Forum, 1989*(1), 139–167. https://chicagounbound.uchicago.edu/cgi/viewcontent.cgi?article=1052&context=uclf

Hillgren, P.-A., Seravalli, A., & Emilson, A. (2011). Prototyping and infrastructuring in design for social innovation. *CoDesign, 7*(3–4), 169–183. https://doi.org/10.1080/15710882.2011.630474.

International Labour Organization. (1999). *Report of the director-general: Decent work.* ILO Conference, 87th Session, Geneva. www.ilo.org/public/english/standards/relm/ilc/ilc87/rep-i.htm.

McKercher, K. A. (2020). *Beyond sticky notes: Co-design for real: Mindsets, methods, and movements.* Beyond Sticky Notes. https://static1.squarespace.com/static/5cc50b947fdcb81f7939668a/t/5efb116985126e27837f1622/1593512343569/Sample+chapter.pdf.

Organisation for Economic Co-operation and Development (OECD). (2018). *LEED forum on social innovations.* www.oecd.org/fr/cfe/leed/forum-social-innovations.htm.

Osborne, N. (2015). Intersectionality and kyriarchy: A framework for approaching power and social justice in planning and climate change adaptation. *Planning Theory, 14*(2), 130–151. https://doi.org/10.1177/1473095213516443.

Schüssler Fiorenza, E. (1992). *But she said: Feminist practices of biblical interpretation.* Beacon Press.

Schüssler Fiorenza, E. (2005). *Wisdom ways: Introducing feminist biblical interpretation.* Orbis Books.

The State of Victoria (Family Safety Victoria). (2018). *Everybody matters: Inclusion and equity statement.* file:///C:/Users/Mary/AppData/Local/Temp/Everybody-matters-inclusion-and-equity-statement.pdf.

United Nations. (2015). *Transforming our world: The 2030 agenda for sustainable development.* Author. https://sustainabledevelopment.un.org/content/documents/21252030%20Agenda%20for%20Sustainable%20Development%20web.pdf.

5 Why We Work

Barry Schwartz

The Gallup Organization regularly polls workers around the world to find out how satisfied they are with their work. Year after year, in nation after nation, Gallup finds that the vast majority of workers are either unengaged or actively disengaged from their jobs. Most workers spend half their waking lives doing things they don't want to do, in places they don't want to be.

Why? Adam Smith (1776/1937) had the view that it is human nature to abhor work, whatever its character. People work for wages, nothing more and nothing less. As he put it in *The Wealth of Nations*, "it is in the inherent interest of every man to live as much at his ease as he can." Smith's view cast a very long shadow. More than a century later, it gave birth to the scientific management movement, which subjected factory production to minute scrutiny with the aim of creating systems of manufacture that maximized output while minimizing the need for skill and close attention.

Today, in factories, offices, fulfillment centers, and other modern workplaces, the details may be different, but the overall situation is the same: work is structured on the assumption that people do it only because they have to. I think that this pessimistic approach to work is entirely backward. It is making us dissatisfied with our jobs—and it is also making us worse at them. For our sake, and for the sake of those who employ us, things need to change.

I am sure that many people do not recognize themselves in Adam Smith's characterization of people's attitudes toward work. Of course, people care about wages and wouldn't work without them. But many people care about more than wages. They want work that is engaging and challenging. They want work that includes a measure of autonomy and discretion. They want work that provides opportunities to learn and grow. And they want work that is meaningful—that makes a difference to other people that in at least some small way is ennobling (see Schwartz, 2015).

Some of us want these things so much that we may even be willing to take home a thinner pay envelope to get them. Lawyers leave white-shoe firms to work with the underclass and underserved. Doctors abandon cushy practices to work in clinics that serve poor populations. Moreover, we regard these

DOI:10.4324/9781003272397-7

desirable aspects of work as more than mere personal preference. When we say of someone that "they are in it for the money," we are doing more than offering a description. We're passing judgment.

You might object that those examples are of professionals—people who have the financial security to care about more than just their paychecks and the privilege of working in fields in which it is possible to find meaning and personal satisfaction. What about the janitor? The phone solicitor? The hairdresser? The fast-food worker?

It may be obvious that professionals care about more than their paychecks. But so do nonprofessionals. Examples are everywhere.

Organizational behavior researcher Amy Wrzesniewski (Wrzesniewski & Dutton, 2001) studied hospital custodians who faced a long list of job duties, none of which included contact with other human beings. Yet, many saw their work to include doing whatever they could to comfort patients and their families and assist the professional staff with patient care. They would joke with patients, calm them down so that nurses could insert intravenous lines, and even dance for them. There was no added compensation for engaging in these "extra role" activities, but these activities are what got the janitors out of bed every morning.

Journalist Mike Rose (2004) found hairdressers for whom the technical skills involved in cutting, coloring, and styling hair took a back seat to the interactions with clients that helped the clients make good decisions about their haircuts and feel good about the results.

In each of these cases, there is ample evidence that when given the chance to make their work meaningful and engaging, employees jump at it, even if it means that they work harder as a result. These feelgood stories tell us that there is a human cost to deskilling and routinizing work. Instead of being able to take pride in what they do, and derive satisfaction from doing it well, workers have little to show for their efforts aside from their pay.

Nonetheless, it is possible that what we lose in work satisfaction, we gain in efficiency. That is certainly what Adam Smith (1776/1937) thought when he extolled the virtues of the division of labor. Our work experience may be poorer, but our bank accounts will be richer. Yet more than 200 years later, there is still little evidence of this satisfaction–efficiency trade-off. In fact, most evidence points in the opposite direction. As Pfeffer (1998) documents, workplaces that offer employees work that is challenging, engaging, and meaningful, and over which they have some discretion, are *more* profitable than workplaces that treat employees as cogs in a production machine. When employees have work that they want to do, they are happier. And when they are happier, their work is better, as is the company's bottom line.

Pfeffer's arguments and evidence have been around for some time (see Schwartz, 2015), and they raise a puzzle. If companies that enable employees to do good work are more successful than companies that don't, surely by now, enlightened workplaces would have driven the benighted ones out of business. But this has not happened. Indeed, the opposite seems to be happening. Instead of enriching the work opportunities of relatively unskilled workers, we are impoverishing the opportunities of highly skilled ones. Teachers are forced to follow scripts that are aimed at producing high scores on standardized tests. Doctors are forced to adhere to "standard and customary practices," in the service of reducing medical costs. Lawyers are held to the single standard of billable hours. Judges are forced to adhere to sentencing mandates or rigid guidelines. In the face of evidence that increased routinization leads to worse performance, we continue to increase routinization. How can this be?

When Adam Smith suggested that people work only for pay, he was making a claim about what he thought was an essential attribute of human nature. What he and his descendants did not realize is that rather than discovering and then exploiting a fact about human nature, they were *creating* a fact about human nature.

This alteration of human nature doesn't happen all at once, like the flip of a switch. People enter occupations with a variety of aspirations aside from their pay. Then, they discover that their work is structured so that most of those aspirations will be unmet. Over time, they either lose the aspirations or leave the work. As this process continues, later generations of employees don't even have the aspirations. Compensation becomes the measure of all that is possible from work, and when employees bargain, they bargain for improved compensation, since nothing else is on the table. When this process goes on for long enough, people become just the kind of creatures that Adam Smith thought they always were. Not everyone, of course. Witness the janitors and hairdressers I described earlier. But in impoverished working conditions, workers like these are regarded as extraordinary, even heroic.

Even Smith seemed to realize the dynamic process by which the work people did change who they were. He said that someone subjected to the conditions of assembly line work "naturally . . . and generally *becomes* as stupid and ignorant as it is possible for a human creature to be." But, what sort of person was the assembly-line worker before he *became* stupid and ignorant? Here is Smith telling us that people are shaped by the image of what work requires of them (see Schwartz, 2015, for a detailed discussion of this process).

The truth is that we are not money-driven by nature. Studies show that people are *less* likely to help load a couch into a van when you offer a small payment than when you don't because the offer of pay makes their task a commercial transaction rather than a favor to another human being (Heyman & Ariely, 2004). And people are *less* likely to agree to have a nuclear waste site in their community when you offer to pay them because the offer of compensation undermines their sense of civic duty (Frey & Oberholzer-Gee, 1997).

If people were always paid to load couches into vans and always paid off for their acquiescence to a social policy, the notions of doing favors and honoring civic duty would soon vanish. Money does not tap into the essence of human motivation so much as transform it. When money is made the measure of all things, it becomes the measure of all things.

To be sure, people should be adequately compensated for their work. Recent efforts across the United States to achieve a significant increase in the minimum wage represent real social progress. But in securing such victories for working people, we should not lose sight of the aspiration to make work the kind of activity people embrace, rather than the kind of activity they shun.

How can we do this? By giving employees more of a voice in how they do their jobs. By making sure we offer them opportunities to learn and grow. And by encouraging them to suggest improvements to the production process and listening to what they say.

But most important, we need to emphasize the ways in which an employee's work makes other people's lives at least a little bit better (and, of course, to make sure that it actually *does* make people's lives a little bit better). The hospital janitor is washing floors but also eases the pain and suffering of patients and their families. The fast-food worker is lifting some of the burden from a harried parent.

Clifford Geertz (1973) once said of human beings that we are "unfinished animals." What he meant is that human beings are not fully formed by their biological endowment. They come into the world a certain way, but their experience in the world then molds them. In a world in which most workers get little or no satisfaction from their work, we risk creating a human nature that matches Adam Smith's assumptions. What modern workplaces show is that people *can* be the kinds of organisms Smith envisioned, but not that they *must* be.

The question we should face as a culture is just what kind of human nature we want to help create. Do we want to help create a human nature in which people seek and find meaning, engagement, and satisfaction from their work, or do we want to create a human nature where work is all about the paycheck? We should not lose sight of the aspiration to make work the kind of activity people embrace, rather than the kind of activity they shun.

The COVID-19 pandemic offers some modest reason for hope. Early in the pandemic, people showed deep appreciation for the efforts of "essential workers" who made it possible for the rest of us to live some semblance of normal lives. We applauded healthcare professionals who left work every day sad and exhausted but then went back the next day to save lives and ease suffering. And we applauded delivery drivers, shopkeepers, and restaurant workers who procured goods, stocked shelves, prepared meals, and found a way to get us access to these goods while keeping us safe. For a moment, these workers, who make life livable while mostly being invisible to the rest of us, were given the attention and appreciation they deserved. Will this appreciation last as COVID recedes and life goes back to normal? I hope so.

References

Frey, B. S., & Oberholzer-Gee, F. (1997). The cost of price incentives: An empirical analysis of motivational crowding out. *American Economic Review, 87*, 746–755.

Geertz, C. (1973). *The interpretation of cultures*. Basic Books.

Heyman, J., & Ariely, D. (2004). Effort for payment: A tale of two markets. *Psychological Science, 15*, 787–793.

Pfeffer, J. (1998). *The human equation*. Harvard Business School Press.

Rose, M. (2004). *The mind at work: Valuing the intelligence of the American worker*. Viking.

Schwartz, B. (2015). *Why we work*. Simon & Schuster.

Smith, A. (1937). *The wealth of nations*. Modern Library (original work published 1776).

Wrzesniewski, A., & Dutton, J. E. (2001). Crafting a job: Revisioning employees as active crafters of their work. *The Academy of Management Review, 26*, 179–201.

6 Great Resignation or Great Transformation?

The Shifting Landscape of Work

Belle Liang, Brenna Lincoln, and Betty S. Lai

At the writing of this essay, the global COVID-19 pandemic has surged on for nearly two years. Among the challenges posed by the pandemic is a growing labor shortage. According to the U.S. Bureau of Labor Statistics, a record-breaking number of people in the United States have quit their jobs since April 2021. This "Great Resignation," largely led by members of Generation Z (Gen-Z; anyone born between 1997 and 2012; under 25 years old in 2022) and millennials (anyone born between 1981 and 1996), has sparked a national conversation about the nature of work, the work ethic of younger generations, and the social safety net (Gerber, 2021).

Generation Z Leading the Great Resignation Movement

Nearly 4.5 million U.S. workers quit their jobs in November 2021 (Bureau of Labor Statistics, 2022). Over a third of all enterprise workers reported that they intend to leave their current jobs within a year, and of these workers, nearly two-thirds said they were motivated to quit simply to gain more freedom to work when and where they want to work (Liu, 2021).

While there are older cohorts of workers who are leaving due to concerns about their health vulnerability and who have challenges getting back into the workforce, the numbers are higher for the youngest members of the workforce. More than half of Gen-Z workers were planning to quit their jobs in response to the pandemic. Of all workers, this youngest group was the most dissatisfied with their jobs. They were especially disgruntled with pressures to work within traditional work structures such as the 9–5 time frame. One in four reported that they work best outside this time frame, and nearly 50% said they often work from bed.

Pundits have offered deficit-oriented explanations for the Great Resignation, such as a lack of resilience, loyalty, and commitment in younger generations. Yet, counter-evidence demonstrates that young people are increasingly purposeful and engaged in leadership in their communities and countries. A new United Nations (UN) strategy for addressing the pandemic suggests that even as they quit their traditional day jobs, young people

DOI:10.4324/9781003272397-8

are not just sitting around while the world is suffering. They are seeking work that is personally meaningful, including social advocacy. This generation is among the most affected by the socio-economic impacts of the COVID-19 response. For example, more than 87% of students around the globe are not able to attend school. Young women and girls have been at risk of increased domestic violence during the pandemic. Young people are especially at risk of mental health problems. They represent more than a third of the world's migrants and refugees who also suffer disproportionately from COVID-19. They will take the biggest hit from a global recession (United Nations, 2020).

Far from being passive victims, young people are serving as caretakers, returning to school, engaging in unpaid work, including global responses to the pandemic (e.g., serving on the frontlines as health workers and advancing health and safety as researchers, activists, innovators, and communicators). In this essay, we explore the motivations and life purpose of young people during this crisis. Lessons learned may be useful for employers and decision-makers as they partner with young employees to create a more dignified and socially just workplace and world for the future.

Purpose in Life

Having a sense of purpose or long-term aspirations to accomplish something that both is personally meaningful and constitutes a contribution to the world is a powerful developmental asset among young adults. Purposeful young people have increased well-being, hope, and even longevity. They are more resilient in the face of adversities, including COVID-19. For example, Gen-Z college graduates engaged in career and purpose planning experienced reduced pandemic-associated employment uncertainty.

Not only are purposeful young people more adaptable in weathering the pandemic, but they also seem to be coping with pandemic adversity by searching for new sources of meaning. In a qualitative study by Todorova and colleagues (2021) on the pandemic experiences of 1,600 respondents (mostly millennials) across the globe, four major themes emerged: the presence of others; rediscovering oneself; the meaning of daily life; and rethinking societal and environmental values. These meaning-making pathways map closely to research in our lab on the 4 Ps of purpose (the characteristics of purposeful youth): people, propensity, passion, and prosociality (Liang et al., 2016). These parallels seem to suggest that Millennials and Gen-Z cohorts may be making meaning and finding purpose through their attempts to navigate the global pandemic.

A willingness to take risks for the sake of personal transformation is integral in purpose development. So, it's not surprising that young people have left their traditional jobs in search of meaningful work. Known as culture creators, Gen-Z'ers seek meaningful jobs that enable them to live out their authentic values. They leave companies with values that conflict with their own values. For instance, organizations in the oil and gas industry have lost scores of their younger employees who have migrated to other industries.

In this light, the Great Resignation might be evidence of a resilient growth response and attempts at meaning-making in the face of adversity. Rather than assuming that they are lazy and disengaged, we might see Gen-Z workers as leading a "great migration" toward authentic and meaningful work. Young people are searching for meaningful work at a time when their help is greatly needed in the areas of health, equity, and innovation.

Some concrete examples of ways companies and organizations could use the 4 Ps to build a better workplace for this new generation of employees is to engage them in meaningful reflection on problems that affect them and work they are motivated to tackle. Questions for reflection include: *What problem upsets me the most? What grabs my attention? Who is working to address this problem? and What are some opportunities for joining these people to do the work I care about?*

Moreover, workplaces can aim to support employees to pursue work that aligns with their purpose guided by the 4 Ps: (1) building supportive mentoring and peer communities where shared purposeful goals are identified, pursued, and celebrated together (people); (2) engaging their employees to "purpose craft" by identifying ways to better align their jobs with strengths and skills (propensity), (3) considering workers' interests and sparks in purpose crafting (passion); and (4) adopting Gen-Z values around societal and environmental challenges and working toward alleviating them (prosocial orientation).

Simultaneous Global Challenges

Despite hopes for a return to life as we knew it, research on disasters outside of the current pandemic indicates that "returns to normal" are mythical and slow. Underscoring this point, societal turbulence has continued amidst this pandemic: our healthcare system is collapsing under the weight of COVID-19. Climate change is increasing the intensity and frequency of weather-related disasters. Education costs are soaring out of control. Unchecked monopoly power of large technology companies threatens our freedom, privacy, and democracy. And systemic racism fortifies policies that perpetuate health, housing, education, and policing disparities.

These relentless global jolts are just the kind of crises that young people find to be worthy causes. As these crises continue unmitigated, more companies are rising to solve them, creating meaningful vocational opportunities for young people. For example:

- Costa Rica transformed their world-class healthcare system by putting public health at the center (Gawande, 2021). This model is likely to be adapted by the United States. *Now would be an excellent time to start a career in Public Health.*

- Guild Education, an organization that partners with companies to provide free access to higher education, is now valued at nearly 4 billion dollars (Wilson, 2021). NYU Professor Scott Galloway raised 30 million dollars to create a more affordable business education to rival six-figure MBA programs (Loizos, 2021). *Now would be an excellent time to start a career focused on reducing the cost of higher education.*
- Run for Something (n.d.) has recruited over 70,000 young people to run for local political office in every single state in America. *Now would be an excellent time to start a career in politics.*
- Ceres manages a network of investors overseeing 37 trillion dollars in assets that are focused on sustainable investment practices (Ceres, n.d.). *Now would be an excellent time to start a career in sustainability.*

Resources and opportunities are being funneled to meet the most critical needs on the planet. An effective response needs to be multidimensional, coordinated, swift, and decisive. It needs to be the result of strong political leadership and buy-in of the population. It needs to foster public trust; be focused on human values; and be supported by solid institutions, technical skills, and financial resources. Every person needs to play their part in the response. No individual country can tackle the global problems alone. Indeed, these times of crisis and adversity have sparked passion and determination in so many Gen-Z-ers and Millennials who are drawn to meaningful work, above all else. Workplaces can be places that nurture and fan these flames.

References

Bureau of Labor Statistics, U.S. Department of Labor. (2022, January 6). Number of quits at all-time high in November 2021. *The Economics Daily.* https://www.bls.gov/opub/ted/2022/number-of-quits-at-all-time-high-in-november-2021.htm.

Ceres. (n.d.). Ceres investor network on climate risk and sustainability. *Ceres.* Retrieved January 31, 2022, from www.ceres.org/networks/ceres-investor-network.

Gawande, A. (2021, August 23). Costa Ricans live longer than we do. What's the secret? *The New Yorker.* www.newyorker.com/magazine/2021/08/30/costa-ricans-live-longer-than-we-do-whats-the-secret.

Gerber, T. (2021, August, 26). Work-life balance in jeopardy: New Adobe research reveals the impact COVID-19 has had on our time. *Adobe Blog.* https://blog.adobe.com/en/publish/2021/08/26/new-research-from-adobe-document-cloud-shows-how-pandemic-is-changing-our-relationship-with-time.

Liang, B., White, A., Mousseau, A. M. D., Hasse, A., Knight, L., Berado, D., & Lund, T. J. (2016). The four P's of purpose among college bound students: People, propensity, passion, prosocial benefits. *The Journal of Positive Psychology, 12*(3), 281–294. https://doi.org/10.1080/17439760.2016.1225118.

Liu, J. (2021, June 9). 4 Million people quit their jobs in April, sparked by confidence they can find better work. *CNBC.* www.cnbc.com/2021/06/09/4-million-people-quit-their-jobs-in-april-to-find-better-work.html.

Loizos, C. (2021, March 11). Professor Scott Galloway just raised $30 million for an online school that upskills managers fast. *TechCrunch*. https://techcrunch.com/2021/03/11/professor-scott-galloway-just-raised-30-million-for-an-online-school-that-upskills-managers-fast/.

Run for Something. (n.d.). *Run for Something*. Retrieved January 31, 2022, from https://runforsomething.net/.

Todorova, I., Albers, L., Aronson, N., Baban, A., Benyamini, Y., Cipolletta, S., . . . Zlatarska, A. (2021). "What I thought was so important isn't really that important": International perspectives on making meaning during the first wave of the COVID-19 pandemic. *Health Psychology and Behavioral Medicine, 9*(1), 830–857. https://doi.org/10.1080/21642850.2021.1981909.

United Nations. (2020). Shared responsibility, global solidarity: Responding to the socio-economic impacts of COVID-19. *United Nations*. Retrieved December 15, 2021, from www.un.org/sites/un2.un.org/files/sg_report_socio-economic_impact_of_covid19.pdf.

Wilson, A. (2021, June, 2). Guild education triples its valuation to $3.75 billion with new $150 million raise. *Forbes*. www.forbes.com/sites/alexandrawilson1/2021/06/02/guild-education-triples-its-valuation-to-375-billion-with-new-150-million-raise/.

Changing Nature of Work

7 Redefining the Health of the Labor Market

Worker Flourishing as a New Index

Blake A. Allan

As most of us experience in our daily lives, the world is rapidly changing. New technology is constantly arising; the world is becoming more interconnected, competitive, and fast paced; economic and political instability are increasingly the norm; and a global pandemic has ravaged the world for two years. These forces have particularly affected the labor market, in terms of both workers constantly adapting to maintain employment and the steady erosion of the quality of work. In this context, workers are in a constant state of precarity. They must routinely update their skills and compete in a labor market where precarious work—work that is insecure, poorly paid, and provides little power to workers—is common. These conditions are contributing to the current mental health crisis, with people unsure if they will be able to meet their basic needs and achieve some level of stability. Underlying these changes in the United States is a culture of individualism, competition, neoliberalism, and a focus on economic growth, which create metrics to assess the health of the labor market (e.g., unemployment rate and GDP growth) that fail to improve the lives of workers. The current economic context during the COVID pandemic, which has placed more power in the hands of workers, provides an opportunity to focus on different metrics to guide decisions and development. These metrics should center on worker flourishing, composed of decent work, human rights and dignity, social justice and equity, a strong social safety net, well-being and mental health, fulfilling work, and worker voice and protections.

Precarious work is not new in the United States. Before labor movements in the 20th century and legislation protecting workers from abuse, precarious work was similarly the norm. Precarious work has also been the norm for marginalized and vulnerable populations who were excluded from laws protecting workers against abuse and unfair treatment. For example, immigrants and people of color—particularly Black Americans with a history of enslavement, segregation, and systemic oppression—have long been forced to work in poor-quality jobs with little pay. However, there is currently a unique proliferation of precarious work in the United States and other regions of the world, and vulnerable populations have experienced the worst of this trend (Kalleberg, 2018).

DOI:10.4324/9781003272397-10

The consequences of this situation for workers are predictable. Workers' mental health is eroding while they experience chronic uncertainty and unsafety, dehumanization, deprivation of their dignity and human rights, and poorer physical and mental health (Allan et al., 2021). Precarious work also disrupts people's sense of self, not allowing a stable work identity to develop over time as people move toward accomplishing their goals. As a result, precarious workers are angry at having their aspirations thwarted and become alienated from their work and society, which results in political instability and vulnerability to populist movements (Kalleberg, 2018).

Among postindustrial nations, precarious work is particularly prevalent in the United States. In recent decades, the social safety net has steadily eroded, wage growth has not kept pace with economic growth or cost-of-living increases, and anti-union legislation has damaged the ability of workers to bargain collectively. This has not occurred in a vacuum. The United States has a long history of rugged individualism shaped by the myth of meritocracy and inaccurate beliefs about upward social mobility. This cultural context has allowed neoliberalism to flourish, which has further moved policies toward privatization, deregulation, an erosion of the social safety net, and increased tax benefits for corporations and wealthy elites.

Because of the neoliberal context of the United States, the dominant metrics the government and media use to indicate the health of the economy and labor market include factors like the number of jobs created, the unemployment rate, GDP growth, wage growth, stock market indices, and the consumer price index. The implicit assumption is that such factors are proxies for the flourishing of workers and society at large, but this is clearly not always the case. For example, GDP growth has certainly lifted many people out of poverty, but it becomes increasingly less relevant as wealth inequality increases. The unemployment rate is similarly important for well-being given that unemployment is a major determinant of poorer mental health; however, *under*employment—employment below the standards of full employment (e.g., involuntary part-time, involuntary temporary work, and poverty wage employment)—is underreported, and underemployed workers often experiencing similar distress to those who are unemployed (e.g., Allan et al., 2020).

In this context, the COVID-19 pandemic has changed workers' relationships to work. The Great Resignation has demonstrated that workers are tired of poor treatment, dangerous working conditions, low wages, and few benefits. And true to society's metrics, this is called a labor shortage instead of a shortage of good jobs. However, the labor movement typified by the Great Resignation offers an opportunity to create new metrics for individuals, organizations, and policymakers to use for work-related decisions—metrics that prioritize human flourishing and mental health.

In 2008, Bhutan famously included Gross National Happiness (GNH) as a core goal of the government, with nine measured domains—psychological well-being, a balance in time use, cultural diversity and resilience, protection

of the environment, community strengths, good governance, quality education, physical and mental health, and good living standards (Ura et al., 2012).
Each domain is assessed with multiple objective and subjective measures that
inform public policy and intervention (Ura et al., 2012). Therefore, GNH
represents an index of human flourishing. However, in the current work
context, a new concept is critically needed—*worker flourishing*: the holistic
health, functioning, and vitality of workers and the labor market. Worker
flourishing provides a goal that is drastically different from the dominant
metrics currently representing the health of the labor market.

Figure 7.1 depicts the seven domains of worker flourishing, which overlap but represent measurable and converging constructs that define the
index. The first component is *human rights and dignity*, which are critical
to worker flourishing. The United Nations Declaration of Human Rights
(United Nations, 1948) clearly articulated the basic rights to employment,
fair work conditions, protection against unemployment, pay equity, a living
wage, union membership, and time for rest and leisure. These aims are also

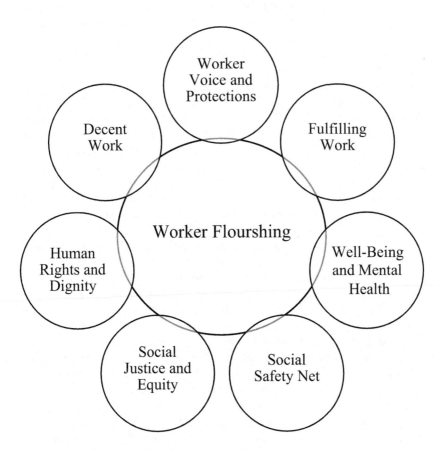

Figure 7.1 The seven domains of worker flourishing.

represented in Goal 8 of the 2030 United Nations Sustainable Development Goals, which includes worker protection and promoting safe and secure work for those with precarious work and other highly vulnerable populations, such as migrant workers (United Nations, 2022). Accordingly, the UN has indices to measure the strength of human rights protections within nations.

Building on this foundation, the International Labour Organization (ILO) created a *decent work* initiative aimed at promoting and measuring productive and sustainable work, social protections for workers, social dialogue among stakeholders, and workers' rights and freedoms (ILO, 2008). Building from this work, psychologists developed the measurable construct of decent work, which represents the basic standards for quality employment, such as a living wage, time for rest, access to healthcare, work that aligns with values, and freedom from harassment and abuse (Blustein et al., 2019). However, critical to maintaining human rights and decent work is having active *worker voice and protection*, which often occurs through collective bargaining. The rise of anti-union sentiment and legislation resulting in the decline in union participation has contributed to the rollback of gains for workers established in the late 20th century. Therefore, metrics such as union participation rates and employment protections for vulnerable workers are a key part of worker flourishing.

However, preserving human rights, decent work, and worker voice is insufficient if societies do not have a strong *social safety net* to help unemployed and precarious workers who need support. As the labor market rapidly transitions due to forces like automation, the exponential growth of technology, and globalization, workers will need robust employment insurance, skills training, housing and nutrition assistance, and other aid. Part of this is also removing unnecessary and harmful obstacles to accessing services and resources, such as work requirements. In summary, the strength of the social safety net, particularly with respect to work-related programs, is another critical part of worker flourishing.

To flourish, workers also need a fair opportunity structure and equal treatment in the labor market, making *social justice and equity* another key component of worker flourishing. As noted previously, marginalized workers have long experienced precarious work, and the pandemic has exposed and exacerbated this inequity. Therefore, worker flourishing must liberate workers from structural oppression in the form of racism, classism, heterosexism, transphobia, ableism, and other systemic forces. These forces create inequities such as income and wealth inequality, pay inequity, racial wealth gaps, employment discrimination, the unfair distribution of good jobs, educational disparities, and many other outcomes that represent inequity in the United States.

Finally, integral to worker flourishing is the subjective experience of well-being. In the work domain, *fulfilling work* means a job that brings meaningfulness, positive emotional experiences, work engagement, job satisfaction, and other experiences. Outside of work, *mental health and well-being* capture both the presence of positive experiences and emotions (e.g., life satisfaction, meaning in life, and self-determination) and the absence of serious mental health concerns that can derive from poor-quality work (e.g., major depression). Ultimately, other aspects of worker flourishing are only meaningful if they promote a fulfilling life.

In summary, worker flourishing is an index that can be the focus of reporting in the media and guide interventions across many domains and levels, including policy and community programs. At the individual level, workers can consider the domains of worker flourishing to direct collective action for change, facilitate exploration of their values, and evaluate organizations and job opportunities. In addition, organizations can adopt these domains as central priorities and outcomes, which has wide-ranging implications for social accountability and promoting stakeholder interests. For example, improving worker flourishing directly benefits workers and contributes to a more sustainable and healthy society; however, it can also directly affect the productivity, creativity, commitment, and citizenship of employees. In conclusion, while providing a comprehensive overview of how different entities can use and measure the domains of worker flourishing was beyond this essay's scope, this essay provides a starting place to refocus on the outcomes that matter to workers and begin building indices that can lead to a better future.

References

Allan, B. A., Autin, K. L., & Wilkins-Yel, K. G. (2021). Precarious work in the 21st century: A psychological perspective. *Journal of Vocational Behavior, 126.* https://doi.org/10.1016/j.jvb.2020.103491.

Allan, B. A., Kim, T., Liu, T. Y., & Deemer, E. D. (2020). Moderators of involuntary part-time work and life satisfaction: A latent deprivation approach. *Professional Psychology: Research and Practice, 51*(3), 257–267. https://doi.org/10.1037/pro0000268.

Blustein, D. L., Kenny, M. E., Di Fabio, A., & Guichard, J. (2019). Expanding the impact of the psychology of working: Engaging psychology in the struggle for decent work and human rights. *Journal of Career Assessment, 27*(1), 3–28.

International Labour Organization. (2008). *Measurement of decent work based on guidance received at the Tripartite Meeting of Experts on the Measurement of Decent Work.* www.ilo.org/wcmsp5/groups/public-dgreports-integration/documents/meetingdocument/wcms_115402.pdf.

Kalleberg, A. L. (2018). *Precarious lives: Job insecurity and well-being in rich democracies.* John Wiley & Sons.

United Nations. (1948). *Universal declaration of human rights.* www.un.org/en/about-us/universal-declaration-of-human-rights.

United Nations. (2022). *The 17 goals.* https://sdgs.un.org/goals.

Ura, K., Alkire, S., Zangmo, T., & Wangdi, K. (2012). *An extensive analysis of GNH index.* Centre for Bhutan Studies.

8 Educating Discerning Jobseekers and Empowered Employees

Nancy Hoffman

In the fall of 2021, I watched the Great Resignation with awe. Why in the greatest crisis in a century were people leaving their jobs in such high numbers? You might think that the need for stability would have ruled when so much else was uncertain. Some reasons had little to do with the quality of jobs: childcare, layoffs, and business closures, contracting COVID. Overwhelmingly, however, many took economic risks out of pure, emotionally raw alienation from what they were doing so many hours a day. And the break gave discontented workers time to imagine a better way to work and live.

The turmoil of the pandemic created a kind of a reverse of cloud cuckoo land where things that seemed impossible have already happened. So why not do the unthinkable and quit? In the film *Network* (Lumet, 1976), the TV commentator, Howard Beale, ranted on air to the world to open their windows and shout: "I'm as mad as hell, and I'm not going to take this anymore!" Workers up and down the pay scale were at that moment as 2022 began.

One group of quitters did "the great reshuffle," as the chief economist of LinkedIn called it, moving from one well-paying sector to another. But hotel maids, baristas, restaurant waitstaff, retail workers, food workers, cleaners, and home health aides had the highest quit rates (Zagorsky, 2022). They were the organizers of walkouts, strikes, and protests with good reason. As their bosses worked remotely from second homes, they put their lives at risk serving others. As a December piece in the *New Yorker* by Lizzie Widdicombe noted: "Covid-19 appears to have lit a match beneath at least a decade's worth of late-stage-capitalist tinder." Yes, COVID highlighted what many workers had endured for years—poor pay, negligible or no benefits, disrespect, lack of safety, and no way to move up or out. America runs on bad jobs. This statistic should be in every policymaker's head: 44% of American workers are living on an income of less than $40,000 a year for a family of three (Harvard Gazette, 2022).

Unfortunately, as of March 2022, the signs were that many dissatisfied workers would be returning to jobs the same or only marginally better than those they quit. A Philadelphia Fed report notes that "the recovery through

DOI:10.4324/9781003272397-11

June 2021 was characterized by a strong rebound in openings for the same types of jobs lost during the recession: lower-wage jobs and jobs requiring lower levels of formal education" (Wardrip, 2022).

I'm an educator, not an economist. These data turn my attention to community colleges, the country's most extensive engine of workforce development. The motivating goal of community colleges is to open the door to economic mobility. While a small subset of students transfers and attains a BA, most do not. Unfortunately, too many community college students believe that a two-year degree alone will boost them into a good job. That is not the case. For example, about 40% of community college graduates end up with a liberal arts degree that has value little better than a high school diploma in the labor market (Schneider & Sigelman, 2018).

Community colleges increasingly recognize that they must do more to prepare their graduates for good jobs that will endure in an uncertain labor market. Community college students, average age 28, are at a critical juncture when they arrive. As a report from the Harvard Business School notes,

> if you're not on a pathway that has some prospect for advancement and economic security by your mid- to late 20s, the deck will get stacked higher and higher against you. Between 18–24 or 25, it's very, very important that you get launched onto something that supports a decent lifestyle, family formation, economic security.
>
> (Harvard Gazette, 2022)

In the old days, workers learned their rights and improved their lot through unions. In addition, many workers supported families quite well with only a high school diploma. Now, union membership continues to decline with only 10.3% of workers unionized. And today's jobs demand more a complex and fluid set of skills than what most learn in high school. College is the primary place to acquire those skills and prepare for the future of work.

Unfortunately, while most students go to college to prepare for a career, too few graduate as discerning jobseekers and activist employees. This absence of labor market savvy is especially damaging for low-income students who lack the connections and social networks that can move them from a low-wage job to a career. Once hired, these students may not feel entitled to be activists—to speak up at work about improvements needed or to call out outright injustices.

What should a discerning jobseeker know? First, she must know the importance of networks in finding appropriate openings. Job description in hand, she can assess and ask questions about benefit packages, flexible hours, and sick and family leave policies. Second, she is also knowledgeable about less tangible signs of job quality like internal training and advancement opportunities, verifiable commitments to diversity, and even less tangible, workplace culture featuring respectful relationships within supervisory structures. Discerning jobseekers also know that if they are Black, Latinx, or working class, they face barriers and must be armed to address them. They are aware of how hiring managers use vague negatives such as "she may not fit" as proxies to disguise discrimination and racism.

College career service offices today help with resumes, cover letters, and interview prep—the basics. But some are doing more: creating career navigation systems and hiring career navigators—professionals in charge of assisting students with career pathways that take them into the future and advance their careers post-graduation. The most innovative community colleges are figuring out how to make students' career preparation everyone's responsibility.

One early innovative initiative in career navigation was developed at Guttman Community College (City University of New York). Guttman's year-long course, Ethnographies of Work (EOW), puts learning about work at the center of the curriculum rather than leaving it to career service offices alone. In EOW, students study theoretical and applied contexts of work as well as observe weekly in diverse workplaces and take notes as fledgling ethnographers. Drawing on lessons from EOW, Bunker Hill Community College in Boston has developed an elegant approach to integrating EOW across the institution. As of this writing, 37 BHCC faculty infuse work-focused ethnographic study into their courses. In addition, incoming students take a first-year seminar that uses EOW as an organizing tool for students to investigate their work values and potential career paths.

Along with understanding how to find and use labor market information, the nitty-gritty of benefits, and how to evaluate career advancement and training opportunities, students should understand the following topics to become successful jobseekers and employees. Knowing these things can be vital to moving out of poverty. These topics are also the substance of liberal arts education.

- *Why do people work?* The answer appears self-evident—to earn a living. Yes, but as Blustein (2019) argues work at best can fulfill human needs "for survival and power," for "social connection," and for "self-determination." Similarly, the Good Jobs Institute drawing on Maslow's hierarchy of needs notes that quality jobs fulfill needs for belonging, achievement, recognition, meaningfulness, and personal growth. Affluent students from professional families feel entitled to fulfillment at work. But working-class students generally see work as to be endured to earn a living. Community colleges help students build confidence that they too can expect a measure of fulfillment and purposefulness from work.

- *Race, class, and gender in the labor market.* Everyone encounters obstacles or bumps in the road to a career; individuals take these on with varying degrees of success. Institutional or systemic *barriers* disproportionately affect people of color and those experiencing poverty; these are systemic, often intangible, and not subject to individual solutions (McGillen et al., 2019). These barriers often hinge on a hiring manager or employer's assessment of soft skills. This is why students need to understand that skills are socially constructed by those in power and determine workplace norms and expectations. Beliefs about skills are operationalized in job requirements and in the "blink" judgment of hiring managers.

- *Networking, building social capital.* It's "I met this guy who knew this woman who was a VP at the place I wanted to work." In 1973, Mark Granovetter (1974) showed how in the job market "influence, information, and mobility opportunities are diffused between groups with different places in the social hierarchy." Who you know higher up in the labor market has become even more important than when information about jobs is passed by word of mouth. Armed with knowledge about how social networks function, and at best, placed in an internship, job shadow, or other situation where they can meet potential employers, community college students are better positioned to make the leap into a good job.

An additional set of topics addresses the issue of fulfillment or satisfaction at work. These come from a scan of new "employee experience" technologies that aim to help young employees Thrive@Work (Swartsel et al., 2021). While most workers cite the following qualities as determining their attitude toward their work, community college students in particular may need encouragement to expect these benefits at work.

Relationships

Are there people at this company—my peers, my manager, and other colleagues—who care about me as a person and make the effort to build authentic, trusting relationships with me? Who can I turn to for information, advice, and guidance?

Agency

Do I feel a sense of ownership over my job and responsibilities, and do I have the skills, tools, and resources I need to carry them out effectively? Do I have opportunities and supports to more fully develop those skills, including through effective coaching and direction from my manager?

Purpose

Am I making a difference? Is my company—and am I—working to address challenges or seek opportunities that are meaningful for me, for my community, and for the world? Can I be an agent of change and social impact here?

The aforementioned topics are examples, but the bigger point that I hope I have made here is that the narrative, "go to college, get a degree, move into the middle class" doesn't work today. And educators, policymakers, and young adults themselves must act on the new reality.

References

Blustein, D. L. (2019). *The importance of work in an age of uncertainty: The eroding work experience in America*. Oxford University Press.

Granovetter, M. (1974). *Getting a job: A study of contacts and careers*. University of Chicago Press.

Harvard Gazette. (2022). *Helping trapped low-wage workers, employers struggling to fill spots*. https://news.harvard.edu/gazette/story/2022/01/helping-trapped-low-wage-workers-employers-struggling-to-fill-spots/.

Lumet, S.(1976). *Network* [film]. Metro-Goldwyn-Mayer.

McGillen, G., Flores, L., & Seaton, G. (2019). Work-related barriers experienced by low—income people of color and indigenous individuals. In N. Hoffman & M. L. Collins (Eds.), *Teaching students about the world of work: A challenge to post-secondary educators* (pp. 113–131). Harvard Education Press.

Schneider, M., & Sigelman, M. (2018, January). *Saving the Associate of Arts Degree*. www.aei.org/wp-content/uploads/2018/01/Saving-the-Associate-of-Arts-Degree.pdf.

Swartsel, A., Ndiaye, M., & Roberts, L. (2021, March). *Thrive@Work*. www.jff.org/what-we-do/impact-stories/jfflabs-acceleration/thrivework-market-scan/.

Wardrip, K. (2022, January). *A moment of opportunity: The COVID-Era job market for noncollege workers*. www.philadelphiafed.org/-/media/frbp/assets/community-development/reports/a-moment-of-opportunity-report-final.pdf.

Zagorsky, J. L. (2022, January). *The 'great resignation': Historical data and a deeper analysis show it's not as great as screaming headlines suggest*. https://theconversation.com/the-great-resignation-historical-data-and-a-deeper-analysis-show-its-not-as-great-as-screaming-headlines-suggest-174454.

9 Re-Building Hopefulness— Co-Constructing Work and Careers in Post-Pandemic Hong Kong

Seung-Ming Alvin Leung

The COVID-19 pandemic started in Hong Kong in January 2020 when COVID-19 was still relatively unknown around the world. In response to the first outbreak, citizens of Hong Kong had their first taste of the "new normal." There were several additional outbreaks in 2020 and 2021 that were effectively contained. Consistent with the approach taken by China, the Hong Kong government adapted a "zero-COVID" policy that translated into aggressive contact tracing, tight border control, and strict quarantine measures. These measures have kept a low COVID-19 infection and mortality rate allowing citizens to maintain a "restricted" regular lifestyle. The "zero-COVID" aspiration collapsed during the Omicron outbreak in the first quarter of 2022 when daily positive cases escalated into the thousands and the healthcare system was overwhelmed. Strict social distancing measures and remote work and learning were re-instituted. The cycles of outbreaks and prolonged infection control measures have caused citizens to feel helpless, exhausted, and disconnected from the rest of the world. There was a sense of hopelessness and that the pre-pandemic way of life will never return.

The COVID-19 pandemic was preceded by a large-scale social unrest that was unprecedented in the history of Hong Kong. The unrest started as a social response to a proposed "Fugitive Offenders and Mutual Legal Assistance in Criminal Matters Legislation (Amendment) Bill 2019" (or known as the Extradition Bill). The protests started in June 2019 and continued into mid-January 2020, right before the start of the COVID-19 pandemic and the introduction of social distance restrictions. The protests started peacefully but evolved into violent encounters between protesters and the police. The long duration of the unrest and sharp social divisions took a heavy toll on the emotional and social well-being of Hong Kong citizens. For instance, Ni et al. (2020) reported that the prevalence of depression and PTSD increased to an alarming level during the social unrest.

The fatigue and helplessness evoked by the pandemic are shared globally, yet in Hong Kong, the intersections between the pandemic and several deep-rooted social problems behind the social unrest have greatly damaged the spirit of the society and have aggravated the psychosocial well-being of

DOI:10.4324/9781003272397-12

individuals. This essay aims to explore these intersections around the following concerns and themes: (a) social inequity and work, (b) sustainable work and work–life balance, and (c) work and mental well-being.

Decent Living: Social Inequity and Work

A recent report from Oxfam on social inequality in Hong Kong (Oxfam Hong Kong, 2018) suggested that Hong Kong has one of the widest resource gaps between the rich and the poor among developed nations, and in 2016, the size of the gap was the largest in 45 years. Property price has remained sky-high and unreachable. Poverty has the strongest impact on low-income workers, women, children, the elderly, and ethnic minorities. The resource gap has left those in the lower economic echelon, the marginalized, and a younger generation to feel forgotten and hopelessly behind. Indeed, many have attributed social inequity and the gaps in housing to be the major underlying causes of the waves of social unrest preceding the pandemic (e.g., Stevenson & Wu, 2019).

The pandemic escalated the economic division that has already divided the city. Social distancing measures have the largest impact on service-oriented industries and businesses. Many workers in these industries are low-wage earners who were struggling to meet ends even before the epidemic. During the pandemic, some lost their jobs, while many others were forced to put in extra work hours to accommodate a reduction of staff. Government stimulus measures to re-boot the economy could only provide marginal support to the poor and unemployed during the pandemic. Workers in service industries such as restaurants, public transportation, cleaning and hygienic services, retail, hospital and health, security, and construction have risked infection to ensure that our community was well-kept and supported. They were instrumental in maintaining our "zero-COVID" aspiration, yet they are likely to be struggling with day-to-day poverty and not having a decent place to live. This is not right and should not happen in an international city such as Hong Kong.

School closures and work-from-home arrangements have a lesser impact on those in the middle and upper classes because they have the digital equipment and social capital to navigate through the new requirements. In contrast, the poor and disadvantaged do not have sufficient resources and home space to support and monitor their children for remote learning. The pandemic has further reduced the social capital of families and children who are economically disadvantaged, making it more difficult for new generations to move upward. The aggravated poverty cycle could create additional long-term impacts (e.g., escalation of the resource gap) and social discontent threatening social progress.

Leaders from the public and private sectors should address the issue of social inequity fearlessly and find decent living solutions for workers and individuals who are supporting the mainstream society but are at the margins of economic resources. A vision to fight social inequity through investing public and private resources in our economically marginalized populations should be an urgent priority now and into the post-pandemic era.

Decent Work: Sustainable Work and Work–Life Balance

People of Hong Kong have been notorious for their long work hours and positive work ethics. In the Kisi's Global Work–Life Balance Index 2021 (www.getkisi.com/work-life-balance-2021), Hong Kong ranked first (among a list of 50 cities) as the most over-worked city, with close to 30% of workers putting in more than 48 hours a week. Relatedly, Hong Kong ranked 45th in work–life balance based on the domains of work intensity, society and institutions, city livability, and COVID-19 impact. In short, Hong Kong workers have been working very long hours, and they have had relatively little time for other life activities and roles. Such a lifestyle is not sustainable.

During the pandemic, some changes in attitude toward work–life balance might be taking place. First, a survey (Wong, 2020) conducted with workers from a number of industries and career roles on May 2020 soon after the first wave of the pandemic revealed that over 80% of workers preferred to work from home for one to two days weekly after the pandemic. The top three reasons given by respondents were having more time to rest, reducing work stress, and improving work–life balance. In addition, many respondents perceived their employers as supportive and positive about remote work, which was unavailable to most workers before the pandemic. Second, Chu et al. (2022) surveyed 500 full-time Hong Kong employees in September 2020 about their work-from-home experience during the pandemic. Workers felt that working from home reduced stress because it enhanced their work–life balance. Increased work–life balance promoted happiness and well-being which in turn increased productivity. These findings suggested that workers perceived work–life balance to be a major advantage of a work-from-home policy. Third, self-employment is becoming more popular in Hong Kong. Self-employment constituted about 6.4% of the workforce in 2019 (Hong, 2021) and was projected to be increasing. The pandemic might prompt more workers to pursue self-employment by choice. Self-employment does not always lead to improvements in work–life balance, but increased flexibility and autonomy could facilitate.

Ranking as the most overworked city around the globe should not be the goal of workers and employers in Hong Kong. COVID-19 showed that human lives are vulnerable, busy work might not be productive, and happiness and well-being are the foundation of good work and good life.

In our small, crowded, stressed-out city, let us re-tune our work and life to achieve a healthy balance. We could draw from the propositions on decent work (Duffy et al., 2016) which includes (a) having a safe work environment physically and interpersonally, (b) having reasonable work hours, (c) supporting family-friendly organizational values and practices, (d) providing adequate work compensation, and (e) providing adequate healthcare provisions. Decent work does not automatically lead to a better work–life balance, but it is a precursor. Along this line, government policies should proactively pursue social and legislative initiatives, such as defining maximum weekly work hours, strengthening family-friendly provisions in organizations to give workers more flexibility to care for family members, and assuring workers of equitable work compensations and benefits, especially for low-wage earners.

Decent Mental Health: Work and Well-Being

Understandably, when citizens were overworked and exhausted from catching up with the ever-increasing living standard, Hong Kong was not a happy city. In the 2021 happiness and well-being survey conducted by the Gallup World Poll (Helliwell et al., 2021), Hong Kong ranked 66th among a list of 95 countries, well behind many of her international peers. The social unrest and the long-lasting pandemic have added tremendous distress to individuals in all walks of the society. Zhao et al. (2020) compared the mental health status of Hong Kong citizens before (2016 and 2017) and during the pandemic (April 2021), and the results showed a large increase in the prevalence of stress-related disorders, depression, and anxieties. Results also showed that the elderly and the economically and educationally marginalized groups were most affected by stress from the pandemic. The authors declared that Hong Kong was in the midst of a mental health emergency requiring immediate interventions, especially among the marginalized.

The mental health concerns aggravated by the pandemic have to be addressed immediately to prepare individuals for recovery and renewal in the post-pandemic society. First, remedial and preventive interventions should be strengthened in scope and staff coverage to meet the needs of citizens, especially for marginalized and high-risk groups. Additional resources are needed to expand service providers (e.g., social workers, psychologists, and counselors) and service modes to reach out to potential clients in sub-communities and districts. Second, measures should be taken to address social disconnection. Whereas political divides could not be bridged easily, cultivating a society grounded in the principles of mutual respect, appreciation of diverse viewpoints, and upholding justice is a good starting point. We can discuss, share, and practice these principles in schools and organizations and in private and public settings. Building a post-pandemic social atmosphere that is fair, just, and open is instrumental in creating a mentally-healthy society and a workforce that is hopeful of the future that they are a part of.

Conclusions—Rebuilding Hopefulness

The pandemic is a watershed event globally and locally. Could Hong Kong and its citizens re-emerge from the abyss of the pandemic and re-ignite their vibrancy and vigor from the past few decades? Resource gaps, overworking, and mental wellness are urgent social issues that could not be tackled by business-as-usual approaches. The citizens of Hong Kong have to recognize the changes that have taken place and to re-invent their niches and uniqueness in the post-pandemic world through their renewed international understanding and know-how. Most importantly, they have to rebuild a sense of hopefulness with courage and compassion, reconcile and embrace differences, and see and believe that there are ways to reconstruct and co-construct an equitable, open, and global Hong Kong.

References

Chu, A. M. Y., Chan, T. W. C., & So, M. K. P. (2022). Learning from work-from-home issues during the COVID-19 pandemic: Balance speaks louder than words. *PLoS ONE, 17*(1), e0261969. https://doi.org/10.1371/journal.pone.0261969.

Duffy, R. D., Blustein, D. L., Diemer, M. A., & Autin, K. L. (2016). The psychology of working theory. *Journal of Counseling Psychology, 63*(2), 127–148. https://doi.org/10.1037/cou0000140.

Helliwell, J. F., Layard, R., Sachs, J. D., De Neve, J.-E., Aknin, L., & Wang, S. (2021). *World happiness report 2021*. Sustainable Development Solution Network. https://worldhappiness.report/ed/2021/.

Hong, J. (2021, September). Will the COVID-19 pandemic replace traditional employment with the "slashie" culture? *Hong Kong Global Service News, BOD Global*. Retrieved February 23, 2022, from www.bdo.global/en-gb/microsites/tax-news-letters/ges-news/september-2021-issue/hong-kong-will-the-covid-19-pandemic-replace-traditional-employment-with-the-slashie%E2%80%9D-culture.

Ni, M., Yao, X., Leung, K., Yau, C., Leung, C., Lun, P., . . . Leung, G. M. (2020). Depression and post-traumatic stress during major social unrest in Hong Kong: A 10-year prospective cohort study. *The Lancet, 395*(10220), 273–284. https://doi.org/10.1016/S0140-6736(19)33160-5.

Oxfam Hong Kong. (2018, October). *Hong Kong inequality report*. Retrieved February 3, 2022, from www.oxfam.org.hk/f/news_and_publication/16372/Oxfam_inequality%20report_Eng_FINAL.pdf.

Stevenson, A., & Wu, J. (2019, July 22). Tiny apartments and punishing work hours: The economic roots of Hong Kong's Protest. *The New York Times*. Retrieved February 3, 2022, from www.nytimes.com/interactive/2019/07/22/world/asia/hong-kong-housing-inequality.html.

Wong, H. K. A. (2020). *Over 80% of HK workers preferred to work from homes for 1 to 2 days per week when the coronavirus crisis is over.* Hong Kong Lingnam University. Retrieved February 23, 2022, from www.ln.edu.hk/research-and-impact/research-press-conferences/survey-findings-on-working-from-home-under-covid19.

Zhao, S. Z., Wong, J. Y. H., Luk, T. T., Wai, A. K. C., Lam, T. H., & Wang, M. P. (2020). Mental health crisis under COVID-19 pandemic in Hong Kong, China. *International Journal of Infectious Diseases, 100,* 431–433. https://doi.org/10.1016/j.ijid.2020.09.030.

10 The Changing Nature of Work and Lifestyle in Southeast Asia Post-Pandemic

Hsiu-Lan Shelley Tien

Since the onset of COVID-19 at the end of 2019, the Taiwan government has devoted considerable effort to keep people safe. People, in a conservative society under collectivism, followed strict precautions for pandemic prevention. However, the confirmed infected cases increased dramatically in mid-May 2021, which is almost a year after when other countries experienced the initial surge. The whole country was promoted to alert level III, which is the next to the highest warning level in times of crises. The schools, from kindergarten to university, shut down, and many commercial activities stopped for two months. The world of work shifted considerably during the past two years.

In the current essay, I present findings from an online survey conducted from October 2021 to November 2021 to understand Taiwanese students' experiences during the pandemic. The survey included the following two open-ended questions: (1) what career difficulties did you encounter in the past year under the influence of the COVID-19 pandemic? and (2) what kind of changes did you perceive and foresee regarding the transition from school to work?

Participants included 379 adults aged between 18 and 58 (M = 22.21, SD = 6.31), 123 men and 256 women. Of the participants, 84.66% were college students (n = 321), 1.32% were graduate students (n = 5), and 13.46% reported that they were currently working (n = 51). The remaining two people graduated and were seeking a job when the survey was conducted.

Difficulties Encountered

College students encountered a lot of difficulties during the COVID-19 pandemic. The students who graduated struggled to find a job; moreover, job opportunities were so limited that many of the participants indicated that they had no other option but to stay at home. The period as a "nibbler," which refers to graduates who depend on their parents because they cannot locate a job, was prolonged in Taiwan. Since many employers stopped

DOI:10.4324/9781003272397-13

hiring new staff members, job opportunities for new graduates diminished considerably. Some of the companies were reorganized and downsized, and the newly hired employees were laid off because of COVID-19, leaving college graduates frustrated in their search for a job.

Life Difficulties Encountered

One of the most common challenges was that people were afraid of dying (n = 86) from COVID-19. It was hard for young adults to believe that a healthy person could die in a few days after a diagnosis of COVID-related pneumonia. Some of the students (n = 6) were planning to travel or begin an exchange learning program but were forced to abandon the plans. Those who were in an exchange program abroad in different countries also decided to fly back home, because it provided them and their families a sense of safety and health. Family love and cohesion emerged naturally during this period.

During the pandemic, students and workers needed to stay at home or stay in the city where they attended school or worked. Some students wanted to go home but could not risk the trip. They feared that they might bring the coronavirus home and cause a family member to be sick, especially elderly parents. Participants also reported feeling uncomfortable and inconvenienced by the restrictions in attending social activities. A response to this sense of constriction was to create a new life mode wherein students sought to enrich their lives, mainly through virtual interactions.

Learning Obstacles

Of the 321 college students, 24 did not want to graduate (7.5%). Nine students indicated that they did not like the virtual learning mode and felt unable to adapt to online learning. At least three students indicated that they wanted to apply for an internship but the chances of locating an internship were slim. It was clear that participants perceived that learning opportunities shrank because of the COVID-19 pandemic.

Job Seeking Barriers

As far as the difficulties in job seeking, 95 out of 321 students indicated that it was very hard for them to find a job (29.60%). Some indicated that their income decreased because they were forced to cut back on their work hours or were laid off (n = 16). For example, many students worked as one-on-one English and Math tutors and were forced to quit their jobs. It was hard for these participants to find another new part-time job (n = 5). Since the availability of job opportunities decreased, the competition for jobs increased significantly. Participants indicated that this caused them to reconsider what their ideal job entailed. They believed that it was necessary to enrich themselves and expand their professional knowledge, but they did not know how to take the next step.

Coping Strategies

The data indicated the following four categories of coping strategies to overcome the academic and work barriers caused by COVID-19: self-preparation; future imagination; family support; and positive thinking.

Self-Preparation

Participants reflected on how to prepare to cope with the difficulties caused by COVID-19. Responses suggested that participants were not sure how long the pandemic would last, so they shifted to setting long-term goals. About one-third of the students in our study intended to apply for graduate school (n = 111, 34.58%). Some professors even encouraged them to pursue doctoral programs. In addition, some students perceived that the time spent seeking a job was prolonged in comparison to the previous few years (n = 97, 30.22%). For those who were unable to find a job, they compromised and tried to find a temporary job or a part-time job (n = 24, 7.48%). In this context, gig work appeared to be a viable option. Working schedules became more flexible, and individuals possessed some degree of autonomy in deciding what they wanted to do although it might not be able to yield a sustainable life.

Nine participants chose to study and prepare for a government job examination. Three chose to be self-employed. Seven participants indicated that they chose jobs that were not related to what they studied at university. Two students chose to stay in college and registered as fifth-year seniors. Some of the students lamented that they were born at a bad time. However, to cope with a hard time, they need to be well prepared to recognize any chances for future job opportunities.

Future Imagination

Future imagination is a kind of entrepreneurship mindset (Rosen, 2016). People might imagine what happens in the future through their past experiences (Schacter et al., 2007). However, the future won't directly replicate the past experiences. In our survey, three students indicated that passion and expectations were two important elements in preparing for this transition. On the other hand, three students indicated that they felt anxious and uncertain about the future. At my university, the Career Center and the Counseling Center provided activities to facilitate the students' positive thinking toward the future. The staff members utilized a variety of activities to support students via online activities after the two-month shutdown in May and June of 2021. Job fairs and job interviews were conducted virtually, and these activities increased students' sense of hope for their future. As a faculty member at the university, I found that the students and staff are getting used to hybrid services.

Family Support

It was mentioned in different studies and reports that COVID-19 evoked a lot of family conflicts, and even domestic abuse when members were forced to work at home (Bullinger et al., 2021; Fusar-Poli et al., 2021; Hwang et al., 2022; Labrum et al., 2022). In our survey, most participants were not married and the quarrels were mainly with parents and siblings. Since the time together at home increased, they were forced to communicate genuinely to relieve the strained relationship. There was no way to escape from the quarrel because they were staying at home and had much time to communicate genuinely. Some of the young adults who failed to find a job could only stay at home. These participants might be symbolized as "nibblers" and depend on their parents for living, which was very frustrating for them. However, if family members could reach a consensus and accept the inevitable crisis, they would be able to build family resilience together. Family support is so important for young adults.

Positive Thinking

Positive thinking is trying to see the best in other people and viewing the self in a positive light. People with positive thinking usually give themselves credit when good things happen (Seligman, 2006). Since it has been almost two years since the advent of the pandemic, the Centers for Disease Control and Prevention went on its press conference every afternoon. From my personal observation, people are getting used to the existence of coronavirus. In my university, some of the students believed that they have to accept what has happened and try a new life mode to cope with COVID-19. They need to live with COVID-19 peacefully. They wear masks, take courses online, exercise at home, meet people through video conference platforms, and create new ways to earn a living. Some of them work for food delivery services. Many of them muster the courage and advocate to serve as a teaching assistant to help professors in handling telecourses. Generally speaking, we found that many students tried their best to overcome the inevitable crisis and to generate a variety of ways to survive under the influence of the pandemic.

What Universities Can Do to Facilitate the School-to-Work Transition

During the pandemic, the Ministry of Education invested money and telecommunication resources for universities to expand electronic and computer equipment. The Career Center and Counseling Center applied and obtained permission from the government to conduct telecommunication services through video-conferencing platforms. The ethical standards for telepsychological services were established very quickly. The university counseling services and community counseling centers reopened for services remotely after they passed the professional ethical review and obtained permission to do online services.

The transitions from university to job market have been so difficult since the start of the pandemic. The career center staff needs to find solutions. Some of the responses to this crisis include reaching out to enterprises, companies, and alumni to increase job opportunities for graduates. The government also provides funding for graduates, encouraging them to create their own businesses.

Conclusion

As a citizen of Taiwan, my view is that the government has indeed done its best to prevent the epidemic. People do not like, but have adjusted to, wearing masks. Now the mask is a necessary habit, not only for preventing COVID-19 but also for preventing polluted air from automobiles and motorcycles. We can expect the urgent needs for mental health services to increase as a result of the emotional strain from the pandemic. The services could be conducted physically or in a virtual way, as is the case for academic learning. Since the students were used to online learning, we need to pay attention to the students' needs and responsibility in reshaping the learning environment and the work/life pattern.

References

Bullinger, L. R., Marcus, S., Reuben, K., Whitaker, D., & Self-Brown, S. (2021). Evaluating child maltreatment and family violence risk during the COVID-19 pandemic: Using a telehealth home visiting program as a conduit to families. *Infant Mental Health Journal, 43*(1), 143–158. https://doi.org/10.1002/imhj.21968.

Fusar-Poli, L., Surace, T., Meo, V., Patania, F., Avanzato, C., Pulvirenti, A., Aguglia, E., & Signorelli, M. S. (2021). Psychological well-being and family distress of Italian caregivers during the covid-19 outbreak. *Journal of Community Psychology, 50*(5), 2243–2259. https://doi.org/10.1002/jcop.22772.

Hwang, P., Ipekian, L., Jaiswal, N., Scott, G., Amirali, E. L., & Hechtman, L. (2022). Family functioning and mental wellbeing impairment during initial quarantining for the COVID-19 pandemic: A study of Canadian families. *Current Psychology: A Journal for Diverse Perspectives on Diverse Psychological Issues, 10*, 1–13. https://doi.org/10.1007/s12144-021-02689-1.

Labrum, T., Newhill, C., Simonsson, P., & Flores, A. T. (2022). Family conflict and violence by persons with serious mental illness: How clinicians can intervene during the COVID-19 pandemic and beyond. *Clinical Social Work Journal, 50*(1), 102–111. https://doi.org/10.1007/s10615-021-00826-8.

Rosen, A. (2016, February 4). Why future orientation is the most important part of entrepreneurial thinking. *Entrepreneur*. Retrieved May 20, 2022, from www.entrepreneur.com/article/254921.

Schacter, D. L., Addis, D. R., & Buckner, R. L. (2007). Remembering the past to imagine the future: The prospective brain. *Nature Reviews Neuroscience, 8*(9), 657–661.

Seligman, M. (2006). *Learned optimism*. Random House.

Inequality and Work

11 International Students

Commodities for Education, Local Employment, and the Global Labor Market

Nancy Arthur

The export of international education is big business, contributing billions of dollars to the national revenue for top destination countries such as the United States, the United Kingdom, Canada, Australia, and Germany (Choudaha, 2019). Securing revenue from international tuition fees, typically four to five times higher than fees paid by domestic students, has been a partial solution to deal with escalating costs and reduced government funding in higher education, fueling an increasingly competitive market within and across major destination countries. However, disruptions due to pandemic conditions and geo-political forces led to an abrupt wake-up call about the risks of overreliance on international student flows. Revenue decreases during the past two years since the advent of the pandemic may not have been as bad as what was expected but still had a serious impact. There were revenue losses in higher education, loss of revenue in the local communities where international students and their families would otherwise spend their travel dollars, and employers lost a labor pool to address vacancies that could not be filled by domestic workers. Those losses were most acutely felt in countries that closed their borders to new and returning international students, whereas other countries seized the moment to increase market share. Although some international students waited to pursue their original program and country choices, many moved on to where they could commence high-quality academic programs and progress their educational plans.

There are many reasons why students pursue education in other countries (OECD, 2020). Common reasons include seeking high-quality education, intercultural experiences, language learning, and travel experiences. Once considered to be the best and brightest from their home countries, expanded markets and programs opened access to students with a wider range of academic backgrounds and abilities. International education may not have been their first choice but was pursued in light of available opportunities in their home countries, particularly when pathways to high-status or high-quality education were not available. Regardless of contextual circumstances, the number one reason that individuals pursue international education is to improve their future options for employment (Nilsson &

DOI:10.4324/9781003272397-15

Ripmeester, 2016). In other words, international education is an investment made by individuals and their families to build capacity for future employment pathways. Among shifting market conditions, international students compare opportunities in their destination and home countries or seek options in other countries.

Linking international education, employment, and immigration policies has shifted views about the perceived value of international students as commodities for education, labor markets, and future trading partnerships (Arthur, 2013, 2014). Once thought of as temporary sojourners, strict visa conditions were imposed to match the expectation that international students would return home when they completed their academic programs. Regulations around international students' work rights have been tightly monitored, progressively shifting from no work rights to limited on-campus hours, and expanded to include off-campus employment. Notably, those conditions have varied across countries according to immigration policies. Elected officials in government have been challenged to preserve access to education and employment for domestic citizens, while also expanding internationalization agendas, revenue generation, and ensuring that sources of labor are readily available.

Presumably, access to part-time work while studying provides an advantage for international students to gain work experience. However, most of the jobs open to new international students are at entry level, and casual labor jobs may neither be related to their academic programs nor enhance professional skills and qualifications. Precarious working conditions emerge when some international students lack familiarity with domestic labor laws or work cultures in a new country and are reluctant to challenge employers, fearing negative consequences. Tolerating difficult work conditions may be necessary to fund their education.

The move by some country governments to expand the post-graduation work rights is aimed at attracting international students as skilled knowledge workers and permanent residents. Countries with low birth rates and aging populations depend on immigration as a key driver of economic growth. International students have been characterized as preferred immigrants because they bring experience and connections from their home countries, they have acquired experience living and learning in the local context and presumably will have smooth transitions to the local workforce. Through leveraging study and work visas, international students are targeted as highly qualified personnel to fill gaps in the local labor force (Berquist et al., 2019).

Although it seems relatively straightforward, the pathways are complex for studying as an international student, accessing valuable work experience, and securing meaningful employment post-graduation. Students experience multiple transitions when they leave their home countries, families, and support networks, move to another country, and quickly have to adjust to new cultural norms (Jindal-Snape & Rienties, 2016). They have to build sources of social capital in the destination county, including friendship networks, mentors, supervisory relationships, and employment references that help them to build their human capital and credentials for employment (Arthur, 2017). Many students have noted barriers to job seeking when their international experience and credentials are devalued by employers who prioritize work experience from the destination country (Nguyen & Hartz, 2020). Microaggressions and more overt expressions of marginalization, such as racism and sexism, are fueled by a lack of information about the cultural and country backgrounds of international students, their qualifications, and/or biases about hiring them. Amidst these experiences, changing immigration policies and visa requirements loom in the background as a source of uncertainty and pressure. With little notice, there can be changes in priority labor market sectors, requirements for permanent residency, and conflicting advice about ways to gain relevant experience. Employers also have to grapple with changing requirements if they choose to pursue hiring international students.

The pause on immigration during the pandemic has created conditions that could increase opportunities for international students. For example, educational recruiters were already strengthening messages about study, work, and stay in destination countries. Some countries offered extended work visas and special considerations for international students living onshore to apply for permanent residency. Just as the in-flow of international students increased for recruitment to international education, the market is increasing to retain students post-graduation. With borders opening and economies recovering, the global race for talent will inevitably heat up as many countries revise plans for immigration quotas. These trends represent several shifts that have occurred over time, as international students are increasingly valued for their contributions to education, local employment, and global labor markets.

In making these arguments, there are important caveats that need to be acknowledged. First, international students are not a homogenous group. The demographic composition and source countries of international student populations vary in different destination countries. There is diversity in their background experiences, motives for studying, access to financial resources, and levels of preparation for living and learning in another country. International students' experiences may be affected by the degree of cultural similarity or difference, and due to the ways that identity markers such as race, gender, social class, and/or how their countries of origin are constructed by people in the destination country. Students may find that they have more or less advantages, freedom, or restrictions in the new cultural context, including experiences of privilege or oppression. Such experiences also pertain to seeking employment due to wide variations in the country and cultural practices, and the degree to which employers are amenable to hiring international students to diversify their labor force.

Second, prior to the pandemic, there were increasing numbers of younger students pursuing international education at the secondary school level

(Arthur et al., 2022). Some families want their children to become established at a younger age and increase their chances of pursuing higher education in the destination country. Along with increases in short-term mobility programs, some families of younger international students are already thinking about the connections between studying, gaining local experience, and pursuing permanent immigration. However, younger international students are at a different life stage and may require additional support for academic planning, career decision-making, and assistance to build local support networks.

Third, prevailing narratives about international students tend to be problem-focused and perceptions about their diversity tend to be framed as deficits. As a result, there is tremendous pressure on international students to assimilate. Although international students may be keen to develop friendships with domestic students and local workers, that interest may not be reciprocated. Consequently, students may gravitate toward interactions with people from their home country or find that they are more accepted by international students from other countries. Although there is a lot that can be gained from interaction between diverse international students, there are missed opportunities for intercultural learning between local and international students.

Fourth, the career development of international students has not been studied as much as other topics, such as their adjustment and adaptation. This may be due to the emphasis on the initial transition to another country, which is a choice that can have profound influences on people's career trajectory. However, international students' career decisions and planning extend beyond the initial decision and involve many contextual influences in both their home and destination countries. Advances in understanding international students' career development would benefit from stronger theoretical foundations to frame research and inform approaches to service provision.

Fifth, the literature on international students is primarily positioned around the flow to major providers in the top destinations of Western countries. Although the recent pandemic has disrupted the flow of new international students, previously established patterns of mobility will only shift if the education sector has succeeded in diversifying source countries and growing new markets. Although not all students choose to stay in the destination countries, most want to, and there are clear signs that international students will have increasing opportunities to turn their study and employment experiences into plans for permanent immigration. With more intense competition for skilled knowledge workers likely to expand in the future, there are serious implications for source countries and loss of human capital, commonly referred to as "brain drain." Destination countries might gain a larger pool of talent, but the loss of talent for other countries rarely figures into narratives about increasing market share of student recruitment and retention (Arthur, 2014). Some may question the ethics of intentionally promoting the recruitment of skilled knowledge workers from emerging countries that are highly dependent on returning international students to advance their economies and improve local conditions.

In summary, international students have been positioned as commodities for increasing the revenue of educational institutions, as a source of casual and part-time labor while they study, and as appealing immigrants due to their long-term potential to contribute to the economic growth of countries where they study. It would seem that the value of international students has been reduced to their human capital for economic gain. This positioning depersonalizes them from the social and cultural contexts of their lives and ignores their multiple and complex transitions. It also discounts their contributions to intercultural learning with domestic students and the value of international perspectives for diversifying workplace cultures. Beyond the hyper-focus on recruitment and filling labor shortages, we need to ensure high-quality learning and work placement experiences and seek reform to streamline work entitlements and protections. Funding and resource allocations also need to be revised to provide seamless career development support for international students during their studies and when they transition to employment in the global labor market.

References

Arthur, N. (2013). International students and career development: Human capital in the global skills race. *Journal of the National Institute for Career Education and Counselling, 31*(1), 43–50. https://hubble-live-assets.s3.amazonaws.com/nicec/redactor2_assets/files/82/NICEC_Journal_31_Oct_2013.pdf.

Arthur, N. (2014). Social justice and career guidance in the Age of Talent. *International Journal for Educational and Vocational Guidance, 14*, 47–60. https://doi.org/10.1007/s10775-013-9255-x.

Arthur, N. (2017). Supporting international students through strengthening their social resources. *Studies in Higher Education, 5*, 887–894.

Arthur, N., Lei, D., & Woodend, J. (2022). From near and afar: International secondary school students' career influences. *Journal of Career Development.* https://doi.org/10.1177/08948453221094309

Berquist, B., Hall, R., Morris-Lange, S., Shields, H., Stern, V., & Tran, L. T. (2019). *Global perspectives on international student employability.* International Education Association of Australia (IEAA). www.ieaa.org.au/documents/item/1586.

Choudaha, R. (2019). Beyond $300 billion: The global impact of international students. *Study Portals.* https://studyportals.com/intelligence/global-impact-of-international-students/.

Jindal-Snape, D., & Rienties, B. (2016). Understanding multiple and multi-dimensional transitions of international higher education students: Setting the scene. In D. Jindal-Snape & B. Rienties (Eds.), *Multi-dimensional transitions of international students to higher education* (pp. 1–18). Routledge.

Nguyen, T., & Hartz, D. (2020). International students in Australia, employability and cultural competence. In J. Frawley, G. Russell, & J. Sherwood (Eds.), *Cultural competence and the higher education sector* (pp. 331–348). Springer. https://doi.org/10.1007/978-981-15-5362-2_18.

Nilsson, P. A., & Ripmeester, N. (2016). International student expectations: Career opportunities and employability. *Journal of International Students, 6*(2), 614–631. www.ojed.org/index.php/jis/article/view/373.

OECD. (2020). *What is the profile of internationally mobile students? Education at a Glance 2020: OECD Indicators.* OECD Publishing. https://doi.org/10.1787/974729f4-en.

12 Essential, Excluded, and Exploited

Undocumented Immigrant Workers Before, During, and After the COVID-19 Pandemic

Germán A. Cadenas and Fiorella L. Carlos Chavez

There are 7 million undocumented immigrants in the United States who are essential workers in a range of industries, including agriculture, food service, hospitality, manufacturing, construction, healthcare, education, science, and technology, among many others. Nevertheless, undocumented workers have been systematically marginalized and excluded from many of the protections and opportunities that are available to workers who hold permanent statuses (i.e., green card holders, naturalized U.S. citizens, and U.S.-born individuals). This leaves them vulnerable as unprotected workers who are prey to exploitative employment practices, providing labor from which U.S. citizens profit and reap most of the benefit. Our goal with this essay is to offer reflections, rooted in personal experience and scholarship, regarding the conditions that marginalized undocumented immigrant workers before and during the COVID-19 pandemic, and our suggestions for changing these conditions through humane policy.

We write this essay from a perspective that we hope is unique, given our positionality in relation to undocumented immigrant workers. Both of us are immigrants from Latin America (Venezuela and Perú), and we have lived, studied, and worked within and alongside immigrant communities since very early in our development. The first author is formerly undocumented and knows first-hand the work-related challenges to which undocumented status exposes individuals who do not have access to a pathway to legal protections (e.g., work permits and citizenship). The conditions of marginalization reviewed in this essay are not at all unfamiliar to him. The second author immigrated to the United States as an international student and has experienced first-hand what it is like to be underestimated and yet expected to excel with limited resources. During graduate school, she became familiar with the struggles of undocumented migrant farmworkers who are *invisible* and *forgotten* in the United States and yet provide essential services and talents to our economy. Our scholarship centers on the experiences of some of the most vulnerable immigrants at the margins of society (e.g., undocumented workers and unaccompanied minors), Latinx families,

DOI:10.4324/9781003272397-16

and other marginalized. We have found that our research lens is crystalized by our lived experiences and personal connection to these issues and communities.

Conditions Marginalizing Undocumented Immigrants Before the COVID-19 Pandemic

For centuries, systems have converged to disenfranchise large groups of undocumented workers, such as racist anti-immigrant policy and the systemic criminalization and stigmatization of immigrants. Many scholars offer in-depth analyses of how these systems function, their history, and their implicit objectives in advancing white supremacy (Goodman, 2020; Sterling & Joffe-Block, 2021). In our view, while these systems negatively impact undocumented immigrants broadly, they are particularly powerfully corrosive in the workplace. For instance, the genesis of immigration policy reserved the right of U.S. citizenship only to White people, hence depriving Indigenous, Black, and other People of Color (BIPOC) of the same rights, and forcing them to be employed by White people, who had the power to write workplace policies and rules. The same workplace dynamics still exist in the present day.

The process of marginalization begins with the migration process itself. Migrating to the United States legally demands the individual to have some type of visa or documentation that grants temporary or permanent status in the country and "empowers the immigrant to seek and secure the most satisfying work arrangement available" (Grzywacz et al., 2018, p. 459), but the availability of such visas is often determined by the immigrant's access to wealth, education, and other markers of high economic status in their country of origin. The lack of available legal immigration options results in a large population of undocumented immigrants (people of color, mostly from Latin American and Asian countries), who are mostly relegated to jobs unwanted by most people in the United States. To illustrate, undocumented immigrants perform essential jobs, including agriculture (Krogstad et al., 2020). In the agricultural sector, responsible for supporting the well-being and nutrition of U.S. families, more than half of farm workers are from Mexico (64%) and 6% of all workers are 14–19 years old (Ornelas et al., 2021). Undocumented Latinx [im]migrant farmworker minors who come to the United States without their parents (also known as unaccompanied minors) confront substantial threats to their health as agriculture ranks among the top three industries for work-related injuries.

The stressors and hardships experienced by unaccompanied [im]migrant youth are substantial, especially by those who leave their families and countries of origin to provide financially for them through remittances. During the second author's fieldwork in the Spring of 2018, Guatemalan undocumented minors working in U.S. agriculture shared that they confronted very hot weather temperatures and lived on their own. These young workers were unaware of the availability of healthcare services, in great part due to isolation and their undocumented status. Perhaps not surprisingly, among unaccompanied Guatemalan [im]migrant youth, loneliness, social isolation, and work conditions were predictors of depressive symptoms (Carlos Chavez et al., 2021). Ironically, despite working in a sector that feeds the country, undocumented migrant farmworker youth experience food insecurity wherein over 70% of [im]migrant farmworker youth experienced food insecurity, based on the second author's fieldwork.

Racism excludes immigrants from opportunities in White-majority fields of employment by procedurally requesting proof of immigration as a work requirement. Furthermore, the "deportation machine" is bloated with resources, such as privately owned detention centers, and laws that allow authorities to fill these detention centers. This deportation machine keeps immigrants in fear, submissive to workplace exploitation by predatory employers. The systematic criminalization and stigmatization of undocumented status discourage undocumented workers from unionizing and seeking worker protections, fair wages, and better treatment. Evidently, these conditions are active and intersect in workplaces.

Undocumented Workers During the COVID-19 Pandemic

While the systems marginalizing undocumented immigrants today have been in existence for centuries, these have been magnified during the COVID-19 pandemic. Indeed, undocumented workers and their families were excluded from federal relief programs aimed at alleviating the economic effects of the COVID-19 pandemic. Undocumented workers have also been overrepresented in essential worker jobs, which expose individuals to the COVID-19 virus at higher rates. Much of our current scholarship focuses on the impact of COVID-19 among Latinx and immigrant communities, through a large research project commissioned by Congress, funded by the National Urban League and its supporting foundations, and implemented through the National Latinx Psychological Association.

Analysis from this action research provides evidence for the concept of "the citizenship shield" (Cadenas et al., 2022). We found that immigrants who held U.S. citizenship were most protected from the negative effects of racist discrimination on their overall health and that this link was facilitated by food insecurity. Furthermore, our research with a sample of Latinx immigrants from low-income backgrounds, where 27% were essential workers, found that three in four immigrants with COVID-19 symptoms who did not get tested for COVID-19 did not have U.S. citizenship, compared to one in four immigrants with citizenship (National Latinx Psychological Association, 2021). Additionally, three in five immigrants without citizenship tested positive for COVID-19, compared to two in five immigrants with citizenship. These gaps were also present when it came to food insecurity and mental health, demonstrating that those without citizenship were most negatively impacted. Lastly, we found that the economic hardships experienced during the pandemic were elevated overall for Latinx immigrants, who reported decreases in full-time employment (from 52% prior to the pandemic to 35% during the pandemic), high experiences being laid off or having to close their businesses (24%), and being unable to pay important bills, mortgage, and utilities (33%). Respectively, swift action is required to alleviate these worsening disparities.

The Way Forward: Policy Recommendations

From our perspective, there is a need for substantial policy change at the federal, state, and local levels to affirm the essential role that undocumented immigrant workers occupy, and to reverse historical patterns of exclusion and exploitation that were inflamed by the pandemic. We make the following policy recommendations to policymakers, advocates, community leaders, scholars, and other stakeholders connected to issues of immigrant workers: (1) Provide a pathway to citizenship for all 10.5 million undocumented immigrants, and have this federal change provide an expedited pathway to the 7 million workers who have provided essential services during the pandemic, as well as their families. (2) Create a community-based process to review immigration policies from an anti-racist lens and enact recommendations to rid immigration policy from its long-lasting racist roots. (3) Expand the family-based migration program, such that the wait time for extended family members becomes shorter, and so that this program becomes more effective at reuniting families within a humane and reasonable time window. (4) Expand the employment-based migration program, such that essential workers' skills are recognized in definitions of "high skill" work, and allow for employers of essential workers (e.g., restaurants, construction companies, and hotels) to provide employment-based sponsorship. (5) Provide a mechanism to report employment-based exploitation in a way that is culturally responsive (e.g., in multiple languages and in community settings), and without requiring immigration documentation. (6) Provide educational opportunities (e.g., legal rights clinics and English language classes) to essential workers. (7) Create funding opportunities for community-based organizations to provide human services and career development and counseling services in immigrant enclaves. (8) Provide economic incentives to employers who hire immigrants, with the purpose of alleviating pay gaps and creating equity in compensation.

We recognize that these policy recommendations are aspirational and that they require collective, organized, and sustained advocacy efforts to help them come to fruition. Anyone may get started by connecting with local or national immigrant-led organizations that are advocating for change. The hub Informed Immigrant has a tool for finding community organizations based on zip code (www.informedimmigrant.com/help/), including groups dedicated to community action and legal services provision. The largest immigrant-led and youth-led organization, United We Dream, has coalition partners throughout the country and many resources to learn about immigrant rights' advocacy (https://unitedwedream.org/). These resources include deportation defense tools, education toolkits, mental health webinars, and opportunities to engage in direct advocacy (e.g., petitions, rallies, and phone and email campaigns).

Employers hoping to support undocumented workers may begin by expressing their support for fairer policies to the workers they employ, connecting them with legal resources in the community, and inviting community organizers to dialogue with workers in an effort to explore pathways for community action and policy change. Additionally, employers may engage in advocacy by meeting with policymakers who represent them at the city/town, state, and Congressional levels. Oftentimes, policymakers find it useful and motivating to hear from the real-life experiences of people in their districts, including employers of immigrant workers. Employers may also join coalitions of businesses that support immigration reform. As an example, the bipartisan organization New American Economy coordinates networks of State Compact & Business Coalition, and chambers of commerce (www.newamericaneconomy.org/state-local-initiatives/). We hope that these recommendations will be helpful in envisioning a way forward, so that we may emerge from the pandemic having created a more inclusive environment that honors the contributions of undocumented immigrants to the U.S. economic prosperity and growth.

References

Cadenas, G. A., Cerezo, A., Carlos Chavez, F. L., Capielo Rosario, C., Torres, L., Suro, B., & Fuentes, M. (2022). The citizenship shield: Mediated and moderated links between immigration status, discrimination, food insecurity, and negative health outcomes for Latinx immigrants during the COVID-19 pandemic. *Journal of Community Psychology*, 1–17. https://doi.org/10.1002/jcop.22831.

Carlos Chavez, F. L., Gonzales-Backen, M. A., & Grzywacz, J. G. (2021). Work, stressors, and psychosocial adjustment of undocumented Guatemalan adolescents in United States agriculture: A mixed-methods approach. *Journal of Research on Adolescence, 31*(4), 1218–1234. https://doi.org/10.1111/jora.12640.

Goodman, A. (2020). *The deportation machine*. Princeton University Press.

Grzywacz, J. G., Gopalan, N., & Carlos Chavez, F. L. (2018). Work and family among immigrants. In K. M. Shockley, W. Shen, & R. C. Johnson (Eds.), *The Cambridge handbook of the global work–family interface* (pp. 454–478). Cambridge University Press.

Krogstad, J. M., Lopez, M. H., & Passel, J. S. (2020). A majority of Americans say immigrants mostly fill jobs U.S. Citizens do not want. *Pew Research Center*. www.pewresearch.org/fact-tank/2020/06/10/a-majority-of-americans-say-immigrants-mostly-fill-jobs-u-s-citizens-do-not-want/.

National Latinx Psychological Association. (2021). *COVID-19 needs assessment of U.S. Latinx communities.* https://www.nlpa.ws/assets/docs/resources/Final%20Report%20 Summary%20-%20COVID-19%20Needs%20Assessment%20on%20U.S.%20 Latinx%20%20U.S.%20Latinx%20Communities%20.pdf.

Ornelas, I., Fung, W., Gabbard, S., & Carroll, D. (2021). *Findings from the National Agricultural Workers Survey (NAWS) 2017–2018: A demographic and employment profile of United States farmworkers (National Agricultural Workers Survey, No. 14).* Department of Labor, Employment and Training Administration. www.dol.gov/sites/dolgov/files/ ETA/naws/pdfs/NAWS%20Research%20Report%2014.pdf.

Sterling, T. G., & Joffe-Block, J. (2021). *Driving while Brown: Sheriff Joe Arpaio versus the Latino resistance.* University of California Press.

13 Envisioning Environments Conducive for the Career Advancement of Individuals in Challenging Mental Health Situations

Tracy S. Woods and Uma Chandrika Millner

> I have had many jobs and a couple of career paths in my life. While my career path may sound like an anomaly, it was fairly typical—go to school, get a job, live independently, just like any other adult. But I've always had a career. Things were just a little different.

Career development is a complex topic for individuals living with serious mental illnesses (referred to as individuals with lived experience). Commonplace understandings of careers presume singular pathways that follow a ladder-like progression. For individuals with lived experience, career development is better compared to a complex jungle gym with sideways, diagonal, and even backward steps. This career jungle gym needs many others on the playground to provide opportunities, support, care, and guidance. But the playground itself is isolating, unkind, unfair, invalidating, and full of grief. For the jungle gym to be accessible, the playground needs to change. We, the authors of this chapter, have been research partners with over a decade of collaboration on participatory research and services related to the career development of individuals with lived experience. The quotes shared in this chapter are the lived vocational experiences of the first author. Here, we ask the question "what will it take for people living with lived experience to thrive at work, not just survive?" and propose an aspirational ideal of employment for these diverse communities.

> When my mental health improved, I felt less than, in so many ways, because I wasn't working. All the stereotypes of people with mental illness seemed to come true.

For individuals with lived experience, employment is crucial for their recovery. Despite significant advances in evidence-based practices and top-class services, unemployment and underemployment within these populations are endemic and the focus of available services on rapid entry into minimal-wage jobs has inadvertently perpetuated a continued cycle of

DOI:10.4324/9781003272397-17

impoverishment and workforce exclusion. These services are limited in their appeal to young adults and ill-suited to older adults (50+) who take longer to return to work (Cornelius et al., 2011; Ellison et al., 2015). Among the lived experience community, transgender individuals are disproportionately affected (Mizock & Mueser, 2014); moreover, Black, Indigenous, and Other People of Color (BIPOC) report greater vocational competencies and interest in a career future than their White counterparts (Nutton et al., 2021).

From treatment and rehabilitation perspectives, work impairments are typically caused by clusters of symptoms that interfere with work functioning. Therefore, services exist to build work capacity and individual-level competencies and then provide supports when necessary. However, interventions solely targeting the individual are expensive and unsustainable. There need to be structural and cultural shifts toward recognizing the primacy of multiple oppressive systems that contribute to complex employment barriers without presuming the applicability of White European cisgender sanist norms to these communities.

> My parents signed me over to the state at the age of twelve and I lived in a children's unit at a state hospital. Within a few months in the system, I began to feel different and less than the average citizen. Soon, I had internalized the experience of myself as "less than" and carried that impact on my vocational identity for decades to come.

Socialization within systems that threaten the safety and self-worth of individuals with lived experience begins early and continues well into their work lives. Individuals with lived experience are not vocational "blank slates." Their vocational narratives and current recent histories of oppression are consequential to their career growth. Furthermore, intergenerational trauma and disenfranchisement contribute to psychological distress. There needs to be a shift toward an *identity-first* model where the mental health identity is borne out of the repeated interactions between symptoms of mental illness and non-inclusive environments. This identity is situated within a matrix of domination (e.g., racism and ableism; Hill Collins, 2000) where mental health systems and other sanist structures contribute to intersectional layers of dehumanization and othering. So far, a very simple heuristic for these experiences is used: *Stigma* is almost ubiquitous in the vocational literature on these populations and is highly problematic. First, stigma is a general and vague construct with little conceptual clarity. Second, stigma is sometimes utilized in reference to individuals' internalization of sanist narratives (self-stigma) without corresponding discourse on intersectional systems of disempowerment. Third, stigma is overused in the context of mental health service underutilization among BIPOC communities. In keeping with neocolonial tendencies, such usage essentializes the concept of mental illness which is, ostensibly, a White, European, middle-upper class, cis male, heterosexist construction. As a result, BIPOC communities become pathologized for their insinuated lack of awareness of mental health, and their sociocultural constructions of mental well-being are erased.

> Throughout my career, I didn't get a lot of support from my mental health providers to work. In fact, I was often encouraged to give up on working because my symptoms were consistently getting in the way. I would end up being hospitalized and sometimes lose my jobs. I never gave up but often questioned myself.

Individuals with lived experience often feel isolated in their desire to work despite the challenges they encounter. While work may interfere with wellness, they benefit when their mental health providers recognize the primacy of work in their recovery. Overall, individuals with lived experience encounter significant challenges within other interpersonal environments (i.e., their living, learning, working, and recovery contexts). These community systems often reduce the individuals to their illness and endorse the narrative that the mental illness needs to be resolved prior to working. Individuals themselves believe that they need to be well enough for work. Their wellness and vocational identity rely on being seen in their fullness and so much more than the illness. Their vocational competencies are supported through positive social messaging, opportunities for mastery (including illness management), vicarious learning, social and familial support, accessible and available work opportunities that are not limited to minimum wage and menial work, and work environments where they experience belonging.

> I had a job in a sober house for women. I lived in a rooming house in what seemed to be a janitors closet with a big mop sink. The place was overrun by roaches, with no kitchen facilities, and I shared a bathroom with numerous people. When I knew there was an upgrade I'd apply. I moved to slightly better rooms until I hit the jackpot and got a room with a kitchen. I did this with employment too.

Restricted access to decent work and employment disparities exists within hierarchical and institutionalized social structures. These communities experience high rates of poverty, incarceration, unaffordable healthcare and housing, inadequacy of services, unjust policing, and discriminatory hiring practices (Interdepartmental Serious Mental Illness Coordinating Committee, 2017). In fact, there is a general acceptance of poverty among individuals with lived experience, and their povertization is further exacerbated by structurally embedded racial and other inequities. An aspirational approach to these structural systems would be to identify pathways for these systems to move toward greater inclusion of individuals with lived experiences in the workforce. These communities need institutional protections, resources, and policies, such as the Americans with Disabilities Act that provide structural "safety nets" and that actively center the voices of those with lived experience (e.g., consulting peer leaders).

> Once I got my training certificate, I found a job at the bottom rung of an electronic company stuffing printed circuit boards. I watched the job boards at the company for postings and would apply for anything that was a step up. I got several jobs. And finally got the engineering technician job I had trained for. I worked hard and kept getting promoted. I went from being a junior engineer to a full-fledged engineer. I had excellent work skills. I showed up on time and got the job done. But then my mental health symptoms worsened, and I would have to call in sick until I got laid off. I didn't have a degree in engineering and could not find a parallel job. This resulted in an intense period of depression.

Work and wellness are closely intertwined entities. This notion has been part of the collective wisdom of individuals with lived experience and has urgently become more apparent and mainstream in recent years. The COVID-19 pandemic illuminated many social and structural vulnerabilities in the general systems of employment and the Great Resignation led to a reckoning, particularly around the interaction of work satisfaction and wellness. This phenomenon highlighted toxic work cultures that have always been challenging and difficult for individuals with lived experience. These achievement-oriented spaces are often non-inclusive where work conditions are disrespectful, cutthroat, unethical, and abusive (Sull et al., 2022).

> Once I felt well enough, I found another training program for women in construction and became one of the first four women to enter the sheet metal union as an apprentice. The work was physically and emotionally demanding and very isolating being unwelcomed by the men on the job. The stress of the work weighed heavy. The lack of support at work and travel time made things worse. Something inside me gave up or gave in. I couldn't see a way out.

For individuals with lived experience, there is the added layer of precarious work situations characterized by nonpermanent, low-wage, and nonunion jobs with risk of loss, uncertainty, and vulnerability without available labor protections, including those accorded to individuals with disabilities (Shuey & Jovic, 2013). Work cultures themselves need rethinking where employee well-being, as a form of social capital, is prioritized over productivity. Managers and supervisors need flexibility and sensitivity to the psychological needs of their employees fostering a work environment where individuals with lived experience feel comfortable disclosing their challenging mental health situations and requesting for accommodations to support their continued engagement. These individuals need equitable access to psychological safety, interpersonal supports, training opportunities, and benefits (e.g., paid time off for mental health) at work.

> I signed up for social security disability insurance. I needed the financial to keep a roof over my head, keep up with medical expenditures, and attend to my mental health.

Individuals with lived experience need psychological and financial safety nets that support their work decisions. Reliance on programs and services to support their livelihood should be a choice, not a matter of survival. These individuals desire meaning, purpose, and relational connections in their work. For some, work is closely intertwined with spirituality rooted in ancestral religious beliefs. Current systems and structures may purport to provide opportunities for meaning and purpose but there is a fundamental obstruction. Structural systems operate within models of scarcity that rely on competition for innovation and progress. Models of scarcity benefit the wealthy and support an accumulation mentality. In contrast, we need foundational philosophies that recognize abundance where plentiful resources can make safety nets available for all. Conducive and inclusive work environments can be nurtured by valuing diversity, developing caring and harmonious communities, rewarding transformational leaders, and honoring autonomy and self-reliance alongside the cultivation of collectivistic ethics. In sum, individuals with lived experience are entitled to the profound joy that comes from working.

> One blessing that moved me forward was the ability to focus on spiritual issues. I didn't know how to make my hodge-podge life have any purpose and meaning until I found the peer specialist training. A way to make sense of all I went through is possibly to help someone else with lived experience. I was able to give back.

References

Cornelius, L. R., van der Klink, J. J. L., Groothoff, J. W., & Brouwer, S. (2011). Prognostic factors of long term disability due to mental disorders: A systematic review. *Journal of Occupational Rehabilitation, 21*(2), 259–274. http://dx.doi.org/10.1007/s10926-010-9261-5.

Ellison, M. L., Klodnick, V. V., Bond, G. R., Krzos, I. M., Kaiser, S. M., Fagan, M. A., & Davis, M. (2015). Adapting supported employment for emerging adults with serious mental health conditions. *Journal of Behavioral Health Services and Research, 42*(2), 206–222. https://doi.org/10.1007/s11414-014-9445-4.

Hill Collins, P. (2000). *Black feminist thought: Knowledge, consciousness, and the politics of empowerment* (2nd ed.). Routledge.

Interdepartmental Serious Mental Illness Coordinating Committee. (2017). *The way forward: Federal action for a system that works for all people living with SMI and SED and their families and caregivers* (PEP17-ISMICC-RTC). Substance Abuse and Mental Health Services Administration. https://store.samhsa.gov/sites/default/files/d7/priv/pep17-ismicc-rtc.pdf.

Mizock, L., & Mueser, K. T. (2014). Employment, mental health, internalized stigma, and coping with transphobia among transgender individuals. *Psychology of Sexual Orientation and Gender Diversity, 1*(2), 146–158. https://doi.org/10.1037/sgd0000029.

Nutton, A., Ashbaker, A. Love, R., Motulsky, S., Becker, B., & Millner, U. C. (2021). *Perspectives on employment among diverse adults living with serious mental health conditions* [Unpublished raw data]. Lesley University.

Shuey, K. M., & Jovic E. (2013). Disability accommodation in nonstandard and precarious employment arrangements. *Work and Occupations, 40*(2), 174–205. https://doi.org/10.1177/0730888413481030.

Sull, D., Sull, C., Cipolli, W., & Brighenti, C. (2022). Why every leader needs to worry about toxic culture. *MIT Sloan Management Review.* https://sloanreview.mit.edu/article/why-every-leader-needs-to-worry-about-toxic-culture/.

14 Building Better Work for Those Released From Prison

Femina P. Varghese

Incarceration in the United States is expensive, estimated to cost from 80.7 billion to 182 billion dollars each year (Wagner & Rabuy, 2017). Even more expensive is the cost of harm to public safety due to recidivism. According to the Bureau of Justice Statistics, nearly half of those leaving prison return within the first five years of release (Durose & Antenangeli, 2021). A major predictor of recidivism is the inability to obtain or maintain a job after release. This high level of recidivism is a drain on the economy and unsustainable. Focusing on helping those leaving prisons to obtain and maintain a job will reduce recidivism and related costs, and gainfully employed persons can benefit the economy through taxes. People released from prison, however, face numerous obstacles to employment, including discrimination due to a criminal record, poor job qualifications, and poor attitudes toward work.

Today, numerous entry-level jobs once widely available are facing permanent closure due to automation and a worldwide pandemic. While many in the United States pursue education to increase job prospects for a changing world of work, one group of people will likely not receive such training to combat the job crisis: people in prison. Prisons in the United States do not provide enough education and training for 21st-century jobs. In addition, less than a third of the people in prison were pursuing degrees or training certificates (Rampey et al., 2016). Most vocational training that is provided in state prisons is in manufacturing, or repair work, with Federal prisons typically offering more options such as cosmetology and medical insurance and billing. Obtaining a GED in prison is typically encouraged, but opportunities for college education are less common.

More access to college education and vocational training is needed. It costs public money to pay for education for inmates, yet that is better and less expensive than spending tax money on building more prisons. Incarcerating one person for one year has been estimated to be $33,274 across state prisons in the United States and in New York, it is as high as $69,355 per inmate per year (Mai & Subramanian, 2017). College education and job training that leads to employment are more cost-effective and increase public safety. RAND reported that people in prison who receive an education are

DOI:10.4324/9781003272397-18

less likely to recidivate and more likely to be employed upon release (Davis et al., 2013). In addition, such education would increase earnings for those released, allowing them to contribute more to society as taxpaying citizens.

Getting a Job

Assessment and Educational and Job Training

For education and training to be most beneficial, the current strengths of the person in prison and his or her willingness to work at the jobs available need to be assessed. Otherwise, evidence suggests that those who leave prison are less likely to pursue work they are unwilling to do or believe they cannot get, thus increasing the likelihood of recidivism. Therefore, prisons would benefit from employing career counselors to provide individualized career assessment and feedback on individual strengths and interests, as well as information on the world of work, including the obstacles people leaving prison face and information on the jobs that are available to them. Career counseling could help the person identify the job they feel they can do and are willing to do upon release to set realistic education and work goals. Counselors could help individuals consider their job obstacles, what it means for them, and their motivation to work. Then, the person can enroll in college education or vocational training to build on the strengths they already possess and work toward their goals. Colleges and universities, including community colleges, might consider partnering with prisons to offer valuable training to inmates. Programs already exist such as the Bard Prison Initiative which has partnered with 15 colleges and universities to offer 160 courses annually and has awarded 600 degrees (Bard Prison Initiative, 2022). Financial barriers are being lifted for more opportunities for college education. For example, in December 2020, the U.S. Congress ended the 1994 ban that prevented those incarcerated from receiving Pell Grants. Further, given advances in educational technology, colleges can provide education and training from a distance and allow people in prison to participate.

Increasing Connections With Potential Employers

All the education in the world will not result in getting a job if no one will hire you. Among the most significant barriers to job obtainment for a person leaving prison is a criminal record. Yet, employers exist who are willing to hire those with a criminal record. Those leaving prison should be provided a list with contact information of viable employers willing to hire them. These lists should be updated regularly. Research has also found that in-person connections can increase employer willingness to hire the person with a criminal record. Therefore, it is essential that job fairs with employers be held within and outside of prison. This will help those who are leaving prison connect with employers personally. Employers could then take part in hiring those who leave prison. Employers who hire a person within one year of release from prison are typically eligible to receive tax incentives of at least $2,400 (Jails to Jobs, 2022).

Keeping a Job

Community Supervision

Many people who leave prison will receive community supervision in the form of parole. People on parole are often required to avoid others with a felony conviction, not use substances, and meet with their parole officer for supervised meetings, along with other requirements. Employment is often a requirement of parole and can help pay for fines and fees typically stipulated for those on parole to offset the cost of supervision. But many on parole cannot keep a job even when handed one upon leaving prison. Yet, job retention is a better predictor of recidivism than job obtainment alone. Therefore, support must be given to those on parole to keep a job. According to best practices in correctional service provision, the Risk Need Responsivity (RNR) model, programming is most effective in reducing recidivism when based in the community versus a prison setting. Career counselors hired by community corrections agencies could provide support to those on parole for work-related issues and prevent a return to old habits and behaviors.

Career Counselors

Many successful people, who have the financial means, obtain support for their careers in the form of counselors, advisors, and executive coaches and find them invaluable. People leaving prison would benefit even more from such support. According to the RNR model, those at the highest risk of recidivism need the most intense services. People on parole will benefit from focused support by career counselors trained to understand their work issues.

Rarely are career counselors employed by correctional agencies, while substance-use counselors and, in some incidences, mental health counselors are regularly employed. This is likely due to funding issues as well as a lack of knowledge that such resources even exist. Yet, counselors with a specialty in career counseling who understand the issues of people who have been in prison could help with job retention issues. Correctional agencies would benefit from information on the value of such counselors in helping those on parole keep jobs and not recidivate. Further, appropriately trained mental health counselors could also provide career counseling to those leaving prison as career and job-related issues can intersect with mental health concerns. People released from prison have trouble keeping a job due to difficulty coping with stress, failing drug tests, anger management issues, boredom, inability to work with others, impulsive behavior, work conflict, and work violations. In addition, they often commit new crimes, quit, or are fired from their job. Thus, criminogenic needs (i.e., risk factors to recidivism that can be changed) could be addressed by career counselors as well as mental health and substance abuse counselors. Career counselors can help released persons keep their jobs and stop committing new crimes by targeting anti-social attitudes and behaviors, decreasing impulsive decision-making, and addressing anger management issues as they relate to work. Career counselors could also increase pro-social attitudes and behaviors, such as problem-solving skills, pro-social motivation, and goal setting. They could also help the person build pro-social supports, and the counselors could model pro-social behaviors.

In addition, to be cost-effective and convenient, career counseling could be provided through a smartphone, before, after, or even during work. Smartphones could provide real-time support for work-related issues for people who leave prison through video calls. Having the chance to talk with someone and gain support, even through a smartphone, has been helpful to those under community supervision. Providing such support can provide a convenient way to help this population and even reduce transportation costs related to in-person visits.

Conclusion

Providing those leaving prison the opportunity to train for, obtain, and maintain 21st-century jobs might appear to some as rewarding criminals. Yet, it is a waste of human capital and societal resources to continue to spend billions of dollars each year to incarcerate people, only to see nearly half return to prison after release. Providing access to college education for work not only reduces monetary costs related to recidivism, but now the released person can be a contributing member of society. Any costs would pay for itself by decreased recidivism and increased tax revenues paid into the community by successfully re-integrated persons. In addition, outcome data should be collected to demonstrate the effectiveness of college education, vocational training, and career counselors for job obtainment and retention of those released from prison. Evidence of effectiveness will allow for continued support for such programs. The benefits to public safety and potential victims should also be considered when allowing those in prison to transform their lives through education and work. Providing college education and vocational training can be an essential step in changing the person leaving prison and giving them the tools to start a pro-social life, affecting their future and their children's future. This would then transform society.

References

Bard Prison Initiative. (2022). Retrieved March 3, 2022, from https://bpi.bard.edu/.

Davis, L. M., Bozick, R., Steele, J. L., Saunders, J., & Miles, J. N. V. (2013). *Evaluating the Effectiveness of Correctional Education: A Meta-analysis of Programs that Provide*

Education to Incarcerated Adults (RR No. 266). Rand Corporation. www.rand.org/pubs/research_reports/RR266.html.

Durose, M. R., & Antenangeli, L. (2021). *Recidivism of prisoners released in 34 States in 2012: A 5-year follow-up period (2012–2017)* (NCJ No. 255947). Bureau of Justice Statistics. https://bjs.ojp.gov/library/publications/recidivism-prisoners-released-34-states-2012-5-year-follow-period-2012-2017.

Jails to Jobs. (2022). Employer incentives to hire you. *Jails to Jobs.* Retrieved March 3, 2022, from https://jailstojobs.org/employer-incentives/.

Mai, C., & Subramanian, R. (2017). The Price of Prisons: Examining State Spending Trends, 2010–2015. *Vera Institute of Justice.* www.vera.org/publications/price-of-prisons-2015-state-spending-trends/price-of-prisons-2015-state-spending-trends/price-of-prisons-2015-state-spending-trends-prison-spending.

Rampey, B. D., Keiper, S., Mohadjer, L., Krenzke, T., Li, J., Thornton, N., & Hogan, J. (2016). *Highlights from the U.S. PIAAC survey of incarcerated adults: Their skills, work experience, education, and training: Program for the International Assessment of Adult Competencies: 2014* (NCES 2016–040). U.S. Department of Education. https://nces.ed.gov/pubs2016/2016040.pdf.

Wagner, P., & Rabuy, B. (2017, January 25). Following the money of mass incarceration. *Prison Policy Initiative.* Retrieved March 3, 2022, from www.prisonpolicy.org/reports/money.html.

15 Calling All *Nepantleras*

Building a More Inclusive Workplace

Ellen Hawley McWhirter

The future of work, like the present, will be encumbered by the neoliberal demand to be efficient, definitive, competitive, adaptive (assimilative), flexible (docile), and compartmentalized. Where profit is the bottom line and driver of decisions, morality and basic human rights may be referenced largely for performative purposes and manifest only as occasional secondary gains. Neoliberalism thrives on categorical divisions, rationalizes hierarchies (e.g., market work above care work, developed world above developing world, and CEO salaries exponentially above those of average workers), and feeds polarities that enable the status quo to persist or that "justify a sliding scale of human worth used to keep humankind divided" (p. 541, Anzaldúa, 2002). To envision and realize a better, more inclusive workplace, we would do well to engage the knowledge and wisdom (hereafter, the *conocimiento*) of *nepantleras*.

Nepantla

The word *nepantla* appears in the Florentine Codex[1] to describe a mountain path between two abysses and also refers to a place in between two bodies of water (Sahagún, 1970). Gloria Anzaldúa (1987, 2002) embraced this word from the Nahua people of Central Mexico to convey a liminal state, a physical, psychological, developmental, and even spiritual borderland. Nepantla is a temporary space for some as they navigate transitions in life, identity, or status, and a long-term residence for many who do not—and will not—fit into existing categories and positions. Anzaldúa herself was a denizen of nepantla, as a queer Chicana neither fully accepted or at home in the traditional Catholic Mexican communities of her origins nor the White liberal feminist spaces of her scholarly career.

The arrangements, norms, and processes that structure workplaces operate without attention to nepantla and those who reside there. Perhaps ironically, given its invisibility, nepantla dwellers are bombarded daily with eviction notices: *Leave your place of in between. Do not call attention to your unbelonging by the questioning of process and purpose, the missed cues of when to speak and be silent, that head wrap, the gender-bending outfit, the loud laughter, and*

DOI:10.4324/9781003272397-19

non-standard language. Instead, belong by being us (well, trying to be us). Accept, produce, and be tolerated.

Nepantleras and Coyolxauhqui

Anzaldúa described nepantla as painful. At the same time, the perspectives born of dwelling in nepantla, rife with its tensions and possibilities, can lead to becoming a nepantlera. A nepantlera forges a difficult path toward *conocimiento* that includes continuous loss, grieving, and healing. A nepantlera shifts from *not being able or allowed* to fully claim identities, to a stance of resisting categorization, claiming the borderland as home, and embracing a neutrality that eludes the politics of division. This neutrality does not ignore the structural roots of marginalization or injustice. This shift enables listening and understanding, without necessarily agreeing or endorsing, across differences of experience, perspective, and belief. Nepantlera identities are forged by realizing the limitations of categories, identities, and worldviews, resisting simplification, finding common aims, and embracing hope. Nepantleras withstand the rejection and tension that occur when they resist the push to align with a particular standpoint. They are bridge-builders who do not "go home" in the evening: They live on the bridge (Anzaldúa, 2002; Koegeler-Abdi, 2013).

The Aztec origin story of Coyolxauhqui, the moon goddess, tells of her dismemberment by her brother Huitzilopochtli, the god of war (Anzaldúa, 2002). Our own contemporary disconnection of heart from head, body from soul, did not start with neoliberalism but has blossomed in its thrall. Those of us who benefit from the current arrangement[2] rarely see how the dismemberment hurts us, and if we see how it hurts others, we put the blame on them: their choices and their lack of necessary qualities. Nepantleras see and feel the damage. Putting Coyolxauhqui back together is the love labor of nepantleras. "Coyolxauhqui personifies the wish to repair and heal, as well as rewrite the stories of loss and recovery, exile and homecoming, disinheritance and recuperation, stories that lead out of passivity and into agency, out of devalued into valued lives" (2002, p. 563). In workplaces fragmented by divides—psychological, social, political, and physical—the conocimiento of nepantleras can foster connection and common aims. Nepantleras can help us usher in a better and more inclusive future of work.

Building a Better Workplace: Calling All Nepantleras

Nepantleras are a counter-current to the forces of neoliberalism: they are complicating, questioning, communitary, resistant, and integrative. Nepantlera *conocimiento*, I propose, offers great promise for transforming workplaces into sites characterized by inclusion, participation, communion, and agency. This requires recognizing nepantleras, engaging and enacting their wisdom, and supporting their efforts.

But how do we find the nepantleras among us? They are not discernable by any identity category. One clue is that they probably make us uncomfortable. They may be doing the work of real (vs. performative) inclusion in our workplaces and education settings (McWhirter & Cinamon, 2021). Yet, especially in this climate of polarity, we often reject nepantlera input. Perhaps it is too complicated or diverges from how things are always done. Perhaps it challenges our viewpoints on the nature of a problem or process. Nepantleras are not playing for our team alone. Just when we think they have signed on to our proposals for change, they make the circle bigger, going beyond our definitions of "us." They see themselves not just in us, but in those we experience as Other. They weave together universal human experiences across our neat categorizations of oppressor and oppressed, powerful and powerless. This does not meet our need to create order out of chaos. We might think of them as troublemakers or accuse them of complicity because they hold all of us responsible for change, whether we consider ourselves enlightened, woke, marginalized, or apolitical. They see themselves and they see us with open, critical, hopeful eyes.

Nepantleras recognize the value of cultural assets and lived experiences people bring to the workplace. They understand the corrosive effects of stereotypes and exclusion. As such, nepantleras are well positioned to enhance the degree to which workers experience *mattering* at work, that is, that workers feel seen and valued, and that workers simultaneously contribute or add value within the workplace (Prilleltensky, 2020). Untroubled by dissonance, nepantleras are poised to cultivate the insights of workers who offer distinct perspectives on a process or problem. Nepantleras' respect for knowledge does not adhere to the confines of roles, degrees, or sanctioned authorities; they will seek workplace ideas and solutions from those unaccustomed to offering input. These capacities can help interrupt and prevent the calcification of toxic dynamics in a workplace, contribute to healthier teamwork, and increase the satisfaction and belonging of workers, particularly those inhabiting nepantla. It is also the case that nepantlera resistance to "us vs. them" conceptualizations and intentional subversion of identity categories may disorient and challenge co-workers.

Workplace tensions and polarization often emerge in relation to policies and practices (official and unofficial) regarding family caregiving leave, dress codes, promotions, pay scales, workplace accommodations, benefits, inclusion and diversity, and decision-making and conflict-resolution processes. Nepantleras can help us understand dissatisfaction, resistance to change, and unintended outcomes because they are tuned in to multiple perspectives and silences. When a new workplace schedule is proposed, a nepantlera will attend to its implications not just for the skilled workers or salaried employees but also for the custodial team. When a policy treats diversity as a purely quantitative outcome, nepantleras will push back, attesting without apology to the distinct and complex nature of inclusion (McWhirter & Cinamon, 2021). Nepantleras will notice and seek to remedy workplace communication processes that silence, ignore, or diminish some perspectives. When workplace transgressions occur (e.g., sexist behaviors), a nepantlera will resist impugning the character of the actor, possibly at the cost of tension with rightfully-offended colleagues. The nepantlera will address the transgression, listening and challenging, and advocate for relevant individual and system change. Nepantleras call people from stances of woundedness and victimhood, denial of privilege and abdication of responsibility, into a shared understanding that makes change possible, aiming that "Where before we saw only separateness, differences, and polarities, our connectionist sense of spirit recognizes nurturance and reciprocity and encourages alliances among groups working to transform communities" (Anzaldúa, 2002, p. 568).

Nepantleras acknowledge the workplace and societal structures and systems that reproduce inequities, while holding individuals, including themselves, accountable to one another. These examples highlight the manner in which nepantlera behavior is consistent with good leadership, but workplaces that ignore or disempower nepantleras fail to reap these benefits.

The goal of engaging nepantlera conocimiento in building more inclusive workplaces is best accomplished if we support the nepantleras among us. Nepantleras are committed to the welfare of the collective, but often experience alienation as they refrain from making static alliances with workplace subgroups. Supporting nepantleras means making time to understand the perspectives they offer, encouraging and respecting their critical input, and prioritizing process and not just outcome. It means sharing the work of fostering inclusivity, rather than allocating this important labor to nepantleras alone. Nepantlera contributions are distinguished from ego-driven, self-serving, or contrarian behavior by their fundamental motivation—putting Coyolxauhqui back together. Publicly affirming the integrity of their commitment can increase understanding and valuing of their role in the workplace.

The global pandemic has magnified our dismemberment, eroding psychological and physical resources, and taxing our capacity to withstand uncertainty and ambiguity. Our nepantleras are also weary. It has never been harder to live on a bridge. Inevitably, trusting nepantlera *conocimiento* means taking steps into nepantla ourselves. For example, to understand nepantlera perspectives, we may have to acknowledge and loosen our grasp on categories (gender binaries, race) and explanations (this group of people doesn't work as hard as my group, those with more education deserve more respect) that protect our privilege. While disorienting and even painful, relinquishing these categories also holds a promise for creating workplaces that are inclusive of all people and that better attend to worker survival, connection, and self-determination needs (Blustein, 2006).

Infusing nepantlera conocimiento into workplaces will be neither smooth nor straightforward. But it runs counter to the strong neoliberal currents of our time, and nepantleras offer a powerful antidote to our present malaise.

We should engage nepantlera wisdom in building a more inclusive work-place as if the future of work depends upon it.

Notes

1 The Florentine Codex is a work of over 2,000 pages presenting the findings of Sahagún's ethnographic study, conducted in the Nahuatl language, to document the language, natural history, religious and cultural practices, beliefs, and social systems of Mesoamerican indigenous peoples. It was written over the course of several decades in the 16th century and based on the accounts of community leaders and elders.
2 In this essay, I use "us" and "we" intentionally (a) to acknowledge my own positional-ity as privileged in numerous and intersecting ways, (b) in recognition of the multiple and intersecting privileges held by many, though not all, readers of this essay, and (c) in an albeit flawed and in-progress attempt to convey and embrace shared responsibility.

References

Anzaldúa, G. E. (1987). *Borderlands/La frontera: The new mestiza.* Spinsters/Aunt Lute.

Anzaldúa, G. E. (2002). Now let us shift . . . the path of conocimiento . . . inner work, public acts. In G. E. Anzaldúa & A. Keating (Eds.), *This bridge we call home: Radical visions for transformation* (pp. 540–578). Routledge.

Blustein, D. L. (2006). *The psychology of working: A new perspective for career development, counseling, and public policy.* Routledge.

Koegeler-Abdi, M. (2013). Shifting subjectivities: Mestizas, nepantleras, and Gloria Anzaldúa's legacy. *Melus, 38*(2), 71–88.

McWhirter, E. H., & Cinamon, R. G. (2021). Old problem, new perspective: Applying Anzaldúan concepts to underrepresentation in STEM. *Journal of Career Development, 48*(6), 877–892. https://doi.org/10.1177/0894845320901797.

Prilleltensky, I. (2020). Mattering at the intersection of psychology, philosophy, and poli-tics. *American Journal of Community Psychology, 65*(1–2), 16–34.

Sahagún, B. D. (1970). *Florentine codex: General history of the things of New Spain.* The School of American Research, University of Utah.

16 Equal Pay for Work of Equal Value

Easier Said Than Done

Ishbel McWha-Hermann

Essay

Better workplaces require better working conditions for employees, including pay that is fair and decent for all employees. But knowing what makes pay fair and decent is not easy. Individual judgments of fairness are subjective, and assessing how others perceive fairness can be particularly difficult. As a blueprint for the future, the United Nations' (UN) Sustainable Development Goals (SDG) emphasize "equal pay for work of equal value" (sub-goal 8.5) as a pathway to fairer more equal societies. At face value, this sounds like a valiant goal; it attends to the gender and racial pay gap, where pay is impacted not only by the job itself but also by personal characteristics—a practice prevalent despite antidiscrimination laws. But dig a little deeper into sub-goal 8.5 and questions begin to emerge about the appropriateness of emphasizing the *value* of different types of work, and whether *equal pay* is the best (or only) way to achieve pay fairness.

I structure this essay around these two considerations, first highlighting the importance of questioning how different work is valued, and second exploring conceptualizations of pay fairness and why recognizing different conceptualizations matters for designing fair and decent pay systems. Asking such questions is crucial for rethinking work, and for finding ways to build better, fairer workplaces in which (all) employees thrive. I am inspired by McWhirter and McWha-Hermann's (2021) social justice framework, which utilizes a critical lens to understand inequality and prompts questions related to the context in which the decisions about what is fair are made, the relative power of those making the decisions, and the underlying (often hidden) ideologies and values underpinning their decisions.

Inequality and the Value of Work

The triple disruptors of the workplace, namely, the COVID-19 global pandemic, the momentum around racial injustice, and the ongoing climate

DOI:10.4324/9781003272397-20

crisis, have given us an opportunity to pause and critically observe the world in which we live. We have had the opportunity to observe those hierarchies and structures within society which have historically helped some to progress and caused others to become stuck in a cycle of poverty. The indiscriminate nature of COVID-19 highlighted the physical consequences of those social structures, where those from lower socio-economic backgrounds were disproportionately negatively impacted. Concurrent with COVID, the growing social movement around racial injustice further highlighted and made visible the differential impact of systems on different racial groups, prompting important discussion of systemic inequality within society more generally. Also at the same time, the climate crisis continued to highlight the uneven impact of climate change on those in some parts of the world, in particular those in the Global South. Together, these disruptors have helped make visible the structural nature of inequality, and in doing so, have made visible previously hidden assumptions underpinning how society is structured. Such visibility provides an opportunity for change. There is an opportunity to question the status quo and pivot to a new normal that attempts to address historic structural and systemic inequality.

In the context of work, pay is one of the more visible manifestations of inequality and hence seems like it should be one that organizational scholars and decision-makers can concretely address. The topic of fair pay continues to gain momentum alongside wider discussions of structural inequality, particularly in terms of the gender pay gap, and increasingly around the ethnicity pay gap. In striving for fair and decent pay, we are guided by the UN SDG8.5's aim of "equal pay for work of equal value"; however, a key question underlying SDG8.5 is why certain occupations are valued more by society than other occupations. COVID-19 highlighted a curious paradox where supermarket workers, care home workers, and childcare staff are considered essential workers but at the same time are some of the lowest-paid workers—suggesting their worth or value is also low. Similarly, primary and secondary school teachers have been some of the hardest hit during the pandemic and are certainly underpaid for the important work that they do.

To understand why occupations are valued differently we need to ask questions of the values upon which (Western) societies are based: neoliberalism, meritocracy, and competition (Bal & Dóci, 2018). These ideals prioritize profit, skill, and individual achievement and assume that attaining these is equally possible (and desirable) for everyone. Those jobs which help to increase profit for companies and organizations are likely to be more highly valued and therefore paid more. Roles that prioritize well-being and caring, and those considered lower skilled, have less impact on the bottom line, and their pay packages reflect this. Despite the pandemic showcasing their *value* for society, these roles are more likely to earn low pay and lack security. They are also more likely to be filled by women, young people, and those from lower socio-economic backgrounds.

Others have written extensively on the link between ideology and structural inequality, but the point I wish to make here is that in striving for "equal pay for work of equal value," we must first question **what value is attributed to different types of work, and why**. Furthermore, there may be important knowledge to be gained from studying approaches to inequality in cultural and geographic contexts different from our own. For example, with its emphasis on social justice and equality, New Zealand's Equal Pay Act has been in place since the 1970s and the country has seen some impressive progress in gender and ethnic pay equity. New Zealand's approach to evaluating pay includes, for example, giving value to skills, responsibilities, effort, and working conditions required by jobs in female-dominated occupations, which are historically not recognized or valued as much as in other occupations.

Is Pay Equity Fair? Cultural and Contextual Boundedness of Fairness

Alongside considering the *value* of different occupations, a second important consideration is whether "equal pay for work of equal value" in itself achieves the end goal of *pay fairness*. To assess this, we are reminded that there is no universal definition for fairness. Our judgments of what is fair are often based on how we feel, and how the actions of others make us feel. But such judgments of fairness are not inherently known. They are learned. Decisions about what fairness looks like are built up over time, based on previous experiences, and on observations of the experiences and reactions of others. They are also heavily influenced by the social and cultural norms of the context in which our observations and experiences occur.

An "equal pay for work of equal value" approach emphasizes a premise of equity as being of key importance for fairness. An equity-based approach suggests that work which is highly skilled, which requires more effort, or which is particularly difficult should be remunerated more highly than that which is less objectively demanding, and less skilled. What you put into your work should align with what you receive—otherwise, feelings of injustice are triggered. Such an approach has clear parallels with meritocratic ideals and assumes equal access to these opportunities for everyone. In contexts dominated by neoliberalism (predominantly Western societies in the Global North), equity-based approaches underpinned by meritocracy are likely to be the norm.

But there are other ways to consider pay fairness, for example, by emphasizing need, equality of outcomes, or basic human rights (Oltra et al., 2013). Some of these approaches argue for the importance of treating people differently in order to have access to basic decent quality of life, or to opportunities for self-enhancement that can help break the cycle of poverty. In some societies and organizations, these values take priority over traditional neoliberal ideals, for example, Scotland is committed to supporting lower-paid staff by mandating living wages and living hours for workers and contractors in the public sector. Furthermore, in many international non-governmental organizations, decisions are made to align pay with social values in order to enhance fairness (McWha-Hermann et al., 2021).

It should not be assumed therefore that achieving SDG8.5's "equal pay for work of equal value" will universally instill feelings of fairness. Judgments of fairness are culturally and socially bounded. ***Considerations of pay fairness should consider the geographic, cultural, social, and even ideological context in which decisions are made as well as implemented.*** Furthermore, it is important to recognize that our ability to relate to injustice experienced by others is limited (at least in part) by whether or not we have experienced similar injustice ourselves. Even with all the best intentions in place, imposing one's own ideas of fair pay on others without checking their perceptions of fairness or being explicit about the basis on which fair pay is based, risks triggering feelings of injustice, and alienating and demotivating employees.

Looking Ahead: Building Better Workplaces With Fair Pay

Achieving fair and decent pay is difficult, but as organizations and institutions look to build better workplaces following COVID-19, critical questions must be asked about how pay structures are defined and why, including whose voices and perspectives are included in the process and reflected in policy. Organizations should engage in regular reflection on the values and assumptions held within the organization, and how this is reflected in the policies or models that are used to guide decisions. Asking questions and engaging in reflection can help to make explicit any hidden ideological values underpinning decisions. In this essay, I have argued that asking critical questions about the UN SDG of achieving "equal pay for work of equal value" (sub-goal 8.5) highlights two key issues: how the *value* of different types of work is defined and whether an *equity-based approach* to fairness is always appropriate. I do not wish to imply that "equal pay for work of equal value" is not an appropriate goal, but rather that it is important to reflect on its *appropriateness in a given context, for a given organization or institution.*

Alternative approaches might include, for example, establishing minimum levels of pay (such as a living wage). A living wage prioritizes needs and respects human rights (the right of everyone to have decent pay which is sufficient for a good quality of life). Establishing maximum levels of pay may also be considered, for example, based on the ratio of highest to lowest earner. Whatever approach is taken, it is important to articulate the values on which pay decisions are made (e.g., equity, equality, and need) and why. Decision-makers must consider the perspectives on fairness of all employees—and especially those who come from different (likely less privileged) backgrounds and cultures to themselves. Finally, questions should be asked about the types of jobs that are most valued (often implicitly). For example, are jobs that increase profit prioritized over those that enhance well-being and happiness? Those setting organizational policies and practices must look critically at their decisions and identify (and question) the hidden assumptions underpinning them. Doing so can help to make explicit any inadvertent implications of policies for inequality and help to create fair and decent pay policies and practices that are appropriate for all employees and that support the thriving of individuals, families, and society.

References

Bal, P. M., & Dóci, E. (2018). Neoliberal ideology in work and organizational psychology. *European Journal of Work and Organizational Psychology, 27*(5), 536–548.

McWha-Hermann, I., Jandric, J., Cook-Lundgren, E., & Carr, S. C. (2021). Toward fairer global reward: Lessons from international non-governmental organizations. *International Business Review, 31*(1), 101897.

McWhirter, E. H., & McWha-Hermann, I. (2021). Social justice and career development: Progress, problems, and possibilities. *Journal of Vocational Behavior, 126*, 103492.

Oltra, V., Bonache, J., & Brewster, C. (2013). A new framework for understanding inequalities between expatriates and host country nationals. *Journal of Business Ethics, 115*(2), 291–310.

17 Empowering Entrepreneurs From Marginalized Backgrounds Through Critical Entrepreneurial-Mindset Training

Alexander Glosenberg

The world in the early 21st century is buffeted by at least three interrelated challenges: rising socioeconomic inequality, accelerating environmental degradation, and an ebb in democratic institutions. These trends are, at least in part, a cause of the severity of the COVID-19 pandemic and leave traditional institutions (multilaterals, governments, and corporations) with a diminished ability, and/or willingness, to bring about positive social and environmental change. The answer to overcoming global challenges must come from grassroots efforts by empowered citizens who both proactively harness the power of free-market systems to sustain their efforts but simultaneously find innovative ways to transform the environmentally destructive, undemocratic, and inhumane aspects of the global capitalist system. In short, *the world needs disruptive, yet sustainable, entrepreneurs*.

As explained herein, I propose that to facilitate the empowerment of such diverse actors, policymakers can rely upon the greater implementation of specific training approaches that help marginalized populations to hone their "critical" entrepreneurial mindsets. Throughout, entrepreneurship is defined as the identification, evaluation, and exploitation of profitable opportunities (Shane & Venkataraman, 2000). In addition, building on existing scholarship (Burnette et al., 2020; Dweck & Leggett, 1988, Mensmann & Frese, 2017), I define an entrepreneurial mindset as a set of implicit beliefs regarding the utility of, and one's potential to, resiliently engage in innovative and proactive behaviors despite barriers and setbacks. Furthermore, I propose a new concept—that of a *critical* entrepreneurial mindset that is uniquely focused on the potential and utility of entrepreneurial approaches to advancing environmental sustainability and social justice.

Despite the need mentioned earlier for more disruptive, yet sustainable, entrepreneurs, certain populations remain underrepresented among the heads of the sort of organizations that might lead to disruptive change in the economy and society. In particular, women and persons from marginalized ethnic/racial backgrounds are relatively less likely to be entrepreneurs (Barr, 2015). While the causes for the underrepresentation of various marginalized

DOI:10.4324/9781003272397-21

populations among the ranks of high-growth entrepreneurs remain disputed (Jennings & Brush, 2013), causes are likely to include macroscopic/institutional-level factors (e.g., cultural/social norms and discriminatory regulations), mesoscopic/organizational-level factors (e.g., discriminatory divisions of labor or discriminatory treatment by key stakeholder organizations like venture capital firms), and microscopic/individual-level factors (e.g., internalized stereotypes on behalf of the entrepreneurial person or the availability of role models).

To facilitate the empowerment of persons from marginalized populations with entrepreneurial interests or potential, it is necessary to understand the psychological processes involved in work-based forms of empowerment. As proposed by Spreitzer (2008), psychological empowerment is dependent on one's sense of meaning in relation to work, one's self-determination or sense of choice in initiating such work, one's competence or capability beliefs in engaging in such work, and one's sense of impact—that is, one's belief that one can influence important outcomes. Seibert and colleagues (2011) illustrate the positive effects of psychological empowerment—prominently including higher task performance. Because entrepreneurs' task performance is likely to impact upon not only their own economic well-being but that of firm employees via firm growth and prosperity, and on communities via the accomplishment of firm goals and the provision of products/services, the psychological empowerment of entrepreneurs from marginalized populations is an important outcome for bringing about social justice and environmental sustainability.

An important tool within a broader set of interventions to benefit entrepreneurs is entrepreneurship training. While an over-emphasis on training can lead to a mistaken and problematic perception that entrepreneurs from marginalized populations are either responsible for their own marginalization and/or in some way deficient (Foss et al., 2019), experimental evidence (e.g., Campos et al., 2017) indicates that training interventions can be of assistance to entrepreneurs. In particular, forms of training that do not only focus on building key business knowledge and skill levels but focus instead on alternative educational outcomes can increase the profits and revenues of businesses (McKenzie, 2021). Such alternative outcomes prominently include helping entrepreneurs to hone their values and behavioral tendencies as it relates to the management and development of their businesses. One such alternative approach, known as personal initiative (PI) training (Campos et al., 2017), broadly focuses on boosting entrepreneurs' self-awareness of, self-efficacy in, and positive attitude toward, certain behavioral tendencies including proactivity, innovativeness, and persistence—often crystallized in new/improved approaches to goal setting, information collection, and self-monitoring/feedback-elicitation (Mensmann & Frese, 2017). In short, promising approaches to entrepreneurship training often tend to focus less on discrete facts and figures and more on an entrepreneurial mindset.

Alternative approaches to entrepreneurship training that address an entrepreneurial mindset hold the unique potential to target and facilitate an entrepreneur's psychological empowerment. This is the case given that psychological empowerment is composed of beliefs regarding self-determination, an entrepreneur's sense of competence in the domain of entrepreneurship, and one's sense of meaning in one's work. Entrepreneurial mindset training's emphasis on proactive work behaviors (see Mensmann & Frese, 2017) is likely to promote a sense of self-determination by highlighting and enhancing a sense of individual agency. In addition, such training's focus on valuing one's own unique skills and strengths as a source of innovation is likely to promote a sense of meaning in one's work. Finally, a focus on personal growth, a concept inherent in entrepreneurship mindset trainings' focus on developing resilient behaviors, would appear to reinforce and sustain an entrepreneur's sense of competence regardless of their current knowledge or skill levels.

Despite the potential for entrepreneurship training that targets the development of an entrepreneurial mindset to facilitate a sense of psychological empowerment among marginalized populations, there are barriers to the success of such training initiatives. First, marginalized populations appear relatively more likely to be skeptical of the power of free-market systems to result in positive outcomes that match their identities and priorities given failures of that system to, for example, benefit women, indigenous communities, and the natural environment. Thus, even if an entrepreneur from a marginalized background possesses a strong entrepreneurial mindset, they might not either possess a sense of meaning and/or impact pertaining to their role as entrepreneurs. As proposed by Spreitzer (2008), both a sense of meaning and impact are important components of psychological empowerment. Consequently, to fully support a sense of psychological empowerment among marginalized populations, alternative approaches to entrepreneurship training must go farther than promoting just an entrepreneurial mindset. Specifically, they must facilitate an individual's sense that entrepreneurship can be utilized to disrupt systems and historic patterns of inequality and injustice.

A second barrier to the potential impact of entrepreneurial mindset trainings on the psychological empowerment of marginalized populations is the likely justified skepticism on behalf of entrepreneurs from marginalized backgrounds regarding the source of such training. Frequently, training interventions like many other policy interventions meant to benefit workforce and economic development are initiated from outside of the community meant to be positively impacted. Because of historic imbalances in power across cleavages in global society (cleavages defined by national origin, race/ethnicity, gender identity, etc.), it is necessary to ensure that entrepreneurial mindset training is not only provided by, but authentically integrated alongside the priorities of, marginalized communities.

To more fully support the psychological empowerment of marginalized populations as entrepreneurs, I advocate for the inclusion of a focus on the development of a critical consciousness—yielding an approach that might be termed, ***critical entrepreneurial mindset*** training. Critical consciousness is composed in part of the reflection of one's social/economic conditions and a sense of self-efficacy in addressing such conditions through social/ political change (Watts et al., 2011). Combined with a focus on the honing of an entrepreneurial mindset, such a critical consciousness might reveal new layers of meaning to entrepreneurial projects (e.g., disruptive entrepreneurial pursuits as potential mechanisms for social/environmental justice). Moreover, the inclusion of critical consciousness development within entrepreneurial mindset training might provide a deepened sense of impact owing to the potential for entrepreneurial methods to help address social, economic, and environmental injustices that are of especially great salience to marginalized populations.

We note that training approaches like PI training center on classroom-based, and frequently group-based, exercises where participants learn and apply principles through heuristics (e.g., the importance of being innovative, proactive, and persistent). These exercises focus on developing key skills including opportunity identification, opportunity evaluation, gathering feedback, setting goals, and developing plans. The unique potential for a critical version of entrepreneurial mindset training resides in three adaptations to entrepreneurial mindset training approaches like PI training. First, while developing strategies to overcome barriers is a topic within PI training, such strategies do not *necessarily* admit to identifying and developing strategies to overcome social and economic forces of marginalization. Thus, critical entrepreneurial mindset training might take a unique focus on such forces and help entrepreneurs to identify social and economic barriers and problems such as racism, sexism, and classism. Second, while the best practice in the widespread implementation of training programs is to use a train-the-trainer model that utilizes local community members as trainers, it is possible to more fully account for the unique perspectives and realities of local communities in entrepreneurial mindset training. For example, it is possible following a train-the-trainer program to hold a localization workshop where ideas are generated by trainers from the local community regarding how best to tailor the content and/or delivery of the training to local priorities and realities. Suggestions for greater localization might include adaptations to the frequency of training sessions, altered scenarios used in the training program, and/or new approaches to training delivery (e.g., integrating trainings alongside existing training and education efforts). Third, the issue of power and identity can be surfaced more explicitly than it might otherwise be in critical entrepreneurship training by, for example, including modules within the overall training on the potential challenges and strengths of relationships between parties supporting/initiating training from outside of the community (perhaps often individuals from higher-income or socially privileged backgrounds) with community members.

As mentioned earlier, an over-reliance on the need for training among marginalized populations might inadvertently signal that such entrepreneurs might be deficient and/or responsible for their underrepresentation (Foss et al., 2019). Thus, interventions to assist entrepreneurially minded persons from marginalized backgrounds should also prominently include systems-level interventions to correct for active biases/discrimination and historic inequalities in access to key resources. Nevertheless, given rising socioeconomic inequality, accelerating environmental degradation, and an ebb in democratic institutions, the need for empowered entrepreneurs from disadvantaged backgrounds has never been greater. As I have outlined herein, a critical approach to entrepreneurial mindset training seems well-fitted, perhaps uniquely so, to accomplish this given such training approaches' likely positive effect on entrepreneurs' psychological empowerment. Entrepreneurs from marginalized backgrounds are likely to possess unique insights into the nature of environmentally destructive and inhumane aspects of the global capitalist system; when empowered, they also appear to hold a unique potential to rectify such failings by harnessing the disruptive power of free-market capitalism to correct those aspects.

References

Barr, M. S. (2015). *Minority and women entrepreneurs: Building capital, networks, and skills.* www.brookings.edu.

Burnette, J. L., Pollack, J. M., Forsyth, R. B., Hoyt, C. L., Babij, A. D., Thomas, F. N., & Coy, A. E. (2020). A growth mindset intervention: Enhancing students' entrepreneurial self-efficacy and career development. *Entrepreneurship Theory and Practice, 44*(5), 878–908.

Campos, F., Frese, M., Goldstein, M., Iacovone, L., Johnson, H. C., McKenzie, D., & Mensmann, M. (2017). Teaching personal initiative beats traditional training in boosting small business in West Africa. *Science, 357*(6357), 1287–1290.

Dweck, C. S., & Leggett, E. L. (1988). A social-cognitive approach to motivation and personality. *Psychological Review, 95*(2), 256.

Foss, L., Henry, C., Ahl, H., & Mikalsen, G. H. (2019). Women's entrepreneurship policy research: A 30-year review of the evidence. *Small Business Economics, 53*(2), 409–429.

Jennings, J. E., & Brush, C. G. (2013). Research on women entrepreneurs: Challenges to (and from) the broader entrepreneurship literature? *Academy of Management Annals, 7*(1), 663–715.

McKenzie, D. (2021). Small business training to improve management practices in developing countries: Re-assessing the evidence for 'training doesn't work'. *Oxford Review of Economic Policy, 37*(2), 276–301.

Mensmann, M., & Frese, M. (2017). Proactive behavior training: Theory, design, and future directions. In S. K. Parker & U. K. Bindl (Eds.), *Makings things happen in organizations* (pp. 434–468). Routledge.

Seibert, S. E., Wang, G., & Courtright, S. H. (2011). Antecedents and consequences of psychological and team empowerment in organizations: A meta-analytic review. *Journal of Applied Psychology, 96*(5), 981.

Shane, S., & Venkataraman, S. (2000). The promise of entrepreneurship as a field of research. *Academy of Management Review, 25*(1), 217–226.

Spreitzer, G. M. (2008). Taking stock: A review of more than twenty years of research on empowerment at work. *Handbook of Organizational Behavior, 1,* 54–72.

Watts, R. J., Diemer, M. A., & Voight, A. M. (2011). Critical consciousness: Current status and future directions. *New Directions for Child and Adolescent Development,* (134), 43–57.

18 A Tale of Two Citizens

Ronald G. Sultana

Philip Larkin, that mischievous poet from England, starts off one of his poems in his typically provocative style, grumpily asking:

> Why should I let the toad work
> Squat on my life?
> Can't I use my wit as a pitchfork
> And drive the brute off?
>
> ('Toads', in *The Less Deceived*, Marvel Press, 1955)

I always liked that poem, even if I have lived a charmed life where work has mostly been a source of satisfaction and serenity, not disgruntlement and despair. Work is one of the quintessential characteristics of humankind, a unifying element that signals a universal identifier of the species: *homo faber*. And yet, the way work is experienced by individuals and groups within and across states, nations, and territories is astoundingly different. For some of us, work is a blessing, an opportunity to feel useful and to be creative, to connect with others, and to do something with passion. For others, however, work is a bane, where for "six days of the week," as Larkin ruefully notes, it "soils with its sickening poison—just for paying a few bills."

This disparity lies at the heart of—and defines—class, profoundly marking one's passage through life. My reflection looks at the chasm that divides the contrasting experience of work of two citizens, arguing that such inequality should fill us with shock, consternation, and dread. That it does not do so signals a reluctance to engage with the world as it is, in order to imagine a world as it could and should be.

Two pen portraits will help highlight the stark reality where work is a blessing for a few and a curse for many. One of the two citizens I portray is my *alter ego*, Greg. I choose to make this personal, for there is little else that affects the person, and one's experience of life, as much as work does. Whether it is an elixir or a venom, work courses through our veins, pumping pleasure or pain, sometimes in equal measure.

The other portrait is of Grace, a woman I once saw in the gloomy shadows of early morning, as she took the bus to work and stared out of the

DOI:10.4324/9781003272397-22

window with that blank and tired look which speaks of a life snuffed out. That woman lives within a stone's throw yet inhabits a world apart. The depiction of her experience at work is a composite representation drawing on an ethnographic study of women in a textile factory, carried out by one of my postgraduate students (Deguara, 2003).

Pen portrait 1: *Greg, the university academic . . .*	*Pen portrait 2:* *Grace, the factory hand . . .*
There he goes to work, smartly yet casually dressed, with a spring in his step, toward a workplace that is as aesthetically pleasing as it is comfortable and welcoming. It is ten in the morning: much of the scholarly work can be done from home, and presence on campus is only required when face-to-face lectures and tutorials, or departmental meetings, beckon. He is mostly master of his own time, which means that he can travel outside rush hours, avoiding the stress and frustration that comes from that, and pick up kids from school, if need be, generally pacing his activities in line with what works best for him. He does not have to clock in or clock out: nobody checks when he enters his office or when he leaves, as long as commitments to students and the institution are kept. Greg is reasonably well-paid, with an income that is on the higher end of the public service salary scale. His monthly wage comes through with the unfailing regularity of a Swiss timepiece, and that is despite the economic predicament caused by the COVID-19 pandemic. Tenure ensures that he does not have to worry about next month's salary, or even that of next year, or the year after that—affording him a sense of stability that makes planning ahead with confidence possible. As long as he fulfills his obligations, he is quite free to do, say and write what he wants, when he wants, and where he wants.	Grace is expected to report to work at dawn. The factory she works for is only a short bus-drive away, and she has got used to waking up early. Getting her children to school in the morning is a daily struggle, but a routine has been established, and the elder children help out. Making it to the factory in time is a serious business: Grace has to clock in and clock out, with punctuality affecting income. Indeed, time is not on Grace's side: it sits, like a toad, on her back, goading her on to meet the targets set by management, to do more with less in the hope of a bonus, to keep comfort breaks short, and convivial interaction with fellow workers to a minimum. Inexorably caught in the cog wheels of time, Grace can only dream of stillness and of the joys of being. Money is a constant preoccupation: a minimum wage does not get one very far, especially with inflation setting in. And yet Grace clings on to her work with tenacity born of dire need. It is, after all, a job, and infinitely better than no job at all. The fear of being laid off makes her count her blessings, knowing only too well that her bosses, despite the friendly smiles at the Christmas gathering, cannot really be trusted. She has seen and heard too many stories about the way corporate greed trumps human need: the ground she walks on is shaky: who knows what tomorrow will bring? Life on the line is marked by the tempo of a continuous flow with which Grace has to keep up. Her task is to attach zippers to jeans, and she dreams of the exotic countries that the pants she handles every day will end up in. She does so under the watchful eyes of the quality controller, who walks up and down the aisle, collecting his dues.

(Continued)

Pen portrait 1: Greg, the university academic . . .	*Pen portrait 2:* Grace, the factory hand . . .

Pen portrait 1:
Greg, the university academic . . .

Leadership at Greg's university has not been overly tainted by managerialism, and since lecturing staff feel trusted and appreciated, most identify with what is, effectively, their second home. They give their best, even in the absence of the micro-surveillance that has crept into some universities, where colleagues have become increasingly proletarianized.

Greg generally feels good about his life at work. He is proud of the identity that he has constructed for himself in a context that is generally enabling. He firmly believes that he has a positive impact on his students, and the fact that he can exert an influence on policy gives him a sense of intense satisfaction. Given his contributions to academia and to public debate, and given the standing that the university enjoys in the community, status and respect follow Greg in most of the social spaces that he inhabits. He feels, and is, acknowledged and respected.

Despite the relational problems that academics the world over are notorious for, Greg's experience with fellow scholars locally and abroad is mostly constructive, marked by reciprocity, mutuality, and conviviality. Opportunities for self-development, growth, and advancement abound, with salary supplements funding attendance at conferences locally and abroad.

Indeed, Greg finds so much pleasure and satisfaction in his work that the boundaries between duty and leisure are not only blurred but also often quite meaningless to him. He moreover has plenty of opportunities to influence the direction of the institution he works for, with well-established structures that encourage participatory leadership. Representative and even direct democracy are prized, and if and when there are problems, he has a strong union to defend him, and colleagues to support him.

Pen portrait 2:
Grace, the factory hand . . .

Sometimes Grace looks back at her life and wonders what went wrong. She remembers her younger days when she would look at her mum and swear that she would never be like her: a worker in the textile industry close by. She still hears her mum telling her: "Study hard, Grace, or you'll end up like me!" However, long-term aspirations had to quickly give in to short-term returns: seeing her family struggling with meager incomes, Grace left school, trading aspirations for a wage, even if the job she found was too small for her spirit.

At times, Grace finds solace in comradeship at work: family stories and prized photos are shared, and encouragement and advice flow freely in the face of life troubles. And yet the milk of human kindness often turns sour: at the end of the day, the achievement of one comes at the expense of another. Divide and rule has long worked as a strategy to keep everybody in place.

Grace lives for the weekend. She hopes to find some time for herself where she can just be. She finds herself wondering whether there is more to life than this, and if jobs can be designed to fit humans, rather than the other way around. Structures and work routines seem to her so firmly established that the very possibility of collective action, let alone collective management, seems remote. And yet she's heard of other work places where this has happened.

These pen portraits are inspired by Dickens, and while they are but pale shadows of his literary brilliance, are nevertheless moved by the same spirit and thirst for social justice that drove him, using his mighty pen as he did to describe the fortunes and misfortunes of class in 19th century Britain. One of his best-known novels, *A Tale of Two Cities*, set in London and Paris and published in 1859, but straddling the period before and during the French Revolution, famously starts as follows:

> It was the best of times, it was the worst of times, it was the age of wisdom, it was the age of foolishness, it was the epoch of belief, it was the epoch of incredulity, it was the season of Light, it was the season of Darkness, it was the spring of hope, it was the winter of despair.
>
> (p. 5)

My tale of two citizens reminds us of this contrasting experience of life, marked as it always is by the reality of the present and the aspirations for the future. Marked also, as always it seems, by the abyss between human beings, dug by none other than fellow humans. The pen portraits remind us, if ever we needed reminding, that class is not some abstract sociological category: it is life itself.

Class speaks to one's experience of work, and hence of life . . . experiences which stand in such deep contrast to each other that they beggar belief. Here we are, ten generations from Dickens' Victorian England, still struggling to design social and economic relations in such a way that all human beings live lives marked by dignity. Access to a living wage, to respect, to knowledge, to quality healthcare and education for oneself and one's family, to a sense of security about one's present and one's future, to the rights of self-determination and of freedom to express oneself at work without fear of consequences . . . one and all are within the grasp of some, but not of many others.

This may be a state of fact, but it is not a state of inevitability. Since Dickens, and in part thanks to him, we have seen a number of workers' rights established in some parts of the world, often at the cost of the blood and tears of those who struggled on behalf of the many.

Historical Achievements of Workers' Struggles Over Time

– Awards (minimum entitlements)	– Meal breaks
– Bereavement leave (paid)	– Paid annual leave
– Child labor rendered illegal	– Paid overtime
– Right of workers to form unions	– Benefits for work injury
– Collective bargaining	– Unemployment insurance
– Equal pay for women	– Paid parental leave
– Establishment of 40-hour week	– Redundancy pay
– Establishment of 8-hour work day	– Rest breaks
– Guaranteed minimum wage	– Shift allowance
– Healthcare insurance for workers	– Sick leave (paid)
– Job discrimination outlawed	– Superannuation/pensions
– Family medical leave	– Unfair dismissal protection
– Health and safety guarantees	– Uniform allowance
– Long service leave	– Workers' compensation

And yet, several of these rights have been challenged, curtailed, and even eroded, under the onslaught of neoliberal economic fundamentalism that puts profit before people, dramatically deepening the gap between the "haves" and "have nots." New forms of exploitation have emerged, impacting not only incomes but also one's experience of work.

And yet this is also the time for new "territories of hope" and for "hope movements"' to emerge and shape the world of the future. Another world *is* possible for Grace, and for all those like her who find themselves struggling in a world that can and should be kinder, gentler, and more caring. The climate crisis and the pandemic are wake-up calls, inviting humanity to rise above greed and self-interest and to embrace the task of being a wise and respectful steward of the earth, in all its surprising beauty. Our very future depends on it.

And to give the last word to Dickens, quoting from the hope-filled tail end of the novel that constitutes the background to this essay:

> I see a beautiful city and a brilliant people rising from this abyss, and, in their struggles to be truly free, in their triumphs and defeats, through long years to come, I see the evil of this time and of the previous time of which this is the natural birth, gradually making expiation for itself and wearing out.
>
> (p. 390)

References

Deguara, A. (2003). *Life on the line: A sociological investigation of women working in a clothing factory in Malta.* Malta University Press.

Dickens, C. (1859). *A tale of two cities.* Penguin Classics (2003 edition).

Larkin, P. (1955). *The less deceived.* Marvel Press.

Precarious Work, Unemployment, and Underemployment

19 The Essential Worker Paradox

Kelsey L. Autin and Gabriel N. Ezema

As the COVID-19 pandemic swept across the globe, the world paid special attention to the *essential worker*. Essential workers were those deemed necessary for society's basic functioning. Ironically, many essential workers earned low wages, no benefits, and had few workplace protections amid life-threatening work conditions. This paradox has the world asking, if our agricultural workers, meatpackers, and cleaners are "essential," why don't they garner the markers of value (e.g., compensation, benefits, and respect) enjoyed by bankers, lawyers, and accountants?

We propose that the essential worker paradox is explained by society's reliance on the neoliberal value system that dominates global labor markets. Boiled down, we assert that the anchoring of value within profit generation, coupled with a high valuing of individualism, drives devaluation of essential workers' contributions. We argue that this is a major social problem and that psychologists, sociologists, economists, career development specialists, and vocational scholars bear responsibility for challenging this inequitable system and promoting new value systems that appropriately support workers who are the backbone of a functioning society.

The Value of Work and Workers

The primary marker of value in Western labor markets is profit generation. The neoliberal ideologies that undergird global markets hinge on the idea that the goal of working is to make money and that more money is always better. As this is played out in our sociopolitical reality, the value of maximizing profit incentivizes low wages and deters fringe benefits and healthy work environments (Crowley & Hodson, 2014). The human cost to individuals and communities remains unaccounted for when determining the value of labor. Further, this lays the foundation for a social value system in which society views income-generating work—and workers—as inherently superior regardless of social impact.

There are a host of assumptions about low-wage workers circulated in the dominant culture. "Low-wage" work is often used interchangeably with "low-skill" work. Consistent with individualistic values inherent in

DOI:10.4324/9781003272397-24

neoliberalism, there is often a failure to distinguish between low-skill work and low-skill workers. Indeed, some argue that the reason for the low wages of essential workers is their low skill level. We see degradation of low-wage workers as "low-skill" workers in a commentary in news media as well as public policies focusing on up-skilling programs (Lowrey, 2021). With interventions focused on improving workers rather than improving jobs, it is clear where policymakers believe the problem lies.

Scholars and journalists have critiqued the "low-skill worker myth." They have argued that many jobs classified as "low-skill" in fact require a high skill level and that designations of low- versus high-skill jobs are arbitrary and laden with biases of powerholders. Likewise, the myth of meritocracy and the related assumption that hard work brings commensurate reward remains a dominant cultural narrative when, in fact, low-wage workers take on the heaviest burdens doing work that is emotionally and physically taxing (Lowrey, 2021). Furthermore, low-wage workers are more likely to work multiple jobs (Lawlor et al., 2009). Thus, experiences of low-wage workers are at odds with cultural stereotypes of a group lacking skill and work ethic.

Researchers have also challenged measures of value defined by profit generation—which often only consider the cost of production and trade—and proposed alternative ways of measuring value grounded in societal benefit. For example, the New Economics Foundation quantified the social, environmental, and economic impact of three low- and high-paying occupations in the United Kingdom. They found that for every £1 spent on wages for waste recycling workers, £12 of societal value is generated. This contrasts with advertising executives, who for every £1 generated, have a societal cost of £11 (Lawlor et al., 2009). This analysis begs the question of the sustainability of this system. Similarly, Graeber (2018) laments the rise of "bull shit jobs"—jobs that garner relative affluence but make no substantive contribution to society. Graeber questions the need for such jobs to exist at all.

Deep flaws and inherent injustice in our current occupational value system are revealed by data showing who is doing the work is more predictive of pay than the work itself. Specifically, work that is dominated by women and people of color is the least valued by neoliberalist metrics. A prime example is care work. Paid direct care workers are 86% women and 59% people of color. They are also some of society's lowest-paid workers; direct care workers in the United States had median annual earnings of $22,200 in 2017 (Scales, 2020). Even more women provide unpaid care work, caring for children and elderly parents, and bearing an unequal burden of domestic responsibilities. Studies examining trends within professions support the idea that the work itself is less important to the ascription of value than who is doing the work. As more women and people of color enter a field, the average pay within that profession decreases (Baron & Newman, 1990). Rampant occupational racial, gender, and class segregation concentrates power among dominant groups, ensuring the imposition of a biased value system.

Impact on Workers and Communities

Contrary to paradigms grounded in wealth generation, growing scientific literature on the psychology of working demonstrates that the benefits of work to individuals go beyond the material. Work is an essential component of human freedom because it allows people to express themselves, direct their own lives, and secure safety and wellness for their families. At its best, work is a pathway to autonomy, connection, and meaning. However, in a society that defines human dignity by productivity and profit, work takes on a new function. It is stripped of its essential principle of being a medium of self-determination for all and instead becomes a pathway to wealth and power for a few.

The absence of value on human dignity in neoliberal practices leads to the erosion of the psychological, physical, and relational health within and outside of the workplace. Research shows that in companies that implement these practices (e.g., worker surveillance, use of part-time employees, and absence of collective worker representation), workers make less money and have more job insecurity; at the same time, they experience meaninglessness and abasement (Crowley & Hodson, 2014). Thus, workers suffer a double tragedy when, after all their toil, they are deprived of both material sustenance and basic psychological needs.

Without sufficient resources to sustain their families, low-wage workers often work multiple jobs or excessive hours, leading to overwork. Physical and mental health challenges associated with overwork among low-earning workers are well documented. People earning below the poverty line are twice as likely to report chronic pain, stress, and worry. They are also twice as likely as higher earners to put off mental healthcare due to cost (Graham, 2015; Jaspal et al., 2018). Finally, neoliberal practices negatively impact health by disrupting supportive relationships among coworkers and with management. Relational connection is the cornerstone of healthy human functioning; thus, when workplace policies disregard the relational function of work, they undermine the most basic aspects of human well-being.

The Role of Scholars and Practitioners

We urge psychologists, sociologists, economists, career development specialists, and vocational scholars to make an active effort throughout their professional work to challenge cultural narratives and systemic forces that degrade low-wage essential workers. At the most basic level, professionals might use their platforms (e.g., scholarly articles, writings for the public, training, and coursework) to spread awareness about the inequities that are embedded in the global labor market and correct misinformation about low-wage work and workers. Amplifying narratives that center on social value, respect, and human rights is essential to shifting cultural norms. While awareness at the societal level is essential for cultural change, it is also important at the individual level; in particular, practitioners working with low-wage workers might promote critical consciousness and reduce self-blame by discussing strategies for navigating and resisting oppressive systems.

As scholars and practitioners, it is also our professional obligation to participate in individual and collective advocacy for policies that support workers. To fully right the inequities embedded in current systems, policies must reflect a cultural shift in values whereby human dignity is prioritized over profit. First, to appropriately assess the value of work, we must assess the true cost—including the social and environmental cost—of goods and services. As such, we recommend policies that ensure workers are compensated according to the societal impact of their work. This might include subsidies for essential work, including unpaid care work and hazard pay for essential work that carries safety risks. Conversely, we must prevent overcompensation of nonessential work, especially work that has a harmful social or environmental impact (e.g., through mandatory maximum wage).

Beyond advocating for pay that is commensurate with the social impact of work, livelihood must be guaranteed regardless of work status. Several nations have implemented building blocks for the strong social safety net needed to make this idea a reality. For example, every industrialized nation (except for the United States) and many developing nations have implemented universal healthcare and paid family leave (Livingston & Thomas, 2019). We advocate for the expansion of these policies worldwide, as well as the implementation of additional supports like mandatory living wage and universal basic income. Some may view these recommendations as unrealistically utopian; we argue that they are not only possible but also absolutely necessary to achieve dignity for essential workers across the globe.

References

Baron, J. N., & Newman, A. E. (1990). For what it's worth: Organizations, occupations, and the value of work done by women and nonwhites. *American Sociological Review*, 155–175. https://doi.org/10.2307/2095624.

Crowley, M., & Hodson, R. (2014). Neoliberalism at work. *Social Currents*, *1*(1), 91–108. https://doi.org/10.1177/2329496513511230.

Graeber, D. (2018). *Bullshit jobs: A theory*. Simon & Schuster.

Graham, C. (2015). *The high costs of being poor in America: Stress, pain, and worry. Brookings Institution Social Mobility Memo*. Brookings Institution. www.brookings.edu/blog/social-mobility-memos/2015/02/19/the-high-costs-of-being-poor-in-america-stress-pain-and-worry/.

Jaspal, R., Da Silva Lopes, B. C., & Kamau, C. (2018). Epidemic of poor mental health among low-paid workers. *The Conversation*. https://theconversation.com/epidemic-of-poor-mental-health-among-low-paid-workers-96754.

Lawlor, E., Kersley, H., & Steed, S. (2009, December). A bit rich: Calculating the real value to society of different professions. *New Economics Foundation*. https://neweconomics.org/2009/12/a-bit-rich.

Livingston, G., & Thomas, D. (2019, December). Among 41 countries, only U.S. lacks paid parental leave. *Pew Research Center*. https://www.pewresearch.org/fact-tank/2019/12/16/u-s-lacks-mandated-paid-parental-leave/.

Lowrey, A. (2021, April). Low skill workers aren't a problem to be fixed. *The Atlantic*. www.theatlantic.com/ideas/archive/2021/04/theres-no-such-thing-as-a-low-skill-worker/618674/.

Scales, K. (2020). It's time to care: A detailed profile of America's direct care workforce. *PHI: Quality Care Through Quality Jobs*. https://phinational.org/wpcontent/uploads/2020/01/Its-Time-to-Care-2020-PHI.pdf.

20 From Unsustainable Jobs to Sustainable Livelihoods

Stuart C. Carr

Great Unfreezing

First let us freeze-frame the world of work right before COVID-(20)19. It was not sustainable. Unemployment, always a scourge on human well-being, stood at 172 million people globally. By comparison, the number of people "in" work with access to a "job" and remunerated with a wage was far greater—at 3.3b globally (ILO, 2019a). This is 19 times greater than 172 m. However, most of the 3.3b were trapped in working poverty, with poor work conditions ranking as the world of work's number one challenge (ILO, 2019b). Two-thirds worked informally—no proper job description, employment contract, protection in case of injury, regular hours, paid leave provision, social protection, or a regular wage. Even in the formal sector, legal minimum wages were failing most workers, with almost 60% struggling to make ends meet (ITUC, 2018). In relation to the other, top end of the wage table, economic inequality was careering "out of control" (Oxfam, 2020). Thus between 2012 and 2019, the UN's World Bank went from advocating "Jobs" as a key for tackling poverty (World Bank, 2012, p. 1) to "Rethinking Social Protection: Protect People, *not* jobs" (World Bank, 2019, emphasis added).

As work, industrial, organizational, and vocational psychologists, surely protecting people is *our* job, if we want to keep it. Facing COVID-19, nobody can go backward to the old world of work. In work psychology, "the job" was ubiquitous, Job Analysis, Description, Evaluation, Selection, Placement, Appraisal, and yes, Security. Sure, formal jobs protected many people in the post-World War II period, and losing one's job, provided it was decent to begin with, was often harmful to mental health. Today, you might even be one of the relatively few who still has and maybe will have in the future a decent formal job. But from the moment the vast majority of the world's workforce ceased/es to have any of those protections from their work, in either a formal decent job or informal employment, "the job" became much less relevant. COVID-19 has since poured accelerant on job insecurities and losses in the wake of recent economic crises. Now is a great *un*freezing moment in work history. Psychologists need to step up and help

DOI:10.4324/9781003272397-25

protect people from jobs. We need a wider, more expansive, and inclusive lens on work.

Sustainable Livelihood

Arguably, the concept of a sustainable livelihood is an ancient one, having been around for as long as people have had to sustain themselves as a species on this planet. More recently, the modern English term *Sustainable Livelihood* was coined in a 1989 report on environmental sustainability, in economically poor rural communities in the "developing" world by the World Commission on Environment and Development. From there, it found an enduring and timely definition:

> a livelihood comprises the capabilities, assets . . . and activities required for a means of living, a livelihood is sustainable which can cope with and recover from stress and shocks, maintain or enhance its capabilities and assets, and provide sustainable livelihood opportunities for the next generation; and which contributes net benefits to other livelihoods at the local and global levels and in the short and long term.
>
> (Chambers & Conway, 1991, p. 6)

During the 1990s, this sustainable livelihood lens widened, extending from rural to urban environments, where most of the world's population now lives. In the 2000s, it was expanded again, to buffering natural and humanmade disasters. In the 2010s, it proceeded in a landmark 2012 United Nations Conference in Rio de Janeiro, where it was linked to sustainable development more widely. Among the first sustainable livelihood, outcomes to be recognized were generating more income and increasing well-being (Department for International Development, 2014). Anchorage points like these connect the concept to humanitarian concerns in work psychology. Policywise, the 2012 Rio Conference and declaration highlighted the need for a concerted plan for all countries to break free of poverty, more multifaceted than any predecessor—including the world of work. In that respect, "sustainable" directly linked the concept of livelihood to the current 2016–30, Sustainable Development Goals (SDGs).

As defined, Sustainable Livelihood reverses a past heavy emphasis on unsustainable "jobs" by looking behind them, to inquire if people's livelihood goals are met, and further still, met sustainably. This means done in a way that does not jeopardize but instead supports the livelihoods of others, either now or, more importantly, in the future. It puts human relations and social connectedness into work and organizational studies, teaching, and services, by stressing that our livelihoods are interconnected, in time and across time, over successive generations. In this time of COVID, such human connectedness—recognizing our shared humanity—are what drove the spontaneous, later informally organized street applause for often poorly waged, frontline care workers that occurred in major cities across the world. It is a magnifying lens through which a revamped humanitarian work psychology can shine.

Literally at the center of the SDGs is goal number 8—Decent Work and Economic Growth. The conjunction makes sense at a macro level, as part of the UN's grand plan for human development. At an everyday work psychology level though, both decent work and economic development can be challenged. Economic development is clearly not something that motivates most people "to" (go to) work or indeed "at" work (when in the workplace). Decent Work conditions are likely to be more relatable. Again though, do people really go to work in search of decent work conditions? Society can aim higher than a hygiene factor. In Goal Setting theory (Latham, 2007), for instance, goals are meant to be more challenging, motivating, and aspirational. In these related senses, seeking a "sustainable livelihood" is inherently relatable, aspirational, and engaging.

Sustaining Wages

Sustainable livelihoods are also a SMART initiative. For example, the most obvious means of living that provides protection against stress and shocks is probably a living wage. Whereas minimum wages were designed to protect against slavery wages by providing a social protection, subsistence floor, living wages aim beyond bare subsistence to afford social participation, inclusion, and opportunity. The concept of a living wage is more consistent with sustainable livelihood than with jobs because it affords social and intergenerational opportunities. The living wage can also become a baseline for setting maximum wages for CEOs (ILO, 2013), thereby addressing wage inequality. It accommodates gig and digital platform work, for example, through contractor rates in city ordinances and along global supply chains. Living wage is compatible with social insurance options like universal basic income, which is now being extensively trialed in the wake of artificial intelligence, automation, and—especially—COVID.

For work psychologists, sustainable livelihood thinking gives us work: who sets it, is it valid, how should it be set, and where? Unlike conventional job evaluation, which sets wages using market sinkholes, living wage evaluation is guided by the quality of work life, and work–life balance, directly *experienced by workers* at naturally occurring wage levels. Research in humanitarian work psychology, for instance, Carr et al. (2018), has found that legal minimum wages and under tend to equate to poor quality of (work) life. Subsistence conditions like these may leave employees caught in poverty traps that are inescapable until wage levels reach a cusp. This cusp tends to be higher, and closer to the voluntary living wage values for which many civil society groups and labor unions worldwide campaign (https://projectglow. net/). The same validating research finds employers are often concerned to reach a living wage value that strikes a balance between decent work and economic sustainability for their organization. Given what we already know about links between work fairness and positive job attitudes, motivational upsides from paying a living wage would thereby offset additional wage costs, enabling shared, more equitable prosperity for all.

Sustaining Well-Being

Addressing the sustainable livelihood concept of shared prosperity could help to counterbalance extant critiques of work psychology that we have served economic power. The most obvious way in which that service has been rendered is by prioritizing efficiency over well-being. To be fair, this is often more inadvertent than deliberate. Training courses to boost resilience among workers may help them in the short term. But in the longer term, they may also enable some organizations to keep demanding more for less from workers. In this way, concepts like resilience, or self-esteem, or job engagement, unless viewed through a wider lens, can become tools for disconnecting people from their own families, relationships with others, and from their well-being.

Work stress, for example, is often viewed through a lens of control and responsibility. No control and lots of responsibility equal high strain and poorer well-being. These ideas of control and responsibility resonate. However, they are also, usually, threaded through the eye of a job, not a social needle, and an individualized job, not a socially sustainable livelihood. They are seen as control over one's own individual work and responsibility toward others at work, on "the job," inside a single formal sector organization. But for millions of lower-paid workers, the primary loci of control and responsibility is much more social. Their radius includes the stress of not being in control of family or household finances, and yet having the responsibility to sustain the same household or family group. It may also include formal and informal occupations, and straddle more than one income stream (as in gig work and portfolio careers). Only by breaking free of narrow assumptions about work that jobs confer will we reach and be able to serve such groups.

Sustaining Earth

The widest possible group we can serve is humanity, under threat from climate change. Organizations make the products and extract the carbon that makes pollution. The concept of sustainable livelihood admonishes work psychology to get real about climate change and the work psychology in it. If corporate social responsibility begins at home, then surely it starts with treating workers with a living wage and other decent work conditions. These may be a prerequisite for being responsible beyond the factory gate to theorize and practicalize the tackling of economic slavery and trafficking, for example, in clandestine fishing and logging industries that are decimating Earth's oceans and forests. In the extractive sector, we can teach students how to safely apply the OECD (2011), via National Contact Points in OECD countries, to call out organizations violating human rights, and non-coincidentally perhaps, environmental responsibilities.

Conclusion

Work psychology has a tradition of being responsive to world changes. We have a responsibility to uphold that tradition by questioning sacred cows. Job, as a concept and institution, is one of these, and a pivot to sustainable livelihood might help us to uphold, and build on, the other. Neoliberal calls for productivity gains before living wages are paid, that is, efficiency before well-being, and for an individual profit before planetary protection, are on the wrong side of history. Work psychology can set a new moral course, toward more sustainable livelihoods.

References

Carr, S. C., Maleka, M., Meyer, I., Barry, M. L., Haar, J., . . . Naithani, A. (2018). How can wages sustain a living? By getting ahead of the curve. *Sustainability Science*, *13*(4), 901–917. https://doi.org/10.1007/s11625-018-0560-7.

Chambers, R. C., & Conway, G. R. (1991). *Sustainable rural livelihoods*. Sussex University.

Department for International Development (DfID). (2014). *Sustainable livelihood guidance sheets*, vol. 2.1. London: DfID.

International Labour Organization (ILO). (2013). *Repairing the economic and social fabric*. Author.

International Labour Organization (ILO). (2019a). *World employment and social outlook—Trends 2019*. Author.

International Labour Organization (ILO). (2019b). *Poor working conditions are main global employment challenge*. www.ilo.org/global/about-the-ilo/newsroom/news/WCMS_670171/lang—en/index.htm.

International Trade Union Confederation (ITUC). (2018). *Global poll: Governments' failure to address low wages and insecure jobs threatens trust in politics and democracy*. Author.

Latham, G. (2007). *Work motivation: History, theory, research and practice*. SAGE.

Organisation for Economic Cooperation and Development (OECD). (2011). *Guidelines for multinational enterprises* (2011 ed.). Author.

Oxfam. (2020). *Time to care*. Author.

World Bank. (2012). *World development report 2013—Jobs*. Author.

World Bank. (2019). *World development report 2018—WDR 2019 presentations*. http://pubdocs.worldbank.org/en/808261547222082195/WDR19-English-Presentation.pdf.

21 Addressing Internalized Stigma

How to Holistically Support Unemployed Jobseekers

Ofer Sharone

In the United States, unemployed jobseekers typically encounter stigma. They are perceived by others to possess an attribute that, in Goffman's (1963, p. 3) words, "reduces them" from a "whole and usual person to a tainted, discounted one." Although unemployment is a social problem, stemming from social and economic forces, stigma means unemployed jobseekers are perceived by others, including employers, as responsible for their unemployment. The persistence of the unemployment stigma is illustrated by audit studies that show employers' reluctance to invite unemployed workers for interviews when compared to employed workers with identical qualifications (e.g., Pedulla, 2020). This essay explores the tendency of unemployed jobseekers to internalize this stigma and how a holistic approach to supporting unemployed workers can help counteract this tendency. This approach to support fosters critical consciousness among unemployed jobseekers which improves their well-being and enhances resilience for continued job searching.

The stigma of unemployment undermines the well-being of jobseekers because it tends to be internalized. Steward et al. (2008, p. 1227) explain that this occurs when "people's self-concept is congruent with the stigmatizing responses of others [and] they accept their discredited status as valid." A line of studies reveals the prevalence of internalized stigma among unemployed jobseekers who report feeling shame, guilt, or blaming themselves for their unemployment (e.g., Blustein, 2019; Sharone, 2013). The internalization of stigma contributes to declines in physical and mental health (McKee-Ryan, 2005), increases isolation, and undermines one's ability to effectively job search (Sharone, 2013).

Support can play an important role in shaping the unemployment experience. How jobseekers interpret their difficulties in finding work is mediated by the messages in advice books, workshops, support organizations, and coaching services (Sharone, 2013). In the United States, the dominant support model focuses on helping jobseekers hone their search skills, such as writing resumes and networking. By emphasizing the importance of search skills and downplaying the role of external obstacles, this form of support ignores the issue of stigma and internalized stigma and encourages jobseekers to see themselves as in control of their search outcomes (Ehrenreich, 2005;

DOI:10.4324/9781003272397-26

Smith, 2001). The implicit message in this form of support is that unemployment is an individual problem—one that can be solved by improved search skills—which can reinforce the stigmatizing assumption that jobseekers are responsible for their own unemployment.

Because internalized stigma poses a significant challenge, and the currently dominant model of support at best ignores this challenge and may exacerbate it, it is vitally important to explore more holistic forms of support that address internalized stigma. Effective support is needed to help individuals resist internalizing stigma by making clear the external forces contributing to unemployment and facilitating "critical consciousness." Blustein (2019, p. 163–164) draws on the work of Paolo Freire to define this as the "capacity to reflect on the causes of social injustice," which in turn helps unemployed jobseekers "not blame themselves for their experience of marginalization." In explaining how critical consciousness works, Brene Brown (2007) uses the compelling analogy of a zoom lens. When the zoom is focused on us as individuals, we tend to only see our own shortcomings, but as we zoom out—with the aid of critical consciousness—we become aware that others face similar challenges, and that underlying these challenges are not individual shortcomings but external forces like stigma and biased hiring practices. In short, critical consciousness enhances "the capacity of individuals to maintain positive self-concepts; dignity and a sense of inclusion, belonging and recognition" (Lamont et al., 2013, p. 130). For example, Hing (2013) shows that for members of a stigmatized group, being aware of potential barriers to employment, such as employer discrimination, means that when facing negative outcomes, they are less likely to blame themselves.

To explore how support may help jobseekers combat internalized stigma, I collaborated with a group of over 60 career coaches and counselors under the umbrella of a non-profit organization I created called the Institute for Career Transitions ("ICT"). We approached the goal of combatting internalized stigma in two ways. First, the support provided by the ICT openly discussed the external obstacles unemployed jobseekers face, including the sobering research findings showing the prevalence of unemployment stigma and other employer biases. Second, this support provided space and time for jobseekers to openly share with peers and coaches the difficulties that they have experienced in their unemployment. The open sharing was meant to facilitate the recognition that they are not alone in their experience and that their challenges do not stem from any individual flaws but from external obstacles and stigmas. The support took different forms—including small coach-facilitated groups that met regularly or large one- or two-day "rebootcamps" which brought together up to 100 long-term unemployed jobseekers—but the common thread was an open discussion of obstacles, stigmas, and challenges that come with feelings like shame and self-blame. Following the receipt of ICT support, 130 unemployed jobseekers were interviewed in-depth about their experience with unemployment and this form of support. In the rest of this essay, I will share some of the key findings from these interviews.

From the interview data, it is clear that the most powerful aspect of the ICT's support for combatting internalized stigma occurred when jobseekers openly shared their experiences with their peers. At the most basic level, this open sharing significantly reduced the unemployed jobseekers' sense of emotional isolation. For example, Daniel explained how previously, "I wouldn't have dared to talk about anything about my unemployment situation with anybody," and this left him "in a situation where I don't have anybody to be open with about this." He explained the importance of the holistic support where "I can let that part of myself out once in a while." Many other jobseekers described the relief that came from recognizing that they are "not alone," especially in experiencing emotional turmoil. The interviewees communicated a palpable sense of relief that they could bring their experiences out of hiding and share them with peers who can fully relate to their experiences.

Breaking jobseekers' emotional isolation required more than simply bringing together people with shared experiences. Prior to the ICT, most interviewees had attended other gatherings oriented to jobseekers, most typically networking events and self-help workshops, but in these settings, the jobseekers were encouraged to keep any experiences of stigma, isolation, or discouragement to themselves (Ehrenreich, 2005; Sharone, 2013). The holistic support, by contrast, gave explicit permission and encouragement to openly discuss these experiences, which then lead to the recognition of the *shared* nature of the experience.

Recognizing that one's experience is similar to others facilitates the development of a critical consciousness that counteracts the internalization of stigma. The shared nature of the experience makes apparent that the obstacles to employment are not necessarily about one's particular qualifications or any other individual-level issue. Lionel put it succinctly: "When in a group you realize it's not you. *Nothing is wrong with you.* Everyone in the same situation. It's amazing how supportive it is to recognize that others are going through the same thing." This powerful experience was reported by a majority of the interviewees.

The process of countering internalized stigmatization often begins with jobseekers openly talking with others in the support setting who are unemployed and struggling with similar issues, but who they perceive as competent and accomplished. The power of this experience stems from the fact that it directly contradicts the core assumption underlying the unemployment stigma, which is that unemployment means something is wrong with the unemployed person. Lionel, who is quoted earlier as coming to realize that "it's not you. *Nothing is wrong with you,*" elaborated on how being in a group with others in the "same boat" helped him feel, in his words "less strange:"

> Being with a group of people who are in the same boat, it's very [pause] what's the word? It makes you feel less strange. . . . When you're with this group of people and you realize there's two lawyers, there's a marketing professional, there's all these *people with all these skills* and they're

also having trouble finding stuff for whatever reason. It just helps you feel better about yourself.

Lionel's experience in the ICT group helped him "feel better" about himself because it challenged the equation of someone being unemployed with someone lacking skills. This experience, in turn, created an opening for viewing his own situation in a new way.

By helping jobseekers push back against the internalized stigma, the holistic support and the critical consciousness it facilitated, improved their well-being. Jobseekers reported that as a result of this support, they experienced less social isolation. Not only were important connections made during the support meetings, but these connections often developed into meaningful and supportive friendships.

Another tangible benefit was enhanced resilience for continued job searching. The critical consciousness facilitated by the holistic support makes the experience of rejections more tolerable because negative employer responses are not interpreted as a sign that something is "wrong" with the jobseeker. For example, prior to the support, Jackie had become discouraged and ceased searching. But the support helped her recognize that "I'm still eminently employable. . . . I just have to keep working at it."

More research is necessary to fully understand the effects of holistic support and critical consciousness on both the well-being of the unemployed jobseekers and their job search results. Fortunately, this holistic approach to support is currently spreading and being evaluated. The "Work Intervention Network" (WIN)[1] program's team of scholars and practitioners is providing trainings for trainers and teaching workforce professionals around the United States how to most effectively support unemployed jobseekers with a central focus on fostering critical consciousness as well as social relationships and self-care. The effects of this form of support are being closely researched by WIN's team of scholars, including this author and the co-editor of this volume. The in-depth interviews discussed in this essay suggest that this holistic approach will help counteract the internalization of stigma and improve the well-being of unemployed jobseekers.

The holistic approach to support discussed in this essay generates the critical consciousness that unemployment is a product of external forces and not internal flaws, which can shield unemployed jobseekers from the assault on the self that comes with stigmatization (Blustein, 2019; Sharone, 2013). By breaking jobseekers' isolation and bringing them into an open discussion with peers, it facilitates unemployed workers' recognition that the emotional turmoil they are privately experiencing is shared by similar others. Along with combating internalized stigma, we see that this support reduces isolation, helps the formation of important supportive social connections, and enhances resilience.

Note

1 www.bc.edu/content/bc-web/schools/lynch-school/sites/win.html

References

Blustein, D. (2019). *The importance of work in an age of uncertainty: The eroding work experi-ence in America.* Oxford University Press.

Brown, B. (2007). *I thought It was just me.* Gotham Books.

Ehrenreich, B. (2005). *Bait and switch: The (futile) pursuit of the American Dream.* Metro-politan Books.

Goffman, E. (1963). *Stigma: Notes on the management of spoiled identity.* Simon and Schuster.

Hing, L. (2013). Stigmatization, neoliberalism, and resilience. In P. Hall & M. Lamont (Eds.), *Social resilience in the neoliberal era* (pp. 158–182). Cambridge University Press.

Lamont, M., Welburn, J., & Fleming, C. (2013). Responses to discrimination and social resilience under neoliberalism. In P. Hall & M. Lamont (Eds.), *Social resilience in the neoliberal era* (pp. 1–31). Cambridge University Press.

McKee-Ryan, F., Song, Z., Wanberg, C., & Kinicki, A. (2005). Psychological and physi-cal well-being during unemployment: A meta-analytic study. *Journal of Applied Psychol-ogy, 90*(1), 53–76.

Pedulla, D. (2020). *Making the cut: Hiring decisions, bias, and the consequences of nonstandard, mismatched, and precarious employment.* Princeton University Press.

Sharone, O. (2013). *Flawed system/flawed self: Job searching and unemployment experiences.* University of Chicago Press.

Smith, V. (2001). *Crossing the great divide: Worker risk and opportunity in the new economy.* Cornell University Press.

Steward, W., Herek, G., Ramakrishna, J., Bharat, S., Chandy, S., Wrubel, J., & Ekstrand, M. L. (2008). HIV-related stigma: Adapting a theoretical framework for use in India. *Social Science and Medicine, 67*(8), 1225–1235.

Race, Culture, and Work

22 The Abolition of Capitalist Work and Reimagining Labor

Sundiata K. Cha-Jua and Helen A. Neville

The COVID-19 health pandemic coupled with the increased awareness of the persistence of anti-Black racial oppression in 2020 after the murder of George Floyd sparked a public discussion about how job and employment inequalities reflect and reproduce other social inequalities. For example, Black Americans were at increased risk of dying from the virus in part because of the nature of the jobs we occupy, and the availability and quality of health benefits associated with those positions. During this time frame, scholars were invited to contribute to decolonizing fields of study and to center the experiences of people most impacted by racial and other forms of oppression. It is in this context that we take the opportunity to reflect on how work in our current political economic system alienates Black workers and reproduces racial inequalities.

Authors Positionality

Where I'm coming from has largely been shaped by where I (Sundiata K. Cha-Jua) came from. I was born into an impoverished working-class African American family in the mid-1950s, in the medium-sized industrial city of Decatur, Illinois. For my first five years, I was raised in a typical African American extended family household. We lived in a four-room shack devoid of indoor plumbing. My grandfather raised chickens and goats, and my grandmother maintained a large garden.

Despite my academic performance, I was tracked into the non-college prep curriculum. Therefore, due to the intertwining of race and class, my route to a Ph.D. included a seven-year stint as a laborer. Except for a 17-month leave to finish my B.A. degree, I toiled at the Firestone Tire & Rubber Company's plant in my birth city, from 1973 to 1979. As a member of the second wave of the Black Power generation, I benefitted immensely from the institutional openings that the 1960s-era (1955–1978) Civil Rights and Black Power insurgencies generated. I participated in two incorporative surges, the movement of Black men into manufacturing and of Black people into colleges and universities. Between 1952 and 1970, the percentage of Black men working as operatives (semi-skilled machine operators) increased

DOI:10.4324/9781003272397-28

from 10% to 26%. Meanwhile, the percentage of Black women and men enrolled in college soared from 5 to 20 and from 4 to 21 percent respectively, between 1950 and 1975.

For the bulk of my employment at Firestone, I worked as an operative building tires. Our contract required members of the United Rubber Workers to work eight hours a day, six days a week, or 48 hours a week. The corporation-mandated tire builders build at least 60 tires a night. The 360 Firestone 500 radial tires I built a week sold for about $105 each. Thus, I helped produce tires worth $37,800 a week. In exchange for my labor, I grossed $210! My 48 hours of labor equated to weekly wages equivalent to the cost of two of the 360 radical tires I produced.

As much, if not more than the exploitation of my labor, I was marked by how the process of production insinuated its way into my inner life. Often, I awoke in the late morning (I worked the graveyard shift) to find my body performing the choreographed movements used to build a tire. Taylorism or scientific management literally had me "working in my sleep." As much as anything having my body hijacked by the rote production performance encouraged my return to school.

I crafted my worldview by reflecting on my lived experiences. It was a dialectical process. I made sense of my labor exploitation and racial oppression, particularly critical race-based encounters in schooling and their opposite, the joy and self-esteem acquired through the affirming aspects of Black culture to construct myself.

My [Helen A. Neville] class position and relation to labor is complicated. Both of my parents were born into impoverished contexts during the Great Depression. My father's whiteness afforded him privileges early in adulthood that allowed him to escape poverty; this included an opportunity to attend college on the GI Bill, making him the first person in his family to receive a college degree. These opportunities were not provided to my African American mother or anyone in her extended family. My mother earned her bachelor's degree at 61, just a year before I graduated college. Although for long stretches of my youth our family's wages were meager, I lived in a middle-class multiracial Los Angeles neighborhood. My mother's hard work and creative problem-solving allowed us to continue to live in the neighborhood while earning a poverty-level income after my father passed away when I was in high school. Like many African American families, my class position growing up and now as a professor is different than my siblings. Growing up I was aware that our family had significantly less capital than our neighbors, and I also recognized that I had access to greater resources than my three much older siblings from my mother's previous marriage. The combination of these dual experiences motivated me to be the only one of my mother's five children to earn a bachelor's degree or higher.

After failing at a work-study job in college, I secured my first real employment as an aide at an independent living (group) home for adults with intellectual and developmental disabilities. I learned about labor exploitation first-hand on this job. My pay was slightly above minimum wage, but when I worked the weekend shift, I earned a nominal stipend as opposed to an hourly wage. I primarily stayed in the job because the work was meaningful, and it allowed me to gain valuable work experience as a psychology major.

I am privileged to have a profession now that pays a comfortable salary and one in which my labor is personally meaningful and rewarding. However, that does not negate the workplace difficulties I experienced as an African American woman in the group home and now in the academy, such as racial and racial-gendered microaggressions, the devaluation of my work, and unequal pay. It is through these experiences that I understand the importance of a living wage, health and related benefits, and a nurturing work environment.

Social Context in Which Black People Have Labored

Black life in the United States has mainly been determined by what Harold Baron (*The Demand for Black Labor*, 1971, 40) called "the demand for Black labor." Baron's concept highlights the knotty fact that Black folks' participation in the labor force exceeded that of white people until 1970. However, Baron's potent phrase references more than just labor participation rate. It also infers where Black folk labored, the type of industry and occupation in which they worked, and the conditions under which they toiled.

In 1860, 89% of the Black folks in the United States were enslaved and all but 2.9% of the enslaved resided in the South. Enslaved Africans worked from "can see to can't see" six days a week. Their coerced labor produced the commodities—tobacco, indigo, rice, sugar, cotton, and hemp—sold by northern mercantile capitalists on the international market. Planters routinized enslaved labor through factory-like discipline. When not harvesting cash crops, enslaved people cleared land, grew foodstuff, tended animals, and labored in a variety of skilled crafts as carpenters, blacksmiths, wheelwrights, tanners, and brick masons constructing and maintaining the buildings and plantation grounds (Nampeo McKenney, "Table 3. *The Social and Ecoomic Status of the Black Population in the United States*, 1979, 11).

To maintain their system of super exploitation, the slaveholding class created an extensive network of force. Their "machinery of control" included routine whipping, mutilation, psychological torment, and starvation. The South was an armed camp. In addition to overseers, the Planters' power was undergirded by slave patrols, police, sheriffs, militias, and ultimately the federal military.

The plantation economy replaced slavery. It was based on a system of rural tenancy in which African Americans labored largely as landless sharecroppers and farm workers. Through the Black Codes and other discriminatory laws, the land and labor barons tied Black folk to the land reducing them to the social status of peons. This new system of Black labor exploitation was undergirded by apartheid or racial segregation. It included "southern etiquette," a system that required deference from African Americans. It was buttressed by revanchist mechanisms of racial terrorism—lynching, pogroms, and convict lease, an arrangement in which incarcerated persons were hired out to plantation owners and governmental entities. Rural tendency lasted a century, from 1865 to 1965.

Partially overlapping the southern plantation economy was another regional system of Black labor exploitation. Located in the urban North, it was based on proletarianized Black labor. Here proletarianization refers to the process by which Black migrants were incorporated into an urban industrial economy, albeit on the bottom rung. They were, however, generally confined to so-called "Negro jobs," the hottest, dirtiest, most dangerous, and lowest paying jobs in each industry (Baron *The Demand for Black Labor*, 1971, 22).

In the prophetic *Who Needs the Negro*, sociologist Sidney Willhelm argued that automation was rendering African Americans obsolete (Willhelm, 1970). "The Future of Work in Black America" by Kelemwork Cook et al. reaffirms Willhelm's thesis (Cook, 2019, 1). It contends African Americans are at considerable "risk from automated technologies in the workplace" (p. 4). Essentially, Black folx are overrepresented in the occupations expected to experience the most displacement and underrepresented in the job categories expected to experience the least. These desperate labor trends occur in a sociohistorical context in which authoritarianism fueled by a surging anti-Blackness is escalating.

The transition to global financialized racial capitalism drastically transformed the demand for Black labor. President Ronald Reagan's regime initiated the marginalization of African Americans from the labor force. Subsequently, from September 1972 to September 2015, the labor participation rate of Black people declined by nearly 12 percentage points, from 78.6 to 66.9. This was because the two sectors, in which the Civil Rights and Black Power movements had solidified African Americans' economic position, unionized industrial employment and public-sector jobs, were the areas most targeted for disinvestment by neoliberal policies (Cha-Jua, 2022, 197).

Historically, African American workers experienced a 2:1 unemployment rate compared to white workers. This pattern persisted into the first quarter of 2022. At 6.4 to 3.2, African Americans experienced an unemployed rate double that of white people in August 2022 (U.S. Bureau of Labor Statistics, August 2022).

In addition to deproletarianization, African Americans have suffered the most from subproletarianization or the rise of part-time and temporary employment. By 2010, Black folx constituted 12% of the civilian labor force but comprised 22% of marginal workers and 25% of discouraged workers. Moreover, 18% of Black workers were employed part-time. Thus, subproletarianization along with deproletarianization characterizes the contemporary demand for Black labor. Therefore, the new information and service economy has rendered Black workers as a superfluous disposable population (Cha-Jua, 2022, 200.).

Racism and the Psychosocial Workplace Environment

Anti-Black racial oppression shapes the types of jobs available to the majority of Black workers. In addition to the material unequal outcomes this stratification produces, Black people are more likely to experience alienation from the labor they engage in and are less satisfied with their jobs and careers (Koh et al., 2016). Black employees have less advancement on the job, are acknowledged less for their work, have fewer training support, and are watched more closely compared to their white counterparts; these psychosocial workplace environment characteristics in turn are related to lower self-reported health status (McCluney et al., 2018). Experiences with interpersonal racial microaggressions also deplete Black employees of energy and resources and subsequently lead to negative consequences including burnout (King et al., 2022).

Reimagining Labor

A meaningful future for the Black people lies in the abolition of capitalist work. Presently, that sounds utopian. The impoverished conditions of the Black working class necessitate immediate progressive reorganization of work in ways that empower and benefit workers. The shift to worker power begins by reconceptualizing work and its social relations. The importance of this shift is to allow Black workers to earn a living with dignity and have opportunities to thrive. The following are five strategies that could initiate this transition:

1. Employment must be reimagined as a human right. The United States must commit to fulfilling the 1978 Humphrey–Hawkins Full Employment Act's comprehensive agenda. The U.S. economy must be restructured to produce full employment which the Humphrey–Hawkins Act defined as "useful and rewarding employment opportunities for all adult Americans willing and able to work." Moreover, Humphrey–Hawkins required the government to act as the "employer of last resort" (Humphrey, 1976).
2. Racial and all other forms of employment discrimination must be abolished. And Black workers must be compensated for decades of deproletarianization and subproletarianization.
3. All workers must be paid the equivalent of a livable wage. This income must be enough for an individual or family to acquire the necessities of shelter, utilities, food, transportation, childcare, and monies for recreation and savings.

4. The workplace and the relationship between workers and management must be reorganized to empower workers in the day-to-day operation and long-term organization of the work process and the distribution of resources.
5. The eight-hour day and 40-hour week without a reduction in pay and time and a half for overtime became the norm in the United States with the passage of the Adamson Act in 1916. Now more than a century later, it's time to similarly reduce work to the six-hour day and 30-hour week. With the rapid advancement in artificial intelligence, it is reasonable that in the foreseeable future, machines could perform menial jobs—this would allow people to work fewer hours and engage in more meaningful work.

In addition to abolishing work as a capitalist institution, we need to reimagine the workplace, whether virtual or in person. In this sense, workplaces are mandated to promote flourishing among all workers and to explicitly challenge racism. The following are five recommendations that could get us closer to this vision:

1. Workers actively co-create workplace environments, paying close attention to instituting practices that (a) foster a sense of belonging to the site, (b) communicate people at the site are respected and their contributions are valued, and (c) ensure quality training opportunities for all.
2. There is racial and ethnic representation across various jobs within the work site, such that Black employees are not segregated into the least desirable positions.
3. Workers enact reflexive practices and institute policies that ensure the work environment is inclusive and adheres to racial justice principles.
4. Work–life balance must be prioritized. Having a shorter work week is necessary but insufficient in aiding in this goal. Additional conscious efforts at worksites are needed to encourage employees to prioritize health, family, community, and leisure as much as they encourage career advancement.
5. Wraparound services to promote health and well-being among employees and their families are provided at all workplaces, including culturally resonate mental health and vocational counseling.

References

Baron, H. M. (1971). *The demand for black labor: Historical notes on the political economy of racism*. New England Free Press.

Cha-Jua, S. K. (2022). Our history is kinky like our hair: The meaning of African American history. Unpublished manuscript.

Cook, K., Pinder, D., Stewart, III, S., Uchegbu, A., & Wright, J. (2019). *The future of work in Black America*. McKinsey & Company. www.mckinsey.com/~/media/McKinsey/Featured%20Insights/Future%20of%20Organizations/The%20future%20of%20work%20in%20black%20America/The-future-of-work-in-black-america-vF.pdf.

Humphrey, H. H. (1976). The new Humphrey-Hawkins Bill. *Challenge, 19*(2), 21–29.

King, D. D., Fattoracci, E. S. M., Hollingsworth, D. W., Stahr, E., & Nelson, M. (2022, April 28). When thriving requires effortful surviving: Delineating manifestations and resource expenditure outcomes of microaggressions for Black employees. *Journal of Applied Psychology*. Advance online publication. http://dx.doi.org/10.1037/apl0001016.

Koh, C. W., Shen, W., & Lee, T. (2016). Black—white mean differences in job satisfaction: A meta-analysis. *Journal of Vocational Behavior, 94*, 131–143.

McCluney, C. L., Schmitz, L. L., Hicken, M. T., & Sonnega, A. (2018). Structural racism in the workplace: Does perception matter for health inequalities? *Social Science & Medicine, 199*, 106–114.

Nampeo McKenney, "Table 3. Black Population by Free-Slave Status and Change in Slave Population, by Region: 1790-1860." *The Social and Ecoomic Status of the Black Population in the United States: An Historical View, 1790*-1978, U.S. Bureau of the Census, United States. (June 1979). US Government Printing Office.

"Employment Situation News Release," U.S. Bureau of Labor Statistics, September 2, 2022, https://www.bls.gov/news.release/archives/empsit_09022022.htm

Willhelm, S. M. (1970). *Who needs the Negro?* Schenkman Publishing Company.

23 Black Women, Work, and Liberation

(Re)Envisioning a More Equitable Workplace

Kerrie Wilkins-Yel and Aisha Farra

On May 22, 1962, Civil Rights leader, Malcom X, described Black women as the most unprotected, neglected, and disrespected group in the United States. Nowhere is this sentiment more evident, 60 years later, than in the workplace. Due to patriarchal and white supremacist practices, work is where Black women are rendered simultaneously invisible and hyper-visible, underpaid yet overworked, and delegitimized yet tokenized.

> *The most disrespected person in America is the Black woman.*
> *The most unprotected person in America is the Black woman.*
> *The most neglected person in America is the Black woman.*
> —Malcom X

These marginalizing experiences at work were evident pre-pandemic, during the pandemic, and continue as we move toward a post-pandemic era. In 2020, nearly one in five Black women (18.3%) lost their jobs between February and April compared to a 13.2% loss among white men (Wilson, 2021). In 2021, Black women's employment was still 5.1% below their February 2020 levels, compared to white[1] men whose employment had rebounded to where they were down only 3.7 percentage points (Wilson, 2021). According to Janelle Jones, the Labor Department's chief economist, "it took until 2018 for Black women's employment to recover from the Great Recession, and now almost all of those hard-won gains have been erased" (Smart, 2021). For far too long, Black women have borne the brunt of disenfranchising work policies and practices. So, with the "great reset" brought on by the COVID-19 pandemic, it is time that we (re)envision and radically transform the future of work to better serve Black women.

Utilizing Black feminist epistemology and ways of knowing, we centered the voices and lived experiences of Black women to best identify the practices that would be foundational to this reimagined future work. We surveyed 107 Black women from across the lifespan who were employed in an array of occupational settings and asked them to describe the specific practices and policies that would support their thriving at work. Participants were recruited using social media platforms, listservs, snowball sampling,

DOI:10.4324/9781003272397-29

and from organizations that serve Black people and women of color. To participate in the study, participants must have been 18 years or older and identified as a Black woman. In the following sections, we describe the four themes that were identified from participants' open-ended responses.

Transformational Strategies for a More Equitable Workplace

Black women in our study identified four workplace practices that would radically transform their experiences at work. These included (1) providing Black women with equitable compensation, (2) promoting Black women to leadership, (3) taking an active and explicit stand against injustices, and (4) supporting Black women's holistic well-being.

Provide Black Women Equitable Compensation

Inequitable pay has been a long-standing concern for Black women for decades. According to the U.S. Census, Black women were paid 63%, on average, to what white men were paid in 2019 (AAUW, 2021). This gender–racial wage gap is inextricably linked to discriminatory employment practices (e.g., de facto and de jure segregation), inadequate legal protections, and persistent gendered racial stereotypes. Given the ramifications of these wage disparities, Black women in the current study overwhelmingly cited equitable compensation as a key practice that would be necessary for a radically transformed workplace. A 63-year-old, tenured professor exclaimed, "I WOULD GET PAID WHAT WHITE MEN GET PAID!!!" Another participant, a 26-year-old, Writing Center Associate, highlighted the importance of transparency in the compensation process. She shared, "It would definitely include equal pay and openness in the process so that I feel rightfully compensated for all the work I do." Given the history of inequitable compensation, several participants described needing multiple jobs to be able to sustain a comfortable life. This tendency contributed to Black women feeling depleted and exhausted. One participant said the following:

> Adequately compensated! (I shouted this): I work three jobs to live comfortably, not luxuriously, comfortably. . . . Financial stress is so real, especially for Black women. To be compensated accordingly and not have to work so many jobs would free me up in so many ways.
> ~ 30-year-old, African/Belizean American woman, Psychologist

Promote Black Women to Leadership

Despite being among the most educated groups in the United States, Black women are the least represented in leadership. In 2019, for every 100 men that were promoted to manager, the first step in the pipeline to leadership, only 58 Black women were promoted to manager (Burns et al., 2021). Consequently, Black women remain significantly underrepresented in senior leadership, particularly in the most elite leadership positions (e.g., Chief Financial Officer). In fact, only three Black women have ever been promoted to the position of CEO of a Fortune 500 company. To build on the metaphor of the glass ceiling, Black women in the workplace contend with what has become known as the *black ceiling*—the "complex attitudinal and organizational barriers that constrain [Black] women from rising to senior leadership" (Erskine et al., 2021, p. 39). Black women are neither white nor men and, as a result, are often shut out from the informal networks that are critical to accessing mentors and sponsors. Consequently, Black women in the current study cited equitable practices that support the promotion and advancement of Black women to leadership as a necessity for future work. For example, a 54-year-old, Contract Analyst stated that a transformed workplace would mean that "more Black women [would] occupy offices in the C-suite (i.e., CEO, CFO, COO, CIO) and drive the conversations." Similarly, a 49-year-old Black woman holding two jobs as both a deli clerk at a grocery store and a certified nursing assistant at a nursing home stated, "I would like to be given the opportunity to become a leader within my field and not be overlooked because of the color of my skin." A 33-year-old post-doctoral research fellow shared, "I want mechanisms to help me get to the same starting point as my white colleagues. I feel like I am starting 5 steps behind."

Take an Active and Explicit Stand Against Gendered Racism

Black women uniquely reside at the intersection of two minoritized identities (i.e., gender and race), and as such, are prey to two interlocking and oppressive forces, racism and sexism [otherwise referred to as *gendered racism* (Essed, 1991)]. For Black women, experiences of gendered racism in the workplace manifest as frequent encounters where their credibility and authority are questioned, where people express surprise at their language skills and other abilities, where they are exposed to frequent comments about their hair or appearance, and where they are held to a higher standard than their white colleagues. The daily onslaught of these experiences has been associated with detrimental effects on health, well-being, and their ability to thrive at work. Despite this toll, Burns et al. (2021) noted that the "allyship gap" persists. Specifically, more than three-quarters of white employees considered themselves allies to Black and Brown women, yet only 10% of white employees stated that they actively mentored or sponsored a Woman of Color. Similarly, only 21% advocated for new opportunities for Women of Color, and only 39% actively confronted discrimination against a Black woman (Burns et al., 2021). Given the emotional taxation levied on Black women in the workplace, and the clear ways in which white employees are falling short in allyship, Black women in the current study stated that an active and explicit stance against gendered racism was a necessity for future work. One participant said the following:

> There would be strict anti-bigotry, anti-racism and anti-discrimination policies that included measures of accountability where the focus would be on holding the perpetrator accountable for their behavior, not their intention or knowledge which is often used as an excuse to evade accountability (i.e., I didn't know that this word was racist or that making fun of someone's culture was offensive).
>
> ~34-year-old, Eritrean American, Doctoral Intern

Support Black Women's Well-Being

To add to the burden of navigating discriminatory workplace practices, Black women are contracting and dying from COVID-19 at higher rates due to systemic health inequities. Black women are also more prone, due to systemic racism and other systems of oppression, to be in a position where their financial reserves are unable to cover the costs associated with emergencies related to COVID-19 (Lopez et al., 2020). Compounding this reality is that more than 60% of Black women have been personally affected by racial trauma in 2020 (Burns et al., 2021). Witnessing the killings of unarmed Black people, including Breonna Taylor, Ahmaud Arbrey, and George Floyd, significantly heightened Black women's experiences of racial battle fatigue. Despite the myriad of factors that are depleting Black women's mental and emotional resources, Black women reported receiving little support from their managers or supervisors. In 2020, Black women were 2.5 times more likely than women overall to report the death of a loved one, yet 1.5 times more likely than employees of other racial and ethnic groups to feel uncomfortable sharing their grief or loss with their supervisor (Burns et al., 2021).

Black women in the current study noted that a key characteristic of a future work environment that truly served them was one that supported their holistic well-being. Participants provided several examples of ways employers could demonstrate this support. This included providing free or reduced-cost mental healthcare services, particularly from therapists of color, offering paid time off to heal from racial trauma, supporting the CROWN Act, and offering flexible working environments (e.g., working remotely). Black women also stated that acknowledgment and validation were other key ways in which their employers could support their well-being. This sentiment was aptly described in the following excerpt,

> I want people to ASK about how I am doing, and to care about me as more than just what I produce. I need . . . someone to say to me "how are things going? what could I be doing better for you? Is there any

help you need?" as opposed to me having to bring up a problem and reveal that I was struggling . . . I want to be in a culture where they are adamant that the goal is not to work yourself to death.

~33-year-old, Guyanese-American post-doctoral research fellow

(Re)Envisioning a Future Work That Serves Black Women

As co-authors who identify as Black and Brown women, we appreciate and honor the Black women in this study who entrusted us with their lived experiences. So, as we look to a (re)envisioned future of work, we aim to center and elevate these Black women's recommendations as the blueprint for a radically transformed workplace. Four key work practices were suggested by those in the study. First, equitably compensate Black women for their labor, effort, and time. Pay audits are a useful tool to identify and monitor pay inequities in the workplace. However, measures must not only stop at audits. Structures must be put in place to actively reconcile pay gaps between Black women and other groups when identified. Second, support the promotion and advancement of Black women to leadership. Implement equitable hiring practices (e.g., anti-racism training) and invest in mentoring Black women into the leadership pipeline. Third, take an active stance against anti-Black racism, gendered racism, and other oppressive experiences at work. Performative statements supporting Black lives are perfunctory at best. So, establish an infrastructure to hold employees accountable and hire Black consultants to create sustainable and transformative company-wide policies that weave anti-racism practices into the fabric of the company. Four, support Black women's mental health and well-being. If implemented, the aforementioned recommendations will undoubtedly contribute to improved mental health for Black women. In the meantime, employers can create work milieus that prioritize holistic wellness by offering paid mental health days, flexible working environments, and discontinuing the "work yourself to the bone" work culture.

It is imperative that we not let another 60 years pass before we radically (re)envision a workplace that disrupts Malcom X's earlier claims. Black women deserve to work in environments where they can bring their full selves to work (including wearing hairstyles of their choosing), where they are free to express themselves in the full array of their emotions, without being characterized as the "angry Black woman" or fear retribution or reprimand. Black women deserve to work in settings free from gendered-racial trauma and discriminatory actions. Most importantly, Black women deserve to be in a workplace where their expertise is adequately recognized and equitably compensated. With this "great reset," let us (re)imagine a liberatory work milieu where Black women are protected, respected, and fully supported.

Note

1 Seeing that the practice of capitalizing white as a proper noun is a practice associated with those who condone white supremacy, we have chosen not to capitalize white when discussing race in this essay. Our choice is supported by the Associated Press style guide and serves to reclaim Black humanity.

References

American Association of University Women. (2021). Black women & the pay gap. *American Association of University Women*. www.aauw.org/resources/article/black-women-and-the-pay-gap/.

Burns, T., Huang, J., Krivkovich, A., Rambachan, I., Trkulja, T., & Yee, L. (2021). Women in the workplace 2021. *McKinsey & Company*. www.mckinsey.com/featured-insights/diversity-and-inclusion/women-in-the-workplace#.

Erskine, S. E., Archibold, E., & Bilimoria, D. (2021). Afro-diasporic women navigating the black ceiling: Individual, relational, and organizational strategies. *Business Horizons, 64*(1), 37–50.

Essed, P. (1991). *Understanding everyday racism: An interdisciplinary theory* (Vol. 2). SAGE. https://doi.org/10.4135/9781483345239.

Lopez, M. H., Rainie, L., & Budiman, A. (2020). Financial and health impacts of COVID-19 vary widely by race and ethnicity. *Pew Research Center*.

Smart, T. (2021). COVID-19 job market wreaks havoc on Black women. *U.S. News & World Report*. www.usnews.com/news/economy/articles/2021-04-15/black-women-suffering-the-most-from-covid-19-job-market-disruption.

Wilson, V. (2021). Black women face a persistent pay gap, including in essential occupations during the pandemic. *Economic Policy Institute*. www.epi.org/blog/black-women-face-a-persistent-pay-gap-including-in-essential-occupations-during-the-pandemic/.

24 Using Power for Good

Learning to Recognize Hidden Biases/Strengths to Improve Workplace Relationships

Margo A. Jackson and Paige Guarino

Biases are differences in how people are unfairly viewed or treated based on attitudes about their group (such as gender, skin color, or ethnicity); some are positive in conferring preference or granting privilege, and some are negative in being discriminatory or causing disadvantage (Carter et al., 2020). While some biases are more openly expressed and harmful, hidden biases are those we may not even know we possess but still affect our behavior and treatment of others. We all have hidden biases *and* potential resources for understanding the influences of prejudice and discrimination in our workplace relationships.

Workers who often face both direct and subtle forms of prejudice and discrimination include people who are women, mothers, older, currently disabled, Black, Asian American/Pacific Islanders, Native American, Latin American, and LGBTQ+ (Johanson, 2021). Many employees hold more than one of these or other marginalized identities. Workplace prejudice and discrimination exacerbate dehumanizing work inequities and hurt both employees and managers with negative costs to health and productivity. These costs may manifest as burnout, reduced ability to achieve personal and professional goals, and higher organizational attrition rates.

To reduce workplace inequities and reap the benefits of interventions to promote diversity, equity, and inclusion (DEI), employing organizations invest significant time and money in diversity training. For employees subject to harmful biases, potential benefits of effective diversity training include countering consequences to their mental/physical health, facilitating engagement and performance, and improving access to professional development and promotion. Potential benefits to employing organizations include increasing tenure and productivity, limiting liability, and improving reputation (Carter et al., 2020). Effective DEI efforts could reduce workplace inequities and include more diverse perspectives in problem solving to improve the quality of services.

Yet, some diversity training is ineffective or, worse, causes more harm. DEI efforts in workplaces too often focus on D without incorporating E and I, for example, increasing diversity in hiring without addressing how to change workplace relations in ways that include, support, and value diverse

DOI:10.4324/9781003272397-30

workers' perspectives. The focus on equity and inclusion in diversity training may be missing, vague, or aimed at what NOT to do in workplace relationships (e.g., do not be sexist or racist). In part, this is because the harmful biases that underlie prejudice and discrimination are often unrecognized and pervasive.

We propose that one promising approach to more effectively promote DEI goals would be to develop and incorporate ongoing diversity training to improve workplace interpersonal relationship skills focused on two core components. One core component should include skill building to communicate well across differences and build on strengths for empathic perspective taking. The other core component should include skill building to develop awareness and understanding about hidden biases and power dynamics of attention, perception, and perspective taking from different social positions of power in relation to prejudice and discrimination.

Hidden Biases of Power in Workplace Relationships

Broadly, prejudice and discrimination persist in hidden biases that impede health and productivity at three levels—individual (intra-personal), interpersonal (relational), and structural (institutional, including policies and practices, and societal) (Jones, 2000). At the structural level, there are promising global efforts to improve equitable access to decent work and reduce discriminatory treatment in workplaces (for example, through the Decent Work Agenda of the International Labour Organization, included in the 2030 Agenda for Sustainable Development of the United Nations). At the individual level (regarding feelings, thoughts, and behavior), evolving theory and research aim to improve our understanding of core psychological aspects (Banaji & Greenwald, 2013; Sue & Spanierman, 2020). Yet fundamental to human health and productivity are relationships at the interpersonal level.

Effective interpersonal communication is the bedrock on which relationships are built in workplaces and beyond (Howell, 2021). Toward working well together, this includes the process and practice of exchanging ideas, information, and emotional experiences through words, cues (e.g., in voice, facial expressions, and gestures), and contexts. Effective interpersonal communication can be built on empathic perspective-taking skills: developing the ability to look beyond one's own frame of reference and to understand and respectfully consider the thoughts, feelings, motivations, and intentions of what another person is experiencing (Israel, 2020). Diversity training should include this core component for cultivating empathic perspective-taking skills in workplace relationships.

Hidden biases may distort and limit empathic perspective taking. We all have biases of which we may not be aware, such as the influences of pervasive stereotypes, automatic assumptions, and systemic injustices; these biases limit our understanding and effectiveness in relationships, communication, and actions. In interpersonal communication, hidden biases are one source of miscommunication and harm, albeit often not recognized or acknowledged.

One hidden bias particularly relates to the power dynamics between managers and employees. Typically, people in social positions of power pay less attention to those in positions of less power (Fiske, 1993) and notice their deficits more than their strengths (Pinderhughes, 1989). Thus, managers may be less likely to get to know their employees as unique individuals, whose assets they might recognize and promote, and more likely to stereotype or discriminate against their employees. Conversely, those in positions of less power tend to pay more attention to and know more about those in positions of more power. Employees' perspectives are likely untapped resources for their potential contributions to more helpful exchanges with managers. Effective diversity training must therefore include developing awareness and understanding of hidden biases in the power dynamics of workplace relationships.

Recommendations

Evidence demonstrates that workplace DEI policies and practices are more effective when they are supported by both managers and employees; helpfully address group differences in beliefs that prejudice and discrimination cause work inequities; and explicitly frame interventions directed toward reducing discrimination and increasing diversity (Scarborough et al., 2019). As part of a broader DEI strategy for structural changes to policies and operating procedures, we offer three key recommendations to develop and deliver effective and ongoing diversity training that focuses on constructively addressing hidden biases in power dynamics and building strengths to improve workplace relationships.

First, skilled facilitators are needed. Whether hired as external consultants or using internal human resources, facilitators must have expertise in DEI training and behavior change, tailored to organizational goals and strategic planning. Foundationally, regarding the need for bias awareness training, "The biggest mistake we make with [hidden biases] is that we think we are the exception to the rule, magically exempt from a lifetime of conditioning, because we are unaware of our biases to begin with" (J. Mathew, personal communication, July 24, 2020). Yet, centering bias awareness in diversity training is necessary but insufficient. In these trainings, defensive reactions from various perspectives are often elicited and must be constructively addressed. For people in social positions of more power (e.g., managers/leaders and employees with identities of taken-for-granted access to resources for decent work), their defensive reactions tend toward avoiding, ignoring, discounting, or silencing bias awareness issues. They may fear acknowledging their part in harmful biases and doubt their ability to effect changes. For people in social positions of less power (e.g., employees with identities subject to prejudice and discrimination), similar defensive reactions may be elicited, alongside anger, mistrust, and fear of repercussions. Their fears are likely based on their risk of being subjected to more harmful biases and behaviors that minimize, discount, or marginalize them, while further reducing their access to resources for decent work and career development.

Therefore, in light of these differing defensive reactions and consequences, skilled facilitators should provide a balance of challenge to and support for developing awareness and understanding of hidden biases in power dynamics and defensive reactions and then practice with participants how to constructively address these biases in workplace relationships. This framework pivotally includes a focus on using power for good. Effective diversity training that takes workplace power dynamics into account can promote agency for individual employees and help organizational leaders develop mechanisms for improving workplace relationships in the long term.

Second, facilitators should coordinate with the executives who choose the organizational DEI goals to tailor diversity training that advances their desired outcomes (Carter et al., 2020). Effective diversity training requires skilled facilitators to persuade employers and employees that discomfort and defensiveness can be expected and managed as an important part of the ongoing process of learning how to better communicate across differences. Furthermore, to address the challenge of demonstrating impact, facilitators and organizational executives should develop and implement plans for evaluating the efficacy of the diversity training (Carter et al., 2020). Evolving evaluation data can be used to inform revisions to ongoing diversity training to constructively improve workplace relationships.

Finally, we propose that diversity training should be an ongoing professional development component tailored to facilitating workplace relationships that promote equity and effective communication across differences in power and perspective taking. This approach should be one component of a comprehensive DEI strategy of the organization's executives who are responsible for strategic planning and accountability structures used to implement applications to everyday practices.

Conclusion

The institution of work continues to be plagued by pervasive prejudice and discrimination that harm workplace health and productivity and impede effective communication in workplace relationships. Hidden biases in power dynamics between and among managers and employees can undermine organizational initiatives to effectively promote DEI. We propose one approach to transforming workplace cultures with diversity training incorporated in a long-term, developmental, constructive process for building workplace relationships that genuinely include, support, and value diverse workers' perspectives. By learning to recognize and mitigate hidden biases in power dynamics—including constructively building on untapped resources for empathic understanding, connecting, and working to advocate for helpful change—we can use power for good.

References

Banaji, M. R., & Greenwald, A. G. (2013). *Blindspot: Hidden biases of good people.* Delacorte Press.

Carter, E. R., Onyeador, I. N., & Lewis, N. A. (2020). Developing & delivering effective anti-bias training: Challenges & recommendations. *Behavioral Science and Policy, 6*(1), 57–70. https://behavioralpolicy.org/wp-content/uploads/2020/08/Developing-delivering-effective-anti-bias-training-Challenges-.pdf.

Fiske, S. T. (1993). Controlling other people: The impact of power on stereotyping. *American Psychologist, 48*(6), 621–628. http://dx.doi.org/10.1037/0003-066X.48.6.621.

Howell, D. (2021, May 22). *Interpersonal communication: How to improve it and why it is a must-have business skill.* www.beekeeper.io/blog/interpersonal-communication/.

Israel, T. (2020). *Beyond your bubble: How to connect across the political divide—skills and strategies for conversations that work.* American Psychological Association.

Johanson, K. (2021, August 5). 10 ways inequity still very much exists in the workplace. *Newsweek.* www.newsweek.com/10-ways-inequity-still-very-much-exists-workplace-1616254.

Jones, C. (2000). Levels of racism: A theoretic framework and a gardener's tale. *American Journal of Public Health, 90*(8), 1212–1215. http://dx.doi.org/10.2105/AJPH.90.8.1212.

Pinderhughes, E. (1989). *Understanding race, ethnicity, and power: The key to efficacy in clinical practice.* The Free Press, Simon & Schuster.

Scarborough, W. J., Lambouths, D. L., & Holbrook, A. L. (2019). Support of workplace diversity policies: The role of race, gender, and beliefs about inequality. *Social Science Research, 79*, 194–210. https://doi.org/10.1016/J.SSRESEARCH.2019.01.002.

Sue, D. W., & Spanierman, L. (2020). *Microaggressions in everyday life.* Wiley.

25 Gender and Racial/Ethnic Disparities in the Workplace

Nadya A. Fouad and Stephanie G. Burrows

One of the most persistent work-related topics in the past 60 years has been a call for gender and racial equity at work. Beginning in the 1960s, many activists argued that the United States needed to create more opportunities for women and racial/ethnic minorities to enter, succeed, and advance in the workforce (Flores et al., 2021; Fouad et al., in press). This has been reflected in legislation, with the Equal Pay Act and Affirmative Action, the creation of governmental agencies, such as the Equal Opportunity Commission, and educational initiatives, such as summer and after-school programs promoting women's interests in STEM. These legislative, governmental, and educational efforts, coupled with economic demands, such as the recession in the 1970s and 1980s that led to a need for dual incomes among White couples, have resulted in consistent increases in the participation of women and individuals from racially and ethnically underrepresented backgrounds in the U.S. workforce. Although women now comprise 55% of the U.S. workforce compared to 43% in 1970, their presence is limited to relatively few occupations. Similarly, racial/ethnic minorities have grown to be a greater percentage of the workforce due to both immigration and higher birth rates but are overrepresented in some occupations and underrepresented in others. Women of color, for example, have always worked, but primarily in lower-wage, service sector positions. The differences in occupations are reflected in overall earnings as women, African Americans, and Hispanics make on average between 55 and 80% of the earnings of their White and Asian male counterparts.

At one level, choosing an occupation is a matter of individual choice, reflecting an individual's abilities, interests, and values around the type of work they want to do. But at another level, the persistent lack of equitable distribution of women and racial/ethnic minorities across occupations, despite 60 years of legislative and educational initiatives, suggests external factors, such as discrimination, limited exposure to occupations, or lack of role models and mentors, may play a role. Indeed, if there was an equitable representation of women and racial/ethnic minorities in the U.S. workforce, their participation would reflect that of their percentage of the U.S. population: approximately 60.1% White, 18.5% Hispanic or Latino, 13.4% African

DOI:10.4324/9781003272397-31

American, 6.1% Asian American or Pacific Islander, and 1.3% American Indian. But Byars-Winston et al.'s (2015) review of 40 years of labor statistics data found disparities across a number of occupations. For example, individuals from White and Asian backgrounds commonly chose professional occupations, although men entered technical positions (engineering or physician) while women chose service and caretaking positions (nursing or teaching). Likewise, Black and Hispanic males commonly entered low-skill and low-wage occupations. Understanding what contributes to these differences in choices would help employers, employees, counselors, and educators know how and when to intervene to better create a more equitable occupational landscape.

Understanding factors related to occupational choice is complicated because of intersecting identities, particularly when focusing on gender and racial/ethnic differences in work decisions and choices. In other words, there are large within-group differences for both groups, and gender and race/ethnicity intersect in ways that may also be different depending on social class and sexual orientation. Research on racial/ethnic differences almost invariably asks individuals to check a demographic box identifying race or ethnicity, but researchers often fail to address how the salience of an individual's identity influences their career decision-making or may change across the lifespan. For example, an African American lesbian who strongly identifies with her gender, racial, and sexual orientation identities may have found her gender to be most salient in choosing courses in high school, her race most salient in choosing a college, and her sexual orientation *and* race most salient as an adult in the workforce.

Gender Disparities in the Workplace

Gender Stereotypes

Some differences in occupational choice are due to **gender stereotypes** that start nearly from birth and influence men's and women's aspirations for different occupations. Little boys' toys are related to building, creating, investigating, and more recently, technology. Little girls' toys are related to caretaking and nurturing. As such, children's aspirations to be in occupations related to the activities they are reinforced for doing, such as engineering for boys and nursing for girls, are unsurprising. There has been some success in creating interventions that alter children's existing gendered career expectations. For example, programs that foster girls' interests in STEM help them to consider careers that use those skills, while fostering interests in caring may help boys consider social work or nursing careers. The messages about what is appropriate for girls and boys to do, however, are remarkably strong, and the biggest barriers start in high school, where both boys and girls choose classes and activities that foreclose non-gender stereotypic occupations. Math classes, for example, have been termed "critical filters" for technical occupations, and girls start to make choices not to take advanced math classes early in high school (Fouad & Santana, 2017). This subsequently leads to barriers in college when girls are less likely to have the preparation to take college-level math classes to prepare them for STEM careers.

Wage Gap

Once men and women enter the workforce, the differences in occupational choices result in a wage gap. This is partially influenced by a complex set of individual and societal factors, including the **unpaid work that women do to care for their families** often resulting in their lower participation in full-time work, but is also influenced by the fact that **women are paid less** and are typically in less senior roles that pay less than executive positions. Calls for action to increase gender equity in employment and leadership have led to changes such as California's required quota for the number of women on the Board of Directors of publicly traded companies. Research has also made the case for having more women in leadership positions (e.g., CEOs and Senior Executive Leaders), arguing that gender diversity has been tied to better business outcomes. Other lines of research explore the effect of gender leadership on innovation and investigate whether diverse teams are more likely to be high-performing teams and whether gender-diverse leadership in companies leads to greater innovation and financial performance. In sum, increasing women in non-traditional occupations and helping them access leadership opportunities may be good for business and innovation.

Racial/Ethnic Disparities in the Workplace

Career Expectations and Choices

Research in the past 40 years has provided some guidance on factors related to racial/ethnic differences in career choices. Although there are few racial/ethnic differences in career aspirations, there are significant differences in career expectations. In other words, there are no differences among racial/ethnic groups when children are asked what job they dream about entering in the future, but there are differences in the job they actually expect to do. What racial/ethnic minority children expected to do was considerably lower in educational achievement, prestige, and wage potential than White children. Internal factors, such as the development of a narrow range of interests, the perception that some occupations are closed to people of their race/ethnicity or gender, or low confidence in pursuing post-secondary education, may contribute to these disparities. Likewise, when considering future choices, some racial/ethnic minority children may not have had the **opportunities to develop a wide array of vocational interests** and/or may have had **limited exposure to opportunities to develop confidence** in various occupations. These external factors may manifest as **discrimination** or lack of mentors or **role models**. For example, racial/ethnic minority children may have limited opportunities to view people who resemble them in a variety of occupations or lack people who could provide encouragement to pursue educational or occupational goals or from whom they could learn coping skills in the face of barriers.

Understanding the barriers that contribute to these disparities and prevent racial/ethnic minorities from gaining occupational equity will allow for the development of interventions to create more equitable workplaces. Offering more opportunities to racial/ethnic minority students may help promote the development of interests and self-efficacy. However, educational opportunities need to be supported by teachers, parents, and counselors and be engaging and long enough in duration to help interests form. Similarly, addressing students' self-filtering out of math classes in high school will help prevent the barriers that come from poor math preparation if a racial/ethnic minority student wants to pursue STEM fields (Fouad & Santana, 2017). At the organizational level, formal policies on hiring and promotion have been shown to counter the unconscious bias that happens when supervisors have too much discretion (Loscocco, 2018). Forced diversity training has not been shown to be effective, but accountability has been effective in reducing racial disparities in hiring. Likewise, while formal mentoring programs are not always as effective as informal mentoring (which happens naturally rather than programmatically), mentoring and strategically building strong networks within and across organizations can help racial/ethnic minorities succeed.

Recommendations

At a policy level, consistent enforcement and re-evaluation of existing policies can help ameliorate occupational segregation. The aforementioned governmental policies were developed 60 years ago; it may be time to assess how well they function in the 21st century. But governmental policies cannot be the only answer to level the occupational landscape. Organizations also need to play a role in changing their policies and practices. One way to do this is by making transparent the number of women and racial/ethnic minorities and their wages, so wage gaps can be studied. Various stakeholders including shareholders, boards of directors, employees, and consumers also need to hold organizations accountable for hiring and promoting women and racial/ethnic minorities.

Organizational interventions must be systemic to be effective and sustainable. Employers need to critically examine barriers to hiring women and racial/ethnic minorities (Flores et al., 2021). Those barriers may come during hiring, where women or racial/ethnic minority interviewees may be subject to implicit bias preventing them from successfully navigating the interview process. For example, when symphony orchestras established blind auditions by having musicians perform behind a screen and, in some cases, remove their shoes so as not to bias jurors, more women were hired. Employers further need to determine the best ways to communicate a welcoming environment for women and racial/ethnic minorities in their hiring advertisements and interview processes (Flores et al., 2021). Once hired, employers need to ensure that individuals are socialized to the company or firm culture. They should also regularly examine their wage structure, including salaries, benefits, and workplace resources to ensure equitable compensation across groups. Employers need to provide both formal and informal mentoring opportunities to ensure that all individuals are provided the resources to be successful and advance within the company. Finally, employers should critically examine promotion criteria to ensure there are no biases in the process of who is selected for leadership opportunities.

Schools can actively create opportunities to build self-confidence to enter different occupations and work to counter the notion that "people like me cannot do" an occupation. In that way, girls and women can counter gendered stereotypes that they cannot enter technical or scientific occupations, and racial/ethnic minorities can pursue occupations in which they are underrepresented. School guidance programs can also create systematic and developmentally appropriate mechanisms to broaden students' interests, create opportunities to develop realistic expectations of various occupations, and support individual efforts to challenge perceptions that some occupations are unavailable to women and people of color. For example, elementary school students may engage in activities focused on learning about the broad array of work and introduce work expectations. In middle school, students can learn about the career decision-making process without pressure about what decision they will make. Then, when they reach high school, students can explore how their interests may lead to various careers and what preparation is needed to reach their goals. Teachers and guidance counselors can also work to counter students' implicit biases that could reinforce occupational stereotypes.

References

Byars-Winston, A., Fouad, N., & Wen, Y. (2015). Race/ethnicity and sex in U.S. occupations, 1970–2010: Implications for research, practice, and policy. *Journal of Vocational Behavior, 87*, 54–70. https://doi.org/10.1016/j.jvb.2014.12.003.

Flores, L. Y., Martinez, L. D., McGillen, G. G., & Milord, J. (2019). Something old and something new: Future directions in vocational research with people of color in the United States. *Journal of Career Assessment, 27*(2), 187–208. https://doi.org/10.1177/1069072718822461.

Flores, L. Y., Settles, I., McGillen, G. G., & Davis, T. M. (2021). Critical contributions to scholarship on women and work: Celebrating 50 years of progress and looking ahead to a new decade. *Journal of Vocational Behavior, 126,* Article 103490. https://doi.org/10.1016/j.jvb.2020.103490.

Fouad, N. A., Kozlowski, M. B., Schams, S. S., Weber, K., Diaz, W., & Burrows, S. G. (in press). Why aren't we there yet? The status of research in women's career development. *The Counseling Psychologist.*

Fouad, N. A., & Santana, M. C. (2017). SCCT and underrepresented populations in STEM fields: Moving the needle. *Journal of Career Assessment, 25*(1), 24–39. https://doi.org/10.1177/1069072716658324.

Loscocco, K. (2018). *Race and work.* Policy Press.

26 Working People

Brown and Black Meat and Poultry Processing Workers in the U.S. South

Keona K. Ervin

In late spring of 2022, just as the COVID-19 global pandemic began to grip the United States, meatpacking facilities across the country captured great attention. With over 500,000 workers in nearly 4,000 plants across the United States, a figure drawn from a *Morbidity and Mortality Weekly Report* of the Centers for Disease Control and Prevention, meat slaughtering and processing plants soon became COVID hotspots (Waltenburg et al., 2020).[1] The virus swept through vulnerable workers and their communities. Workers at meat and poultry processing plants, the overwhelming majority of whom were Latinx and Black, were especially affected. For instance, in Hall County, Georgia, home to several poultry processing plants, Latinx workers were infected at approximately double the rate of the rest of the population, according to an *NPR* report (Green, 2020).[2] High infection rates and the working conditions at meat and poultry processing plants made for a dangerous combination. The *Morbidity and Mortality Weekly Report* found that crowding, poor ventilation, long work periods, and exploitive policies defined the work for low-income workers of color, many of whom lived, commuted, and often gathered outside of work hours on a communal basis (Waltenburg et al.).[3] Gary Ward Black, Sr., Georgia's Commissioner of Agriculture, blamed workers when asked by Atlanta-based journalist Emily Green (2020) about the high infection rates among plant workers.[4] "You can see that where there have been some elevated cases," he explained. "The facts are it's not happening at work. It's happening after hours."[5] Such an observation reflects both a long-standing partnership between local and state government officials and big industry leaders and also a routine tendency to name low-income communities as sites of communicable disease and squalor. It was clear, however, that plant conditions were driving rates of infection. Black assured that plant managers were following safety protocols but workers told a different story. Instructed by management to apply for unemployment, symptomatic employees continued to work because as one Georgia employee put in an *NPR* news story, "If you tell the boss you don't feel well, the response is, keep working."[6] Likewise, poultry industry giant Tyson Foods had almost 600 workers test positive at just one of its facilities, according to the same report. One worker there shared, "I'm scared, but

DOI:10.4324/9781003272397-32

if I don't work, who will."[7] Of course, migration status profoundly shaped access to care and the paltry benefits of the social safety net. The *NPR* found that undocumented workers most often did not qualify for unemployment benefits and were understandably reluctant to get tested for COVID because they feared deportation.[8] In much of the coverage, southern meatpacking and poultry processing plants emerged as a central focus for understanding the disastrous outcomes brought about by the clash of a highly contagious and deadly virus and the devaluing of "essential work."

In the U.S. South, meat packing and poultry processing industries function as significant anchors of regional and national economies, a fact intimately tied to the understanding that southern plants were and continue to be deeply marked by race, ethnicity, nationality, and migration status. A pillar of Georgia's economy, poultry processing pours approximately 18 billion into the state's coffers each year, as reported in the aforementioned *NPR* account.[9] Roughly, since the turn of the 21st century, Mississippi's poultry plants yielded the highest income-generating product in the state based on a 2017 Mississippi State University Extension report (Tabler & Wells, 2017).[10] According to the same study, the Magnolia State reached more than $2.7 billion in sales in 2012 and more than $2.87 billion two years later (Tabler & Wells).[11] Although Arkansas, home to the headquarters of industrial giant Tyson Foods, made up just 1% of the total U.S. population, the state accounted for 12% of poultry processing jobs nationwide in 2014.[12] Two years earlier, Arkansas ranked third in US broiler production and second in 2013.[13]

Across the second half of the 20th century, assistance from federal fiscal policies favoring mechanization and the underproduction of cotton pushed Black farmers out of their jobs, forcing them to find positions in industrial employment. As a result, white workers had the racial benefit of being able to abandon poultry work to land jobs at new state-constructed industrial plants. What is more, adopting vertical integration made it more possible for companies to control costs and output. As Stuesse and Helton (2013) demonstrate in "Low-Wage Legacies, Race, and the Golden Chicken in Mississippi," their study of poultry processing plants in the Magnolia State, such deeply impactful structural shifts were the result of the relation between corporate and state partnership and "strategic" decision-making, which moved toward centralization and standardization, and Black protest. The southern-based Black struggle for freedom, one marked by the effort to build economic self-determination, was, in part, a political response to changes in the employment landscape of the South, which resulted in the expansion of precarious labor practices more broadly. Stuesse and Helton (2013) put it this way, "By the end of the 1960s most of Mississippi's chicken plants were run by white management, overseen by white supervisors, and staffed by line workers who were almost entirely African American," Stuesse and Helton (2013) observe.[14] Within this context, as early as the late 1970s and more intensely in the 1990s, meat and poultry processing plant managers began recruiting Latinx workers, creating a predominantly Brown and Black workforce as white working-class workers gained the capacity to secure relatively "better" jobs.

Beginning in the late 1970s and accelerating in the 1990s, Stuesse and Helton (2013) note, plant managers began recruiting Latinx workers from El Paso and Miami and, as other companies did so, recruited Cuban, Mexican, Peruvian, Argentinian, Uruguayan, El Salvadoran, and Guatemalan workers. Forwarding old, racist and misogynistic notions of Black workers—namely, that they were "lazy" or "bad" workers—company officials ramped up their recruitment of Brown workers, punishing Black workers for daring to challenge companies through self-organization, coalition work, unionization, walkouts, and strikes. New migrants lived in inadequate makeshift company housing because private rental managers refused to make their properties available and generally earned under approximately $10 per hour. Cries of labor shortages joined the chorus, too, as companies rapidly expanded. Latinx migration to the U.S. South, then, was intimately bound up with Black, southern-based struggles for working-class justice during the civil rights and immediate post–civil rights eras. Industrial expansion, companies' expanding fiscal power, wage reductions, speedups, deskilling, and the concentration of Black and Brown workers across the latter decades of the 20th century set the conditions for intense battles for economic justice. The changes described by Stuesse and Helton (2013), along with the broader histories of race, gender, and poultry processing in the South, as analyzed by historian LaGuana Gray (2014), for example, are generally applicable to transformations in the South's meat and poultry processing industry.[15]

The vulnerability of Brown and Black poultry and meat packing workers in the South did not go without challenge. A tradition of worker organizing among this group has exposed the routine abuses practiced by corporations and the state and won partial victories that merit widespread attention. Southeast North Carolina, for example, among the poorest regions in the country and home to Smithfield Foods, one of the world's largest meatpacking companies, was the stage for a 15-year unionization battle that began just one year following Smithfield's opening in the Tarheel State. *Union Time: Fighting for Workers' Rights*, a film by Matthew Barr (2016), tells the story of the long-term struggle to organize employees at a facility in which working conditions were beyond horrific. Employees were rendered temporarily or permanently disabled because of a lack of safety measures; and, some were even killed, as was the case with Glenn Tony Birdsong, a supervisor from Fayetteville who died in November 2002 after falling into a tank filled with toxic chemicals. Investigations revealed that the company had not trained Birdsong and had violated multiple Occupational Safety and Health Administration regulations. Even following Birdsong's death, which ended in settlement, workers were hit, knocked over, or trampled by hogs; they worked on poorly ventilated shop floors under temperatures that were either too hot or too cold, and they used extremely sharp knives that resulted in routine cuts and scrapes, maiming, and partial amputation. Rates of repetitive motion injury from speedups that required thousands of fine, repetitive precision at a machine-like pace were consistently high. Worker disposability made it relatively easy for company officials to continue to threaten and abuse workers with impunity. After many failed attempts that were due in large part to the power of the company to resist organizing efforts through violence, intimidation, tampering, raids, and even the creation of a deputized Smithfield Foods Police Department that had the power to detain and arrest workers, workers found favorable outcomes. A May 2006 Court of Appeals ruling found Smithfield Foods in violation of 20 separate labor policies and workers eventually won their union election in 2009.[16]

This brief overview of some of the recent history the southern meat and poultry processing industry and worker organization within it is by no means exhaustive, but it can offer some recommendations for ways to better protect vulnerable workers. Pay increases; safety protocols; eliminating speedups; breaks; access to facilities; full and complete access to healthcare, sick pay, and other basic work benefits for all workers, especially undocumented employees, is a good place to start. Establishing mechanisms for eliminating discrimination against Black and Brown workers and providing clear and transparent paths toward economic mobility is also desperately needed. Finally, as the labor organizing examples in Mississippi and North Carolina suggest, workers' ability to collectively bargain without intimidation must be protected. And for those involved in efforts to organize workers, drawing upon coalitions and sharing workers' stories far and wide are crucial to the fight to build an influential labor struggle.[17]

Notes

1 Michelle A. Waltenburg, Tristan Victoroff, Charles E. Rose, et al., "Update: COVID-19 Among Workers in Meat and Poultry Processing Facilities—United States, April-May 2020," *Morbidity and Mortality Weekly Report*, vol. 69, no. 27 (July 2020): 887–892.

2 Emily Green, "The Coronavirus Hits Poultry Processing Plants in the South," *National Public Radio*, Atlanta: WABE, May 22, 2022.

3 Waltenburg, Victoroff, Rose, et al., "Update: COVID 29 Among Workers in Meat and Poultry Processing Facilities."

4 Green, "The Coronavirus Hits Poultry Processing Plants in the South."

5 Green, "The Coronavirus Hits Poultry Processing Plants in the South."

6 Green, "The Coronavirus Hits Poultry Processing Plants in the South."

7 Green, "The Coronavirus Hits Poultry Processing Plants in the South."

8 Green, "The Coronavirus Hits Poultry Processing Plants in the South."

9 Green, "The Coronavirus Hits Poultry Processing Plants in the South."

10 Tom Tabler and Jessica Wells, "Economic Impact of Mississippi's Poultry Industry," *Mississippi State University Extension*, Publication 3048 (POD-06-17), 1, 2017. http://extension.msstate.edu/sites/default/files/publications/publications/p3048.pdf.

11 Tabler and Wells, "Economic Impact of Mississippi's Poultry Industry," 1.

12 Nina Ebner, Jessica Halpern-Finnerty, Saru Jayaraman, Miya Cain, Amber Moulton, and Chris Benner, "Wages and Working Conditions in Arkansas Poultry Plants," The Northwest Arkansas Workers' Justice Center Report, February 1, 1016, 1.

13 Ebner, Halpern-Finnerty, Jayaraman, Cain, Moulton, and Benner, "Wages and Working Conditions in Arkansas Poultry Plants," 8.

14 Angela Stuesse and Laura E. Helton, "Low-Wage Legacies, Race, and the Golden Chicken in Mississippi: Where Contemporary Immigration Meets African American Labor History," *Southern Spaces*, December 31, 2013. https://southernspaces.org/2013/low-wage-legacies-race-and-golden-chicken-mississippi-where-contemporary-immigration-meets-african-american-labor-history/.

15 Stuesse and Helton, "Low-Wage Legacies"; LaGuana Gray, *We Just Keep Running the Line: Black Southern Women and the Poultry Processing Industry*, Baton Rouge: Louisiana State University Press, 2014.

16 *Union Time: Fighting for Workers' Rights*, directed by Matthew Barr, released in 2016.

17 Ebner, Halpern-Finnerty, Jayaraman, Cain, Moulton, and Benner, "Wages and Working Conditions in Arkansas Poultry Plants," 35–36.

References

Barr, M. (Director). (2016). *Union time: Fighting for workers' rights.* The Video Project.

Gray, L. (2014). *We just keep running the line: Black southern women and the Poultry Processing Industry.* Louisiana State University Press.

Green, E. National Public Radio, All Things Considered (2020, May 22). *The coronavirus hits poultry processing plants in the South.* Atlanta: WABE. https://www.npr.org/2020/05/22/861202489/the-coronavirus-hits-poultry-processing-plants-in-the-south.

Stuesse, A., & Helton, L. E. (2013, December 31). Low-wage legacies, race, and the golden chicken in Mississippi: Where contemporary immigration meets African American labor history. *Southern Spaces.* https://southernspaces.org/2013/low-wage-legacies-race-and-golden-chicken-mississippi-where-contemporary-immigration-meets-african-american-labor-history/.

Tabler, T., & Wells, J. (2017). *Economic impact of Mississippi's poultry industry.* Mississippi State University Extension, Publication 3048 (POD-06-17), 1–8. http://extension.msstate.edu/sites/default/files/publications/publications/p3048.pdf.

Walternburg, M. A., Victoroff, T., Rose, C. E., et al. (2020, April–May). COVID-19 among workers in meat and poultry processing facilities—United States. *Morbidity and Mortality Weekly Report 2020, 69,* 887–892.

Practice, Systematic, and Policy Perspectives on Work

27 Women's Leadership and Advancement in a Kaleidoscope World

Opportunity Awaits

Donna E. Schultheiss

Just how much of a problem is gender equity at work? Recent data indicate the United States ranks 30 out of 156 countries in a global gender gap report (Work Economic Forum, 2021). Gender equality is the fifth of 17 United Nations Sustainable Development Goals aimed at promoting an inclusive and sustainable world (United Nations, n.d.). As the proportion of women in skilled professions continues to increase, income disparities are largely driven by the low percentage of women in leadership positions. Globally, women hold only 33% of managerial positions and 42% in the United States (McKinsey & Company, 2020). Data reveal the COVID-19 pandemic has impacted women more severely than men, suggesting stark cumulative effects on future economic opportunities, inferior re-employment prospects, and a persistent decrease in income. The pandemic has disproportionately affected vulnerable workers (e.g., women, underrepresented groups, younger workers, less educated, and low earners), and without proactive intervention, the deeply unequal recovery for workers will further exacerbate inequality.

The disproportionate burden of unpaid domestic and care work on women, exacerbated during the pandemic, has created untenable circumstances for women and led to a reduction in working hours or exit from the workforce. This creates a motherhood penalty from which women rarely recover. Expectations to work long hours, paired with a lack of access to work–family policies and stigma for those who use it, add to even greater gender career inequality (Kossek et al., 2017). During this work-from-home era, women are less likely to be visible—a key advantage on the path to leadership. To mother or matter (Schultheiss, 2009) has never been more apparent than it is now.

The pandemic has created the largest reorganization of work in recent history, challenging the rigidity of corporate America which has had punishing effects on workers, mostly women, who ask for flexibility outside of traditional norms. Disruption, friction, and change can create radical transformation. Is this the disruption we need for positive change? The World Economic Forum (2021) report which asserts that gender-positive recovery policies and practices have the potential to counter these challenges, suggests it is.

DOI:10.4324/9781003272397-34

Theoretical Underpinnings

Role congruity theory points to the perceived incongruity between the female gender role and leadership roles which have been perceived as characteristically male (Eagly & Karau, 2002), resulting in perceptions of successful leaders as those who possess characteristics aligned with masculine stereotypes. This creates a double-bind from two forms of prejudice which contribute to women having less access and more obstacles to leadership roles than men: (1) evaluating women less favorably than men as potential leaders because leadership ability is more stereotypical of men than women and (2) evaluating leadership behavior of women less favorably than men because such behavior is perceived as less desirable in women (Eagly & Karau). Leaders from multiple diverse identity groups feel added pressure to conform to the leadership styles of the dominant group and often feel isolated and unsupported. Gender inequality in selection and leadership development, discussed next, are of critical importance in identifying an opportunity to attain equitable leadership prospects for women.

Gender Inequality in Differential Rates of Selection

Trailing percentages of women in ascending leadership positions (from 48% at the entry level to 26 and 21% at the senior vice president and chief corporate officer, respectively) suggest that women are disadvantaged from the start (McKinsey & Company, 2020). Institutional barriers—such as being offered fewer challenging leadership tasks, fewer opportunities to learn and develop leadership skills, less visibility in the organization, smaller networks, and fewer leadership role models, mentors, and sponsors—accumulate over the course of women's careers. Women tend to be selected for leadership positions that are risky and precarious, a phenomenon referred to as a "glass cliff" (Ryan et al., 2016). Selection bias (i.e., when organizations are performing well, they tend to hire men, and when performing poorly, they tend to hire women) is an underlying process contributing to this phenomenon. A second underlying process occurs when women are hired at greater rates than men during times of crisis or transition, or when the rate of failure is high, referred to as "think crisis, think female" (Ryan et al., 2016). In times of crisis, interpersonal characteristics stereotypically associated with women are more salient in leadership selection, while in times of success, agentic characteristics associated with men are more highly sought.

Gender Inequalities in Leadership Development

The lack of leadership development opportunities for women has been well-documented. Women's development programs provide impactful opportunities to strengthen skills and networks. Alternative approaches suggest leadership programs take an all-inclusive approach, encouraging the involvement of dominant group members as allies to support women and intersectional group identities.

Similar to career development, leadership development is increasingly understood as a dynamic lifespan developmental process. Everyday experiences provide an opportunity for intervention to enhance leader development. Gender role stereotypes and expectations take hold early in life, discouraging girls from self-advocacy, risk-taking, and ambition, propagating negative expectations about girls and women in male-dominated endeavors. Researchers have examined the relationship between the developmental origins of gender stereotypes, and the characteristics believed to be necessary to be a leader, otherwise known as implicit leadership theories.

Millennials now make up the largest generation in the labor force. This cohort of leaders is more people-oriented and gender-neutral in how they view women in leadership. Millennial women tend to have professional aspirations in line with personal values and expect challenge and flexibility from the workplace. Equality and fairness are of paramount concern for these leaders, and respect for equal rights and opportunities and collaboration over competition (characteristics typically associated with women) are now seen as congruent with good leadership. Is generational change upon us?

Recommendations for Socially Responsible Organizations and Policies

Research that quantified the relationship between women's representation in leadership and the organization's financial performance emerged to substantiate the diversification of upper ranks of organizations, otherwise known as the business case (Hideg & Krstic, 2021). Profoundly, the value of men in leadership positions has not been analyzed—or otherwise questioned—by examining their representation and organizational financial performance. The business case obstructs and undermines the significance of social responsibility, endorsing a double standard in which women are held to higher standards than men. A provocative trend is a move toward solutions motivated by corporate social responsibility, as opposed to the business case. Opportunity lies in corporations making public data dashboards of the gender and racial composition of senior leadership, rates of workplace gender-based violence and harassment, and workplace climate metrics. Holding senior leaders accountable for DEI communications and behaviors provides further opportunity. Leaders have the power to disrupt and advocate for national policies supporting flexible paid family leave, child and elder care, and equitable healthcare, including coverage for sexual and reproductive health. Instead of examining what women can do for organizations, the focus rotates toward what organizations can do for women (Hideg & Krstic).

The United States lags behind most major industrialized countries in adopting national work-life policies, viewing work-life issues as an individual problem, instead of a threat to public health and economic well-being.

Countries (e.g., United Kingdom and Sweden) with mandatory parental leave for both parents, nontransferable paternal leave policies, and policies to promote women's leadership have been associated with gender equality and economic growth (Allen et al., 2016). To achieve gender parity, concurrent attention to organizational and societal factors is crucial. What can be done to promote gender equity in leadership?

- Intervene early to mitigate the development of gender stereotypes and the constraining outcomes associated with them for women and society.
- Senior leaders must advocate for structural and policy changes that promote equity, inclusion, and public health in the workplace.
- Develop provocative models to disrupt the alignment of masculine leadership templates and pathways to increase inclusion and challenge norms (Kossek et al., 2017).
- Eliminate implicit bias by using selection criteria based on evidence of effective leadership such as self-awareness, desire to learn, adaptability, humility, and ability to seek and accept feedback and coaching.
- Improve leadership development for women to reflect a deeper understanding of issues women face in leadership, such as the double bind.
- Address the relative lack of understanding of leadership careers embedded within family, personal, and community life.
- Grant lifespan leadership development a prominent focus in vocational and career development theory, research, and practice.

Summary

The 20th century saw an influx of literature on women's career development as women entered the workforce in large numbers (Flores et al., 2021). Contemporary data point indisputably to gender inequities in leadership. The time has come to address 21st-century working women's advancement and leadership development (Schultheiss, 2021). An epistemological turn in career development theory toward the inclusion of leadership development would reflect current realities and present possibilities for greater career equity. The more the world of work changes, the more we can not let it stay the same.

References

Allen, T. D., French, K. A., & Poteet, M. L. (2016). Women and career advancement. *Organizational Dynamics, 45*(3), 206–216.

Eagly, A. H., & Karau, S. J. (2002). Role congruity theory of prejudice toward female leaders. *Psychological Review, 109*, 573–589.

Flores, L. Y., Settles, I., McGillen, G. G., & Tangier, M. D. (2021). Critical contributions to scholarship on women and work: Celebrating 50 year of progress and looking ahead to a new decade. *Journal of Vocational Behavior, 126*, 103490.

Hideg, I., & Krstic, A. (2021). The quest for workplace gender equality in the 21st century? Where do we stand and how can we continue to make strides? *Canadian Journal of Behavioral Science, 53*(4), 106–113.

Kossek, E. E., Su, R., & Wu, L. (2017). "Opting out" or pushed out"? Integrating perspectives on women's career equality for gender inclusion and interventions. *Journal of Management, 43*(1), 228–254.

McKinsey & Company. (2020). *Women in the workplace.* Retrieved January 24, 2021, from https://womenintheworkplace.com/.

Ryan, M., Haslam, S. A., Morgenroth, T., Rink, F., Stoker, J., & Peters, K. (2016). Getting on top of the glass cliff: Reviewing a decade of evidence, explanations, and impact. *The Leadership Quarterly, 27*, 446–455.

Schultheiss, D. E. P. (2009). To mother or matter: Can women do both? *Journal of Career Development, 36*(1), 25–48.

Schultheiss, D. E. P. (2021). Shining the light on women's work, this time brighter: Let's start at the top. *Journal of Vocational Behavior, 126*, 103558.

United Nations. (n.d.). *Gender equality: The unfinished business of our time.* Retrieved December 11, 2021, from www.un.org/en/global-issues/gender-equality%20.

World Economic Forum. (2021). *The global gender gap report 2021.* Retrieved December 6, 2021, from https://www3.weforum.org/docs/WEF_GGGR_2021.pdf.

28 Coming to Terms With the Limits to Vocational Training Within Helping Professions

Ryan D. Duffy

Every year I teach a seminar on vocational psychology to about six doctoral students who are training to enter a helping profession, in this case, counseling psychology. What I like most about the course is connecting with students around their own career process. My first major assignment is for each of the students to present an extensive career lifeline to share how they got here and where they see themselves going. We build off the centering of our own stories to connect to vocational theory and research, and in the best-case scenario, the semester discussions blend personal narrative and academic scholarship to build knowledge and enthusiasm about work and careers. The class is not always successful, but when it is I believe that this blend nicely positions students to feel confident addressing vocational concerns in therapy.

Recently, I decided to add an additional component—bringing in graduates from counseling psychology programs to share what their jobs and careers actually look like. Considering my students were at a place of making major career decisions, I thought it would be a good idea to hear from the source itself, people actually doing the careers students may be considering. These included graduates in research-intensive academic jobs, teaching-intensive academic jobs, veterans affairs hospitals, medical centers, counseling centers, and private practice. For each speaker, we spent an hour asking them questions, learning about how they got there, what their day looks like, and their compensation. We got about halfway through our lineup, and I thought they were going great. But the class as a whole had a major critique and request.

None of these guest speakers was doing the type of work many in this class were interested in—advocacy work to change systems at large which are harming marginalized individuals. On top of this, our class readings also heavily skewed away from understanding how work and jobs are constructed within larger systems and leaned toward an understanding of how individuals make career choices and move through the world of work. Of course, this critique of being individually versus systems focused is not entirely new to psychologists (Blustein et al., 2019; Vera & Speight, 2003), but Brewster and Molina's (2021) recent article on intersectionality in vocational

DOI:10.4324/9781003272397-35

psychology cemented how much of a gap this tends to be in our training. They noted, "no student should leave an applied psychology training program without a working knowledge of direct-action strategies, labor laws, and community-based organizations that they can share with their clients" (Brewster & Molina, 2021).

For full disclosure, I edited the Brewster and Molina (2021) paper published in the *Journal of Career Assessment* and, despite that, the students in my class were still going to leave the course with little to no knowledge of a systems approach to understanding work and tools to change the world of work through advocacy within these larger systems. It is not that these ideas weren't brought up in our materials or course discussions, but they were often tacked onto the end of scholarly articles or represented small parts of our guest speaker's full-time jobs. The critique and requests from the students were valid and on point.

For about three weeks, I consulted with close to a dozen colleagues and former students in an attempt to find a guest speaker who graduated with a Ph.D. in counseling psychology that was primarily doing advocacy work. It was a struggle and very few folks had anyone in mind from often very large networks of graduates. I was eventually able to find a guest speaker who devoted a considerable amount of time to educational and organizational consulting—someone who was working within larger structures to address issues around diversity, equity, and inclusion. She was excellent and inspiring. However, I knew she still wasn't exactly what the students were looking for.

These experiences as a whole pushed me to reflect on the role—writ large—of a system level and advocacy focus when it comes to (a) teaching graduate students in helping professions about vocational topics and (b) training students to have the knowledge and expertise to secure jobs postgraduation where this is the primary focus. In the following, I detail three possible approaches to this issue, which mirror my own reflective thought process as I went through the semester.

That's Not What We Do Here

Most of my workdays are spent researching, reading, writing, teaching, editing, and thinking about vocational issues, most often from more of an individual perspective. As such, I am naturally biased to feel like this approach to understanding work is valuable. I am also somewhat familiar with fields outside of vocational psychology, which do have more of a system's focus on work, including scholarship in the sociology of work and labor relations. So, my immediate reaction to the criticism was—that's not what we do here. This is a counseling psychology program where our focus is on working with individuals or small groups. Yes, systemic factors may have a large role in people's experiences, but this training program is not the place where we focus on changing those factors. Rather, we focus on what clients need right now to make better career decisions and be happier at work. Of course, I did not voice any of these defensive reactions to my students—they mainly lingered in my mind for a little while—but I have to be honest that these were my initial reactions.

What Are We Doing Here?

It did not take long for my defensiveness to turn into soul searching. I had incorporated a few articles in the class written by sociologists and—along with the student criticism—I started to wonder about the efficacy of attending to work issues within counseling psychology as a whole. It wasn't that doing work with individuals wasn't valuable or needed. But did that work only exist because enough work wasn't being done at systematic levels to minimize individual problems? I wondered about the focus most helping professions put on individual clients and why that focus was so ingrained. One piece of this explanation may stem from scholarship in the management literature focused on the concept of beneficiary contact, where work is more meaningful when we have more direct contact with the person benefiting from that work (Grant, 2012). As such, it is not surprising that myself and probably many people who enter helping professions are drawn to it because of the ability to work with individuals face to face. When we put in the time to help someone, we actually see the results of this help and this makes us feel good about ourselves.

However, although it probably feels better to think about careers from the perspective of helping individuals, if we want to have the greatest positive impact on most people, shouldn't our time and energy be directed toward changing society at large? If the answer to this is yes, what then have we been doing with our training all of these years? I began to reconsider the entire way our field taught about work and careers and the types of jobs we should be encouraging our students to pursue. I then proceeded to question my own expertise in this approach and acknowledge how much I would need to learn to actually feel confident training students from a systems approach.

Where Is a Middle Ground?

Certainly, there is a middle ground between these two positions. From a learning perspective, it seems essential that a system's and societal view of work be taught, and at the very least given as much attention as the individualistic perspective. At the end of the semester, several students gave me specific suggestions of needing to incorporate more readings on capitalism, its origins, and how it has shaped the world of work that currently exists. I nodded along with the suggestions while at the same time realizing, embarrassingly, how very little I know about capitalism and work and wondering where I would even try to find scholarship on that. Growing that knowledge base will take time for me and I suspect most faculty who teach vocational courses. We have to be honest that often our own training and learning come to a halt after we finish graduate school and people like me need to take more accountability for continuing to learn. In my opinion, the largest target area for learning is around systemic factors influencing the world of work.

For training, I see this as being a bit clearer. Training programs in all helping professions have a long history of training students to work directly, face to face with clients. I do think there is a strong argument to be made that having hundreds of thousands of therapists and counselors who work directly with individuals on their career issues is not the most efficient way to change the world of work at large. But individuals do need help even if the root cause of many of these issues may be systemic. Individual therapy and counseling is still good, valuable, and important work. As such, I would contend that helping profession programs should not be expected to trans- form into those that primarily produce system-level advocates; there already exist programs in community psychology, social work, and sociology where people can go to get this specialized training. Additionally, there are specific programs that exist within the helping professions—several in my specific field—with an added focus on advocacy and social justice training (Alexan- der & Allo, 2021; Goodman et al., 2004; Miles & Fassinger, 2021)

However, considering helping professions as a whole, our training pro- grams still need to move from where they currently are, especially consider- ing the workforce data on what graduates actually end up of doing. We need to, at a minimum, give students the opportunity to connect with agencies and organizations that are doing systemic work. Some programs like Boston College's counseling psychology program have doctoral students do a social justice/advocacy practicum within their first year (Goodman et al., 2004). Other programs (i.e., University of Tennessee) have this type of practicum and also require a course in intergroup dialogues, with the aim of facilitat- ing a greater awareness of systems and exposure to differing opinions and experiences (Miles & Fassinger, 2021).

I would contend that making the world of work more equitable is a primary way to make the world as a whole more just. We need to educate our students not only about self-exploration and assessment but also about capitalism, labor laws, unions, and the broad ways the world of work is changing quickly. We need to expose students to scholars focusing on that type of work. We need to offer the tools and knowledge to students who might come into our courses with some interest in doing full-time advocacy work to feel confident in pursuing that as a full-time career. I believe doing these things will serve to make as many students as possible passionate about vocational psychology and, in particular, appeal to those students who want to be system-level advocates.

References

Alexander, A. A., & Allo, H. (2021). Building a climate for advocacy training in professional psychology. *The Counseling Psychologist, 49*(7), 1070–1089. https://doi.org/10.1177/00110000211027973.

Blustein, D. L., Kenny, M. E., Di Fabio, A., & Guichard, J. (2019). Expanding the impact of the psychology of working: Engaging psychology in the struggle for decent work and human rights. *Journal of Career Assessment, 27*(1), 3–28. https://doi.org/10.1177%2F1069072718774002.

Brewster, M. E., & Molina, D. A. L. (2021). Centering matrices of domination: Steps toward a more intersectional vocational psychology. *Journal of Career Assessment, 29,* 547–569. https://doi.org/10.1177%2F10690727211029182.

Goodman, L. A., Liang, B., Helms, J. E., Latta, R. E., Sparks, E., & Weintraub, S. R. (2004). Training counseling psychologists as social justice agents: Feminist and multicultural principles in action. *Counseling Psychologist, 32*(6), 793–836.

Grant, A. M. (2012). Leading with meaning: Beneficiary contact, prosocial impact, and the performance effects of transformational leadership. *Academy Management Journal, 55,* 458–476. https://doi.org/10.5465/amj.2010.0588.

Miles, J. R., & Fassinger, R. E. (2021). Creating a public psychology through a scientist-practitioner-advocate training model. *American Psychologist, 76*(8), 1232–1247. https://doi.org/10.1037/amp0000855.

Vera, E. M., & Speight, S. L. (2003). Multicultural competencies, social justice, and counseling psychology: Expanding our roles. *The Counseling Psychologist, 31,* 253–272. https://doi.org/10.1177%2F0011000003031003001.

29 Job Quality and Workforce Development

Jerry Rubin

Why Does Job Quality Matter?

It's being called "The Big Quit" or "The Great Resignation." But whatever the headline, U.S. workers are not flocking back to workplaces as the pandemic recession eases. In fact, job resignations are the highest in recorded history, labor market participation is historically low, and employers across many sectors and most regions of the country are having great difficulty securing the talent that they need to serve their customers and grow. The causes of this phenomenon are many: concern about workplace safety, limited childcare options, and accumulated financial cushions, to name just a few. One consistent theme is that American workers are frustrated with the quality of their jobs and are not willing to go back to the conditions they faced prior to the pandemic.

For the three decades following World War II, American workers could count on steadily rising standards of living, fueled by consistent robust economic growth and public and private policies that supported shared prosperity. Beginning in the 1970s, those trends, which propelled millions of Americans into the middle class, began to change dramatically, and in the four decades since, American workers have seen their wages stagnate and their standards of living steadily decline.

Six years ago, the nation began recovering from the Great Recession, the most significant economic decline since the Great Depression. But, despite robust job growth, wages continued to lag productivity growth. Low wages aren't the only element of job quality that has changed since the 1970s. Reducing benefits, manipulating scheduling, and eliminating training were only a few of the ways that employers sought to reduce costs and increase profitability.

That said, in many regions of the country, wages and broader job quality have improved modestly over the past six years, and despite a brief spike in unemployment early in the pandemic, labor markets continue to be very tight, and employers are being forced to consider the quality of their jobs. This is producing a "once in a generation" opportunity for workforce development organizations, when the interests of employers, who are desperate to secure talent, and the interests of workers are more aligned.

DOI:10.4324/9781003272397-36

Changing Our Framework and Narrative

To successfully leverage the current opportunity, workforce development organizations will need to adopt a narrative and operating framework that recognizes the common interests of employers and workers, especially in a tight labor market. JVS Boston, an innovative, 84-year-old workforce development organization has adopted this strategy and is helping other workforce development organizations do the same.

In a tight job market, employers that change their practices to improve job quality and more effectively attract and retain workers will be the most successful "employers of choice." Employers who do not will be left behind. Jobseekers who can position themselves most effectively to be hired by employers of choice—by improving their job-related and job search skills as well as by making the right connections with good employers—will find better quality jobs.

In this changing landscape, both employers and workers may find navigating the new reality challenging. Employers may not easily change job quality practices to become "employers of choice." Workers may find it difficult to understand the exact skills employers of choice are looking for, attain those skills, and get a foot in the door with those employers. This intermediary role—helping employers become "employers of choice" and helping workers become "employees of choice"—should be the focus of sophisticated workforce development organizations in this historic moment.

Workforce development organizations should adopt a consultative and strategic partnership perspective, in which they work closely with employers to develop and implement policies that will make them employers of choice and improve their competitiveness. Of course, that requires that workforce development organizations have the skills, knowledge, business-savvy staff, and relationships with employers to be given the opportunity to provide genuinely valuable assistance, and then effectively deliver that help. The remainder of this essay addresses four important strategies that workforce organizations can adopt to become effective intermediaries between employers of choice and employees of choice:

1. Crafting a Dynamic Definition of Job Quality
2. Applying a Dynamic Definition of Job Quality
3. Transforming Job Training
4. Moving Beyond Job Training

1. Crafting a Dynamic Definition of Job Quality

Before we can effectively help employers and workers take full advantage of job quality opportunities, we need to clearly define what we mean by "job quality." Most of us think about job quality primarily in terms of pay and benefits, but it is far more complex. At JVS, we surveyed our own employees and clients about what they valued most about a job. One worker's definition of what makes a great job is not the same as another's. Some may value predictable and flexible hours more than wages. Others may put a premium on proximity to home, while others may place more value on the culture of the company or how they are engaged, valued, and empowered. And, as workers attain higher quality jobs, their priorities change. From our surveys, we identified five common factors that our clients consider for their own definition of job quality: salary, stable scheduling, benefits, supportive managers, and career ladder opportunities. And we identified that as the foundation of job quality—wages and benefits—improves, workers may prioritize more aspirational elements such as career ladders, organizational mission, and company values.

Employers' definition of job quality also varies significantly from one industry to another and even from one employer to another within the same industry. Employers in one industry do not have the same constraints and opportunities as an employer in another industry. Acute healthcare organizations, for example, tend to have more wage flexibility than most long-term care organizations, which are more dependent on fixed reimbursement rates. Fixed-shift organizations may have less scheduling flexibility than others.

Recently, JVS has turned our definition of job quality into a practical tool known as the "Job Quality Benchmarking Index." The Index helps employers know where they stand and improve by comparing themselves to other companies with similar jobs in their industry and region across five key elements: Wages, Benefits, Scheduling, Access to Career Ladders, and Supportive Environment. (For more information on JVS's job quality strategy and the Index: www.jvs-boston.org/for-employers/job-quality-initiative/.)

2. Applying a Dynamic Definition of Job Quality

A flexible definition of job quality can be used by workforce organizations to determine how much to invest in employer relationships. Beginning five years ago, JVS began seeing more employers attend graduations and job fairs than graduates and realized that "first come first served" was not the most strategic approach to use. Our staff have limited time, and clients have choices, so we are now prioritizing companies based on the quality of their jobs.

The tight job market is giving us important opportunities to use these tools in real time. Recently, our team was approached by a long-term care organization to explore creating a Talent Pipeline recruitment and training program (explained later) for them. We had received information from graduates of our Certified Nursing Assistant (CNA) program who had worked there, as well as their JVS coach, suggesting that the company's pay was comparatively low and that there were internal challenges around supportive management. After analysis of our database, we determined that the company's pay rate was $2.50 below the average hourly earnings of our CNA graduates. With that information in hand, JVS's staff explained that we would not be able to successfully recruit and train for them with their current pay level and delicately brought up internal management challenges. The company will continue trying to recruit on its own and is considering purchasing coaching services from JVS to supplement its retention efforts.

3. Transforming Job Training

Job training is the traditional bread and butter of the workforce development field. In this very tight labor market, we have an opportunity to transition to new models of job training that more effectively tap market forces, better serve lower-income and lower-skill workers with higher-quality jobs, better serve employers, and are far more sustainable and scalable than traditional approaches.

Turning Job Training Upside Down: The Talent Pipeline Model

When workers are hard to find, employers may be willing to pursue approaches to recruiting talent that they would not consider in a softer job market. JVS is actively taking advantage of the opportunity by re-designing our traditional job training programs into a new "Talent Pipeline" model. Traditional job training programs train jobseekers and then introduce them to prospective employers, while training costs are paid by public sources or philanthropy. In the Talent Pipeline model, trainees are either pre-hired at a training wage or guaranteed a position upon graduation by an employer partner who pays for their training on a per-trainee basis. The employer partner also provides JVS with real-time skill and hiring requirements for curriculum development, and our staff shadow the roles they are recruiting for and conduct in-depth interviews with hiring managers. JVS recruits and screens to the company's specifications and narrows the field of candidates to a small, curated cohort. Utilizing JVS staff recommendations, the employer partner makes the final selection of candidates who will go through training to be hired upon successful completion or be hired at a training wage during training.

The Talent Pipeline model is an important tool for improving job quality. For example, to attract high-quality applicants and impact retention, a large healthcare organization piloting the Talent Pipeline model with JVS for nursing assistants agreed to offer program applicants higher wages, full-time hours, predictable schedules, and benefits packages. Beginning this year, JVS delivers Talent Pipeline projects for employers offering full-time, benefited positions, paying at least $16/hour.

Tapping the Un-Tapped Labor Market

Another advantage of tight job markets and new job training strategies is that they allows us to secure good jobs for individuals who might not have been considered by employers of choice in a softer job market. For example, six years ago, JVS's traditional pharmacy technician program graduates were hired exclusively by retail pharmacies, which have different hiring requirements than their hospital counterparts. Hospitals were not interested in considering our candidates. Now, not only are several of the largest hospitals in Boston hiring our pharmacy technician graduates, but they are also paying us to recruit and train them.

The Talent Pipeline model also gives us the opportunity to work closely with employers we have built trust and credibility with to consider a wider range of candidates whom we stand behind, giving us the opportunity to leverage our trusted relationship with them to change hiring standards that were not essential for job performance but were habitually applied. Recently, we convinced a hospital partner, who hired us to recruit for a very difficult-to-fill position, to reduce the required English language skills for the position, increase the hourly wage, and consider dropping the requirement for a high school diploma.

4. Moving Beyond Job Training

Creating a great workplace goes far beyond skills training. Strategies can include more supportive human resource policies, career ladder opportunities, re-designing jobs to tap employees' talents and creativity, more transparent sharing of financial information, or even sharing profits and creating employee stock ownership opportunities more fully. Workforce development organizations, which have credibility, knowledge, and meaningful employer relationships, can provide expertise and knowledge about how companies can effectively recruit, retain, and advance their employees. By doing so, they will have an important opportunity to affect job quality.

Not all employer policy changes are complicated or require sophisticated human resource or job re-design knowledge. In an early Talent Pipeline pilot project, we convinced an employer partner to offer participants guaranteed full-time positions, with predictable and fixed schedules at specific locations, which are not the typical conditions for long-term care workers. Another employer partner worked with JVS to re-design physically demanding jobs so that older nursing assistants, with many years of experience, can continue to work for the company. JVS is now using the Job Quality Index to provide companies with insights into their ineffective practices and practical solutions for improving the quality of their jobs.

Changing Policy

Improving job quality one employer at a time is critically important, but not sufficient if we want to change the societal dynamics that have helped undermine job quality and economic equity since the 1970s. Employer and public policy changes led to this dire situation, and they can lead us out of it. To that end, JVS has increased its engagement in both state and federal public policy and urges other workforce development organizations to do the same. We see several important public policy changes that can have an enormous effect on job quality and economic equity:

- Increase federal and state minimum wage levels.
- Increase the federal and state Earned Income Tax Credit.
- Adjust federal and state public benefit regulations to reduce the "cliff effect" that ends all public benefits beyond strict wage limits and dis-incentivize greater earnings.
- Increase investments in workforce training and adult education.

The workforce development field cannot solve the job quality conundrum alone. But, under the current labor market conditions, workforce organizations can take full advantage of this historic moment to substantially expand their impact, deliver better quality jobs for their clients, and deliver better results for their employer partners.

30 The Importance of Not Working

Paid Time Off as a Right Not a Privilege

Saba Rasheed Ali and Allison R. Bywater

The legend of John Henry is a tale that most kids in many parts of Appalachia learn at a very young age. John Henry was an African American railroad worker during the late 1800s who is lionized for his willingness to sacrifice his own life to prove that human labor is better than machine labor. Of course, the legend is also celebrated within Black communities as a tale of John Henry's defiance of White oppression since Henry was a freed slave "who proved his worth." The African American folk ballad sung about John Henry "describes a contest with a steam drill, in which John Henry crushed more rock than did the machine but died 'with his hammer in his hand'" (The Editors of Encyclopedia Britannica, 2020). The tale also illustrates much of the United States' relationship to labor and in particular to valorizing individuals (especially individuals of color) who sacrifice their own health, well-being, or lives for the sake of their work.

The socialization of the Protestant Work Ethic (hard work as a means to salvation and laziness connected with evil) infiltrates even the youngest members of society. I (Saba) remember hearing this tale every year in music class when I was in elementary school in West Virginia, and it is only after studying humans' relationship to work that I began to have a new understanding of the tale. In our neo-liberal capitalist society, we celebrate working and often demonize individual need for time off to rest and recuperate. Yet, this is largely class-based with most "professional class" workers able to take paid time off (PTO) as a benefit built into their employment, while most low-wage workers never receive this benefit. Currently, PTO is seen as a privilege reserved for salaried employees whose jobs often come with negotiated benefits. We argue that PTO is a pillar of dignity and is a right that should be extended to all, regardless of occupation or social class.

In 1910, then President Taft proposed that U.S. workers should have two to three months of vacation time per year. He viewed this extended vacation as essential to the worker's well-being and necessary for future productivity. One hundred twenty plus years later, despite many attempts at legislation, PTO is still not afforded to U.S. workers on a federal level. Without a federal policy, we are leaving the question of who is worthy of PTO to employers. Statistics show a grave discrepancy in who employers are choosing to allot PTO to: fewer than

DOI:10.4324/9781003272397-37

20% of low-wage earners have access to PTO compared to over 78% of high-wage workers (Glynn et al., 2016). We cannot rethink work without generating policies to combat the deeply ingrained biases and stereotypes that lead to stratification within the workforce. What are the covert messages perpetuated in the pervasive phenomenon of not affording low-wage workers PTO? *Your work is not worthy of respite or break.* In a society that continues to tie identity with employment, the covert message may be *you are not worthy of leisure.*

I (Allison) think about the years I spent nannying in Southern California. Caretaking is a unique profession in that you are intimately, socially and emotionally, intertwined with others' lives. To be perceived as a good caretaker means to give yourself generously and selflessly to those you are caring for; to ask for time off directly conflicts with the perception of this position. Similar to John Henry, we lift these positions up on a pedestal to idolize while we, on the surface, appreciate the selflessness involved in the position. However, dissimilar to John Henry, these workers often do not literally die in the name of their work. Instead, these low-wage workers burn out, and then we, on a nation-wide scale, demonize their identity. The covert message? *You do not deserve respect or admiration unless you are quiet about your needs.* We saw this during the 2018 Arizona teachers' strike, and we saw it on a large scale with nurses during the COVID-19 pandemic.

These hidden messages lead to burn-out among workers who internalize their exhaustion as a moral failing rather than externalizing their burnout as a consequence of the unrealistic expectations pressed upon them. Many of the strategies suggested for preventing burnout at both an institutional level and an individual level rely on solid work/life balance strategies including individual ways to manage stress such as taking long walks, mindfulness practices, or taking a vacation (Henderson, 2022). While widely supported by literature, these strategies are not only ineffectual but also insensitive to many low-wage earners because they rely on the assumption that one has the ability to leave work for walks or to take a vacation.

The traditional argument for universal paid leave policies suggests documented benefits encompassing personal health, public health, and economic gain (Hruska et al., 2020; Kim, 2019; Mansfield, 2019). The AAUW (2020) advocates for paid leave and touts the benefits for businesses which they suggest will help retain workers and reduce the high costs of turnover by offering PTO. They cite California as an example of a state that has a successful family leave insurance program, where workers in low-wage, high-turnover industries are much more likely to return to their jobs after using the state's program. The AAUW strongly supports the passage of the FAMILY Act which would implement paid family and medical leave for workers in the United States. More specifically, it would provide workers with up to 12 weeks of partial income when they take time for their own serious health conditions and would cover workers in all companies regardless of the size of the company. Those arguing for this legislation suggest that providing PTO would actually retain workers as those who take PTO are more likely to remain in the workforce.

However, making an argument solely based on how PTO benefits employers and the economy ignores the humanistic argument: beyond family and medical leave, all workers should have access to PTO for leisure and vacation purposes which are implied within the definitions of decent work (Blustein et al., 2019). It should be a right of all employees to have time to rest, recuperate, and relax. A reframing of federally mandated PTO policy as a fundamental need and right of all workers would steer the conversation more toward a justice-oriented perspective. A conversation of PTO that encompasses the principles of dignity, respect, and leisure would center the humanistic interests of the workforce. When we include the ethical reasons for which a worker is entitled to PTO, we might be able to move away from viewing workers as commodities whose rights can only be justified through a risk/benefit analysis of the employer and economy. This perspective would be more consistent with focusing on the dignity of the worker (Blustein, 2019). PTO for low-wage workers can in the long run benefit the economy and employer bottom lines. However, rethinking work should include policies and perspectives that align with the decent work and human rights agenda put forth by Blustein et al. (2019) where workers have the rights to their own time without jeopardizing their financial security.

References

AAUW. (2020, March 27). *Policy recommendations: Paid leave.* www.aauw.org/resources/policy/paid-leave/.

Blustein, D. L. (2019). *The importance of work in an age of uncertainty: The eroding work experience in America.* Oxford University Press.

Blustein, D. L., Kenny, M. E., Di Fabio, A., & Guichard, J. (2019). Expanding the impact of the psychology of working: Engaging psychology in the struggle for decent work and human rights. *Journal of Career Assessment, 27*(1), 3–28.

Glynn, S. J., Boushey, H., Berg, P., & Corley, D. (2016). *Fast facts on who has access to paid time off and flexibility* (Report). Center for American Progress.

Henderson, J. D. (2022). Self care is not the solution for burnout. *The Beautiful Truth.* https://thebeautifultruth.org/life/mental-health/self-care-is-not-the-solution-for-burnout/.

Hruska, B., Pressman, S. D., Bendinskas, K., & Gump, B. B. (2020). Vacation frequency is associated with metabolic syndrome and symptoms. *Psychology & Health, 35*(1), 1–15. https://doi.org/10.1080/08870446.2019.1628962.

Kim, D. (2019). Does paid vacation leave protect against depression among working Americans? A national longitudinal fixed effects analysis. *Scandinavian Journal of Work, Environment & Health, 45*(1), 22–32. https://doi.org/10.5271/sjweh.3751.

Mansfield, A. (2019). Mandatory paid vacation and mental health leave for all employees: Better for the economy, employers and employees. *University of Baltimore Law Forum, 50*(1), Article 3.

The Editors of Encyclopedia Britannica. (2020, August). John Henry. *Encyclopedia Britannica.* Retrieved December 25, 2021, from www.britannica.com/topic/John-Henry-folk-hero.

31 Work Is a Four-Letter Word

Secondary Schools, Employers, and Transitions Into Early Employment

Anthony Mann

Don't waste your life
There is so much I know you can do
Let me see you wide awake
And take on the world that is waiting for you

(Black & Wolfenden, 1968)

When the conversation dries in gatherings of new friends, you can be sure to generate a lively hour by asking what people wanted to do when they were young and the career advice they received at secondary school. Everyone has a story, often a negative one. My own sole experience of guidance: as a shy 16-year-old, we were told to avoid wasting the time of a guidance counselor who had come into the school by having nothing to say. We needed to come up with a career aspiration and discuss it for ten minutes. Being obsessively engrossed in international politics, I mumbled an interest in the diplomatic service and my plan to focus my studies on French, English, and History. For nine of the ten minutes, I was encouraged to choose instead Biology, Chemistry, and Physics. At the last minute, it dawned on us both that she had heard me say medical service and our time was up. I am sure the reason why I spoke so hesitantly was that people from my school simply didn't go on to work in the national government. We joined the army or police, became nurses, and worked in local financial institutions or for the council. A few might become lawyers or even a doctor, but living hundreds of miles away from the nation's capital, it seemed absurd, even arrogant, to imagine one of us representing the country abroad. When years later at a second attempt, I did finally end up working in the department of education rather than the diplomatic corps, I chalked the success down to having had the good fortune to sit next to someone from a similar background at a wedding. He had just succeeded in getting a job in government and showed me the ropes. Serendipity, rather than public policy, I felt was responsible for my success.

DOI:10.4324/9781003272397-38

There are lots of stories like this. They are common in biographies of successful figures who often share the feeling that their aspirations were not nurtured or enabled by their schools. However, you can also find heartwarming stories of unique and unforgettable sources of encouragement and support from their teachers and counselors. These are experiences that stay in our minds. They speak both to the rarity with which futures are sometimes discussed at school and how fundamental our journeys through education and into employment are to our self-conceptions.

Forty years after my own short interview with a counselor, career guidance has changed considerably, but often it is still not fit for purpose, and concerns over the lack of student career preparation are growing. In 2021, at the height of the COVID-19 pandemic, six international organizations did something rather unusual. They published a joint statement on the importance of guidance, arguing essentially that never before in human history has guidance been so important (Cedefop et al., 2021). Across the globe, greater numbers of teenagers now progress to upper secondary and university education. Consequently, young people have more decisions to make than ever before (not only about what and where they study, but how hard to apply themselves), and they do so in the face of labor markets and education systems that are undergoing radical change. Digitalization and automation are fundamentally changing work processes. The Organisation for Economic Co-operation and Development (OECD) estimates that over the next decade, nearly half of all jobs will change substantively due to technological innovations. And then, there is the pandemic and the response to climate change. New jobs emerge, old jobs disappear, and huge numbers of jobs change in some important way, often becoming more precarious with less access to ongoing training. In many countries moreover, continuing education and training is increasingly marketized and costly, making early decision-making still more challenging and more stressful. It is also now well-known that long-term penalties can be expected to follow poor starts to working life. The economists call it scarring: early experiences of youth unemployment, and work at skill levels lower than qualifications, can have long-term negative economic and psychological impacts on young workers.

Finally, there is one further important reason why career guidance is more important than ever. There is substantial new evidence that it works. In 2021, I led a review of longitudinal datasets in 10 countries, including Australia, Canada, the United Kingdom, and the United States (OECD, 2021, see www.oecd.org/education/career-readiness/). Following young people from adolescence (typically age 15) to early adulthood, the study found considerable new evidence that career-related teenage attitudes and experiences are positively linked to better employment outcomes at age 25, including lower levels of unemployment, higher wages, and greater career satisfaction. Employment boosts, such as earnings 5–10% higher than expected, are meaningful and commonplace. The data show that schools have it in their power to help students to do better and be happier in work than would be anticipated given their qualifications and backgrounds. David Blustein reminds us of the stakes at play:

> Work has the potential to add a great deal of meaning and richness to our lives; at the same time, it has the capacity to wither our souls in a way that few other life activities can match.
>
> (Blustein, 2019)

As the British song (and saying) goes, for many at different times, work can best be characterized by a four-letter word, a pseudonym for a short profanity. While education systems do not have it in their power to transform the labor market into careers that consistently add meaning and richness to people's lives, primary and secondary schools have the capability to reduce the risks that students face in transitioning. By so doing, a rare quadruple win in public policy can be achieved: students gain easier and more rewarding early employment; schools gain through more motivated students; employers gain by finding new recruits better matched to available jobs; and, society gains as the social and financial costs of youth unemployment and underemployment reduce.

Looking across the new analysis and building on a wide research literature, the study identifies 11 indicators of greater teenage career readiness. Students who **explore their potential futures in work**, **gain first-hand experiences of workplaces,** and **actively think about their aspirations** can be expected to attain better outcomes in their entry into the workforce. It is not apparent in every analysis, but clear patterns can be seen and clear guides do emerge for policy and practice. Direct engagement with people at work, for example, clearly matters. Data from multiple countries show that teenagers who **work part-time** or who **volunteer** in the community often gain later benefits. While at school, the confirmed indicators include **participation in career talks and job fairs**, alongside **visits to workplaces** and episodes of **job shadowing**. Young people who take part in **occupationally focused short programs,** as are common in Australia, Canada, and the United States, can also typically expect to do better by age 25 than peers from comparable backgrounds with comparable academic records who did not engage in these programs.

One of the most interesting findings relates to how teenagers think about their potential futures in work. Students who have clear and high ambitions at 15 which align well with their education plans, and who see a connection between their studies and adult employment, can commonly anticipate better outcomes. Such thinking is more frequently found when students take part in guidance activities or experience the workplace firsthand. They are becoming more adept at visualizing and planning their futures. With the help of their families, friends, and schools, they are developing the agency that is increasingly expected of them (Covacevich et al., 2021).

Too Few Students Are Career Ready

Every three years, the OECD Programme for International Student Assessment (PISA) study collects data from teenagers in dozens of countries about their attitudes and experiences in and out of school. From the 2018 questionnaire, we learn that across participating OECD countries, only 50% of students by the age of 15 had spoken to a career advisor in school, and fewer than 40% had taken part in a job fair or visited a workplace. We also find that the career thinking of young people is increasingly narrow. In the United States, 59% of 15-year-old girls and 47% of boys say that by the age of 30, they expect (not *hope*) to work in one of just 10 jobs—22% of American girls say that they will become a doctor. In other countries, figures are comparable or still more concentrated. We find moreover worrying evidence of the ways that social class impacts on career planning. Across OECD countries, looking only at those students who achieved the highest scores on the PISA science test, socially advantaged students were twice as likely as their more disadvantaged peers to plan on proceeding to university. What's more, disadvantaged students were three times more likely than their more advantaged peers to plan on entering a job typically requiring a university education, but planning to leave education at 18. Across all the data, consistent concerns are found among the lowest achievers. At 15, they are often approaching the end of their compulsory secondary schooling with a poor understanding of what they need to do to achieve their job ambitions.

So what can be done? It is time to recognize fully the central importance of career guidance in the development of young people. Secondary schools are the democratic vehicle for ensuring that *all* students are actively encouraged and helped to imagine and plan their pathways through education into fulfilling employment. Effective schools create cultures of career curiosity and exploration from a young age and track the ways in which such engagement influences career thinking. Indeed, one of the predictors of better outcomes is simply whether students at 15 were engaging in **conversations** with people around them about their futures in work. Career development is a social process. In later years, effective schools help students to test out their interests in real-life settings, embracing the powerful learning tool that is the simple process of seeing first-hand what different trades and professions are really like. First-hand employer engagement is at the heart of effective guidance because it enables students to gain insights from working professionals and visits to workplaces that cannot be so easily or authentically replicated in schools.

Consequently, effective guidance and effective employer engagement will be **often, early,** and **integrated** within a student's school career. Like throwing mud at a wall, we don't know what will stick, but we can be confident that the more that is thrown, the more things of value will—especially if it is hurled within a learning culture of preparation and reflection. We need to picture students beginning their school lives with narrow and poorly informed understandings of work. Effective guidance will broaden and enrich their knowledge, preparing them academically as well as psychologically for the modern reality of the labor market. An excellent question to ask students after guidance interventions is if they learned anything that was new and useful?

The OECD Career Readiness longitudinal study identifies international indicators of better employment outcomes. By breaking down the barriers between education and employment in a supportive, exploratory context, schools can add substantial value to young people's lives and expectations of the future. Now, as the world adjusts to a period of profound disruption, the need is greater than ever to help all students to focus on other four-letter words, to **plan** their futures with **hope** for fulfilling futures based on a deeper, more authentic understanding of the perils and opportunities provided by the world of work.

References

Black, D., & Wolfenden, G. (1968). *Work is a four-letter word [recorded by C. Black].* On *Completely Cilla (1963–1973).* EMI Records.

Blustein, D. (2019). *The importance of work in an age of uncertainty: The eroding work experience in America.* Oxford University Press.

Cedefop, European Commission, European Training Foundation, International Labour Organisation, OECD, UNESCO. (2021). *Investing in career guidance.* Cedefop.

Covacevich, C., Mann, A., Santos, C., & Champaud, J. (2021). Indicators of teenage career readiness: An analysis of longitudinal data from eight countries. OECD Education Working Papers No. 258. OECD Publishing.

OECD. (2021). Indicators of teenage career readiness: Guidance for policy makers, OECD Education Policy Perspectives No. 43. OECD Publishing.

32 Career Preparedness and Safety Nets as Hedges Against an Uncertain Work Future

Robert W. Lent

In observing trends in artificial intelligence (AI), machine learning, corporate mergers and monopolies, workforce downsizing, and related developments, some economic forecasters anticipate that many workers will face a precarious occupational future—one characterized by increasing work instability, especially for those who perform work routines that can be readily replaced by cheaper alternatives (e.g., algorithms, robotics, and outsourcing). While this bleak view of the future of work is neither entirely new nor universally shared (Ford, 2015), it behooves policymakers, workforce observers, and career development specialists to consider preventive strategies that might buffer workers against the worst-case scenarios.

In this essay, I consider two sets of proactive, damage-limiting strategies, one focused on systemic, government-level interventions and the other on devising better psychoeducational methods for preparing individuals to enter, and plan for changes in, the world of work. First, it may be helpful to consider conflicting views on the magnitude of the problem.

Is There a Cause for Despair or Optimism?

As I have pointed out previously (Lent, 2018), there is anything but consensus among forecasters about what awaits future workers. One can certainly spot many pessimistic trends over the past few decades, such as the erosion in middle-class jobs and the rise of gig work (Friedman, 2016), that may fuel worries about future large-scale work instability. On the other hand, expert predictions of any sort, including those involving economic and geopolitical events, can be wildly inaccurate (Epstein, 2019; Kahneman, 2011). Some writers envision something akin to a "robot apocalypse," while others foresee a future in which technological advances will create a wealth of new work possibilities that can offset one's loss (Lent, 2018).

Ford (2018) reported that many leading AI pioneers acknowledge the potential for significant work disruptions, though there was a considerable range of views on the timeframe in which these might occur. Many also saw a role for government regulation to protect workers—though, again, there were differing views on what such regulations might look like and when

DOI:10.4324/9781003272397-39

they should be enacted. Part of the peril in making these sorts of forecasts is that advances in AI, especially in human-simulating general AI, may prove to be sudden and exponential rather than resulting from linear, incremental advances. Moreover, no one knows precisely when an inflection point might occur or what sorts of new jobs could be created.

There are some trends that seem likely to continue (e.g., more loss of stable, middle-income jobs and creation of more temporary, and contractual positions), yet the magnitude or timing of the instability problem cannot be forecast with any certainty. Who, for example, expected the arrival of COVID-19 in Spring 2020, the rapid transition of many workers to telecommuting, or the emergence of the "Great Resignation" in Fall 2021? By their nature, one-of-a-kind or extremely rare "black swan" events tend to defy prediction. Yet it may be wise to prepare for plausible adverse work scenarios under the old adage of "better to be safe than sorry." In dealing with the potential for large-scale work disruptions, I focus on two levels of primary or secondary prevention: (a) systemic, government-level responses and (b) upgrades in individual and group-level career development interventions.

Systemic and Policy Responses

At the systemic level, I would highlight proactive repairs to the social safety net aimed at preventing large-scale unemployment and underemployment—and the psychological, social, and financial damages they may inflict. Such strategies include changes in tax policy (e.g., "robot taxes"), inception of a universal basic income, and government work projects. These are ideas that have been proposed by many writers and deserve to be part of an arsenal of options for anticipating and forestalling economic (e.g., loss of income), psychological (e.g., lack of purpose, depression), and social (e.g., crime) problems that could, and probably would, be caused by a widespread absence of adequate work. "Robot taxes" involve imposing a tax on technology that has been used to replace human workers. Other tax schemes, such as negative income taxes (Brynjolfsson & McAfee, 2014), may also be used to assist persons who have been made redundant by technological or other circumstances (e.g., off-shoring).

Government-funded work projects, such as those created during the New Deal era, offer a viable path to paid work for many unemployed workers. Recent proposals for infrastructure funding by the U.S. federal government may provide new work and training opportunities, along with the potential to stave off the personal and community ills that can accompany unemployment. Universal basic incomes represent a compelling, if controversial, option (Brynjolfsson & McAfee, 2014; Ford, 2015). These might replace many current safety net programs with a modest guaranteed basic income for all citizens that would guard against poverty, allow workers to seek education and training, and facilitate the pursuit of entrepreneurial efforts. Their controversial nature stems from the conservative view that individuals should "pick themselves up by their own bootstraps" rather than rely on government assistance; there would also most certainly be resistance to the wealth taxes or other schemes needed to fund such an ambitious agenda. Given the current political climate in the United States, the universal basic income concept does not seem likely to gain traction anytime soon, unless mass unemployment on the order of the Great Depression becomes a reality.

Expansion and Updating of Career Services for Work Sustainability

I would like to see government policies and employment programs be accompanied by a host of innovations in the career-related services that are offered to individuals and groups, principally by school counselors, career counselors, and vocational psychologists in school and work settings. In particular, I envision a greater emphasis on career-life preparedness (CLP) programs and choice architecture strategies (defined later) to help students and workers to make more sustainable work choices—choices that, for example, incorporate labor market projections regarding which forms of work will be more and less vulnerable to technological obsolescence over a reasonable timeframe. Though such projections are, of course, susceptible to the same inaccuracies as other types of expert judgment, they at least have the advantage of reliance on actual labor market data and have demonstrated their utility as career exploration tools (Gore & Leuwerke, 2021).

What do I mean by CLP programs and choice architecture? As I have argued elsewhere (Lent, 2013, 2018), three-step Parsonian interventions that match people to occupations based on person–environment compatibility data still have considerable value, at least as a starting point. However, because they offer a static solution to a dynamic problem (i.e., neither persons nor environments are likely to remain the same over the long haul), they may be woefully inadequate at preparing students and workers to manage their work lives in the face of later career-disrupting events, such as layoffs due to technological developments in AI and robotics.

I would like to see vocational psychologists, in collaboration with other social scientists and practitioners, develop state-of-the-art CLP programs that offer "Parsons on steroids" guidance to career planners. The ideal location of such programs would be in schools, colleges, and other training settings, modularized within developmentally appropriate segments to deal with the challenges of (a) selecting an initial work or career path, (b) finding work, (c) anticipating changes that could disrupt one's occupational path, (d) learning proactive career behaviors (e.g., continuous planning, skill development, and networking) to enhance work viability, and (e) developing financial, psychological, and social plans as a hedge against possible periods of unemployment and underemployment. Fuller versions of such programs could be offered as required career preparation courses in educational settings and, as implied earlier, their purview would extend far beyond the typical Parsonian model. The last element (planning for major setbacks) may arguably fit best as a part of work adjustment interventions once students enter the workforce. Because employers may or may not wish to invest in such programs, they might be offered as part of the Department of Labor's suite of online and job center services.

Importantly, CLP programs would be founded on the assumptions that career and work options are not likely to remain stable over time, that change in jobs and whole career paths is likely to be the norm (indeed college graduates often make numerous job changes by age 30; Epstein, 2019), and that workers cannot rely with any certainty on their current employers to protect their economic well-being over the long run. In short, the notion of the protean career, which is by no means new, deserves to gain much more traction among career development professionals, as the image of the stable, linear career is about as timely as a Model T Ford. Fostering the notion of "Me, Inc."—which is to say seeing the self as the primary agent of career development—may be long overdue. We as career development specialists need to truly accept career or work change as a necessity for most workers rather than as a sign of personal failure, and we need to convey this to our clients as readily as many of us now dispense Holland scores.

Choice architecture represents a largely untapped resource in the provision of career services. Pioneered by cognitive psychologists and behavioral economists (e.g., Thaler & Sunstein, 2009), it involves making changes to the context of decision-making in order to help individuals make complex choices in the face of uncertainty. Choice architecture interventions have been used, for example, to help workers engage in company-supported savings programs. Career/academic choice represents a clear instance of decision-making under uncertainty, given the large volume of information to be processed and the high stakes involved. Yet it also poses far more complexity (e.g., evolving knowledge of the self and a wide range of shifting choice options) than is the case with typical choice architecture applications.

While space considerations permit only a brief mention of this topic, I can imagine creative, coordinated efforts by a range of career service providers and educational policymakers to redesign the conditions under which students make consequential educational and career decisions. The current situation is one in which students typically spend very little time in career exploration (Gore & Leuwerke, 2021) yet are expected to slot themselves into fairly specialized academic or vocational niches in high school or college. One choice architecture option would be to use assessment data proactively to provide all entering college students with information about majors at their institution that are compatible with their work personalities, linking the majors to relevant career paths, and highlighting paths with high-demand projections. Choice architecture interventions could also be infused into high school or training curricula for work-bound students. Such programs might leverage assessment and occupational data to encourage consideration of work options that feature favorable labor market projections, along with the development and maintenance of job skills that are likely to be reasonably transferable, at least over the near term.

Conclusion

Though I remain uncertain about whether there is more cause for concern or hope regarding the future of work, I am cautiously optimistic that government planners and policymakers will be able to devise strategies to strengthen the safety nets protecting those facing work disruptions due to changing technologies and world economic markets. I remain even more optimistic about the creative steps that social scientists and career practitioners can take to modernize programs that foster work sustainability.

References

Brynjolfsson, E., & McAfee, A. (2014). *The second machine age: Work, progress, and prosperity in a time of brilliant technologies.* W. W. Norton & Company.

Epstein, D. (2019). *Range: Why generalists triumph in a specialized world.* Riverhead Books.

Ford, M. (2015). *Rise of the robots: Technology and the threat of a jobless future.* Basic Books.

Ford, M. (2018). *Architects of intelligence: The truth about AI from the people building it.* Packt Publishing.

Friedman, T. L. (2016). *Thank you for being late: An optimist's guide to thriving in the age of accelerations.* Farrar, Straus, & Giroux.

Gore, P. A., & Leuwerke, W. C. (2021). Occupational information and guidance systems. In S. D. Brown & R. W. Lent (Eds.), *Career development and counseling: Putting theory and research to work* (3rd ed.). Wiley.

Kahneman, D. (2011). *Thinking, fast and slow.* Farrar, Strauss, & Giroux.

Lent, R. W. (2013). Career-life preparedness: Revisiting career planning and adjustment in the new workplace. *Career Development Quarterly, 61,* 2–14.

Lent, R. W. (2018). Future of work in the digital world: Preparing for instability and opportunity. *Career Development Quarterly, 66,* 205–219.

Thaler, R. H., & Sunstein, C. R. (2009). *Nudge: Improving decisions about health, wealth, and happiness.* Penguin Books.

33 Toward a *Squared* Sustainable Work

Placing Ecological and Human Sustainability at the Heart of the Future of Work

Shékina Rochat and Jérôme Rossier

Thinking of the future of work makes sense only if humanity itself has a future. With the publication of the sixth assessment report of the Intergovernmental Panel on Climate Change (2021), it is becoming clear to everyone that humanity is facing a global crisis that forces us to consider and act with determination to meet the challenge of ecological transition. Moreover, the sustainable development goals unanimously adopted in 2015 by the United Nations assembly in its resolution, "Transforming our world: The 2030 agenda for sustainable development" (UN, 2015), emphasize that the challenges of our time are not only ecological but also concern many social aspects, such as access to education, healthcare, and decent living conditions. Thus, we propose that the preoccupation with environmental and human sustainability should be placed at the heart of reflections on the future of work.

In particular, it seems essential to question how work can contribute to a more sustainable world, both socially and ecologically. In fact, the dominant economic forms of work play a key role in phenomena such as resource depletion, global warming, overconsumption, and increasing social inequalities, each of which poses a real threat to the future of humanity (Cohen-Scali, 2018). Considering that social and ecological sustainability is needed to ensure the future of humanity and the promotion of a fair society, policymakers and all actors of this economic system such as organizations, associations, and unions have to question themselves about their impact on our ecological and social environment (Bal et al., 2020). Thus, the future of "work must be examined in relation to far broader issues, such as how it affects the planet and what kinds of human beings and what world it contributes to constructing" (Guichard, 2016, p. 186).

Until now, in the field of work psychology, the term "sustainable" is mostly used as the opposite of precariousness to describe career sequences that allow individuals not only to access decent work but also promote perceived continuity over time, agency, and meaning (De Vos et al., 2020). Despite the tentative efforts of this model of sustainable careers to incorporate more distal ingredients, this conception of sustainable career overlooks

DOI:10.4324/9781003272397-40

the fact that "work is only decent if it contributes to a sustainable society and environment" (Cohen-Scali, 2018, p. 299). This shortcoming is well evidenced by the absence of ecological concerns within this model or previous agendas about the future of work such as the *Manifesto for the future of work* (Bal et al., 2019). Moreover, such a model does not consider the fact that an individual's career sustainability can come (or be built) at the expense of the sustainability of the nature and of other living beings. Yet, the current social and ecological crises can be partly traced back to humans' tendency to overuse environmental resources to pursue happiness and stability (Kjell, 2011).

These considerations underscore the urgency of defining the future of work as an institution that promotes sustainability at both individual and societal/ecological levels. In this sense, the notion of "sustainable career" needs to be expanded to involve a commitment to invest in the long-term development of our entire ecosystem. To fill this gap, Di Fabio and Bucci (2016) propose the name "green decent work" to describe work that goes beyond traditional sustainable career development by, among other things, attempting to address the needs of the present while preserving environmental and ecosystem resources, so as to ensure the ability to meet the needs of the future. However, the use of the term "green," which is mainly associated with ecological issues, tends to obscure the many social challenges of our time.

Epistemologically, "sustainable" originates from the classical Latin "*sustinere*" meaning "to endure." Therefore, this adjective seems appropriate to talk about a career that is sustainable for the individual, humanity, and the planet. We thus propose to use the term "squared" sustainable work (or sustainable² work) to envision the future of work in a way that reconciles these two understandings of sustainability (Bonzon & Rochat, 2022). Here, the idea of squaring sustainability consists in not only considering both individual well-being and the social and ecological environment but rather considering the synergies and interactions between them. This approach would also affirm that everyone's pursuit of sustainability does not lead to exploit other people or the planet's resources yet instead can contribute to fostering their very preservation and flourishing (Kjell, 2011).

To develop such a squared sustainability for the future of work, we claim that career counseling interventions can play a crucial role. In particular, the concept of "green guidance" has been introduced to describe career counseling practices that encourage people to consider the social and environmental implications of their vocational choices and aim at achieving a balance between individual's aspirations and the needs of the planet (Plant, 2014). Such interventions notably consist of helping clients to establish links with their career plans and the UN's goals for sustainable development (e.g., Rochat & Masdonati, 2019). However, such avenues should not result in over-emphasizing the individual's responsibility for sustainability². Instead, squared sustainability should not be envisioned as an individual liability, but rather as a collective and shared responsibility.

With respect to these considerations, green guidance practices should also encourage companies to acknowledge their ecological and social responsibility seriously and to act accordingly, especially in their human resources policies (Di Fabio & Bucci, 2016). One way to do so is to promote "dignity at work," which consists in placing the intrinsic value of all living beings and the planet at the heart of the organization's economic system, instead of treating them as objects to achieve an end (Bal et al., 2020). The enactment of such dignity is mostly attained through dialogue and collective action: two necessary ingredients to formulate ways of working that are sustainable for individuals, organizations, and the planet.

Financial profit can still remain a central preoccupation for companies, as it is essential for them to be stable to positively impact their wider environment (Bal & de Jong, 2017). However, it is possible that workers and managers fear that attempts to reduce carbon emissions will negatively affect the labor market and the financial health of companies (and thus lead to more precariousness for workers). Therefore, it is good to keep in mind that, according to the OECD (Dussaux, 2020), it is possible to reduce CO_2 emissions by 10% without hurting the labor market or the financial performance of companies. In fact, corporate governance and policymakers would benefit from seeking "sustainable economic growth," which is a resilient, low-carbon economic growth that prevents or combats pollution and supports healthy and effective ecosystems, while reducing poverty and social exclusion (Global Green Growth Institute, 2019).

To move in this direction, we suggest that companies proceed to an overall carbon footprint analysis or life cycle assessment to estimate the greenhouse gas emission caused by their different sectors of activity. Such an endeavor will aid in locating potential areas of improvement and facilitate the adoption of targeted, concerted, and truly effective change. A similar analysis can also be supplemented by an individual assessment of the carbon footprint at the worker level, which is easily achievable thanks to the means of tools made available by various non-profit pro-climate organizations, such as the World Wide Fund for Nature. Moreover, the procedure could be enlarged to assess companies' contribution to all of the UN's goals for sustainable development, including humane and societal ones.

Delineating good practice for a squared sustainably should thus fundamentally be part of the agenda for building a better workplace. We hope that this simultaneous concern for the well-being of the humans and the planet could serve as a guiding light to navigate the unpredictable changes that will inevitably shake up the current landscape of work. Setting the course toward these ethical standards will then help to reduce the harmful impact of future crises for the most vulnerable and for the planet, rather than continuing the path of greater damage to both the planet and the people who optimally can serve as caregivers to their natural home.

References

Bal, P. M., & de Jong, S. B. (2017). From human resource management to human dignity development: A dignity perspective on HRM and the role of workplace democracy. In M. Kostera & M. Pirson (Eds.), *Dignity and the organization* (pp. 173–195). Palgrave Macmillan.

Bal, P. M., Dóci, E., Lub, X., Van Rossenberg, Y. G. T., Nijs, S., Achnak, S., . . . Van Zelst, M. (2019). Manifesto for the future of work and organizational psychology. *European Journal of Work and Organizational Psychology, 28,* 289–299. https://doi.org/1 0.1080/1359432X.2019.1602041.

Bal, P. M., Kordowicz, M., & Brookes, A. (2020). A workplace dignity perspective on resilience: Moving beyond individualized instrumentalization to dignified resilience. *Advances in Developing Human Resources, 22,* 453–466. https://doi.org/10.1177/1523422320946115.

Bonzon, S., & Rochat, S. (2022). "Durabilité au carré ": La logique effectuale au service des carrières individuelles, du bonheur et des besoins du monde ["Squared sustainability": Effectual logic for individual careers, happiness and the world's needs]. *Sciences & Bonheur, 7,* 60–82. Retrieved from https://sciencesetbonheur.files.wordpress.com/2022/08/bonzon-rochat-2022-sciences-bonheur-volume-7.pdf.

Cohen-Scali, V. (2018). Life and career design interventions to help people direct their active lives toward human-sustainable development: The case of young people interested in the social and solidarity economy. In V. Cohen-Scali, J. Pouyaud, M. Podgórny, V. Drabik-Podgórna, G. Aisenson, J. L. Bernaud, I. A. Moumoula, & J. Guichard (Eds.), *Interventions in career design and education* (pp. 285–302). Springer.

De Vos, A., Van der Heijden, B. I. J. M., & Akkermans, J. (2020). Sustainable careers: Towards a conceptual model. *Journal of Vocational Behavior, 117,* 103196. https://doi.org/10.1016/j.jvb.2018.06.011.

Di Fabio, A., & Bucci, O. (2016). Green positive guidance and green positive life counseling for decent work and decent lives: Some empirical results. *Frontiers in Psychology, 7,* 261. https://doi.org/10.3389/fpsyg.2016.00261.

Dussaux. (2020). *The joint effects of energy prices and carbon taxes on environmental and economic performance: Evidence from the French manufacturing sector.* OECD Environment Working Papers. https://doi.org/10.1787/b84b1b7d-en.

Global Green Growth Institute. (2019). *GGGI strategy: A low carbon, resilient world of strong, inclusive, and sustainable growth.* Author.

Guichard, J. (2016). Life-and working-design interventions for constructing a sustainable human(e) world. *Journal of Counsellogy, 5,* 179–190.

Intergovernmental Panel on Climate Change. (2021). *Climate change 2021: The physical science basis.* Author.

Kjell, O. N. E. (2011). Sustainable well-being: A potential synergy between sustainability and well-being research. *Review of General Psychology, 15,* 255–266. https://doi.org/10.1037/a0024603.

Plant, P. (2014). Green guidance. In G. Arulmani, A. J. Bakshi, F. T. L. Leong, & A. G. Watts (Eds.), *Handbook of career development: International perspectives* (pp. 309–316). Springer. https://doi.org/10.1007/978-1-4614-9460-7_17.

Rochat, S., & Masdonati, J. (2019). Sustainable Career Cards Sort (SCCS): Linking career choices to the world needs. In K. Maree (Ed.), *Handbook of innovative career counselling* (pp. 505–520). Springer.

United Nations. (2015). Transforming our world: The 2030 agenda for sustainable development. General Assembly 70 session. Retrieved from https://documents-dds-ny.un.org/doc/UNDOC/GEN/N15/291/89/pdf/N1529189.pdf?OpenElement.

34 Decent Work in America?

Caroline S. Fawcett

As America begins recovering from the COVID-19 pandemic, there is a collective need to ask—what has the COVID-19 pandemic shown us about our policies and institutions? The health system, the economy, and the social and governance institutions offered a wide range of support and assistance. Yet the COVID-19 pandemic revealed the weakest links within this system, particularly as it relates to the relationship between psychological factors and policy response. To examine this system, I turn to the concept of "decent work" to identify the weaknesses and strengths within the system and identify policies and practices that can help us in the future.

The concept of "decent work" offers a broad definition of work, including psychological and economic factors. Developed by the International Labor Organization in 1999, decent work states that "work is central to an individual's well-being." Decent work starts with job stability, establishing a stable contract of 40 hours and a fixed schedule (ILO, 2014). It establishes a fair wage and social benefits, ensures workplace safety and wellness, and promotes respect, social connection, and engagement—including psychological aspects of work. It also creates educational and training opportunities for workers. Decent work is not just another job, but it is also a labor standard to be used to capture quantitative and qualitative aspects of work.

The COVID-19 pandemic affected every American worker and their family. Approximately 16 million American workers lost jobs, due to the sharp, immediate contraction of the U.S. economy. The essential workforce, representing around 70% of all workers, was exposed to unimaginable stress, risks, and constraints, as they performed their jobs in safety, health, essential products, or infrastructure sectors. Remote workers, averaging around 25% of the workforce, attempted to balance work and their caregiving roles, placing emotional stressors on every household, particularly those with elderly or young members. Each of these groups profoundly experienced a dramatic change in their work lives and faced uncertainty and precariousness in their employment (Bauer et al., 2020).

The economic and social uncertainties cut deeply for three specific groups of workers: women, people of color, and youth (Oddo et al., 2021), who have the highest levels of precarious employment—that is work that

DOI:10.4324/9781003272397-41

is uncertain (temporary or irregular hours), unprotected (lacking health and social security protections), or economically insecure. These structural trends existed well before COVID-19, and the epidemic deepened precariousness among these groups. Women have borne the brunt of COVID-19 job loss, due to the fact that women, particularly women of color, are most likely to be a part of the essential low-wage workforce.

So why did the U.S. do so poorly in protecting its workers during the COVID-19 pandemic? The U.S. follows an economic approach to protecting employment, emphasizing wages, income, and benefits. Yet 40% of U.S. workers today do not have these "good jobs," they have no binding contract with an employer that ensures these benefits. Second, the current employment system pays little attention to well-being and psychological aspects of work, such as trust, social connection, consensus, and engagement. The value of work is so much greater than simply its economic value; work also has deep and complex levels of psychological value (Blustein, 2019). Work includes being with others, being part of something bigger, being motivated and able to care, and being able to be respected. Take away the work or create uncertainty regarding work, there will be a reduction of the psychological bonds that tie us together, as well as eliminate the structure of the daily behaviors and patterns of a person's life. With this loss of employment, the COVID-19 pandemic triggered a deeply troubling psychological and social crisis that cuts across the country. As explored in the following, the U.S. unemployment policies increased precariousness and psychological loss during the COVID-19 pandemic.

The main employment support program during COVID was the federal-state unemployment insurance (UI) program. It provides a portion of the wage of a worker for a fixed period and requires that the worker is actively searching for another job (Kovalski & Sheiner, 2020). This program was re-designed as a worker income support program during COVID-19, offering additional income benefits. The main requirement of the program was that all workers were laid off by their firm. For any worker, this was a cruel condition. Should the main government message to the private sector be that they should lay off their workers? What are the psychological effects on workers due to their separation from their job? The UI requirement contributed to a sense of precariousness for all workers. It set an expectation that if workers did not perform, they would lose their jobs, contributing to the psychological stress of the COVID-19 pandemic.

The alternative model is a wage subsidy to workers, used by most other developed countries. This model provides partial wage support to workers that are retained at the firm, with support in the range of 75–80% of wage income. Job retention is the main outcome of the process. While the U.S. did provide some wage support through two small programs—the Workshare program and the Paycheck Protection Program loan program, the UI program supported the large majority of support to workers. The UI policy, the main worker policy of COVID-19, contributed to the psychological distress of workers, and this policy issue remains outstanding in terms of research and policy guidance. In short, U.S. employment policy revealed its weakest links in terms of decent work. Policy reform of the UI system that benefits and centers the psychological well-being of workers should be a priority.

Decent work in the U.S. is often discussed as the "good jobs" that include social protections—such as social security and health insurance benefits. The "good jobs" include stable contracts, negotiated wages, occupational health and safety, and training and education opportunities for workers. Missing from this discussion is the issue of psychological wellness. Yet the weakest link is that the low-income workforce does not have basic work conditions, often referred to as decent work. These basic labor protections should extend to all workers, offering the fundamental conditions of decent work, such as the 40-hour work week, stable hours, and basic psychological wellness.

Second, the priority for psychological health is job stability. Getting fixed hours of employment and eliminating precarious employment is an important feature of decent work which contributes to the psychological stability of the workforce. The message is clear: *decent work requires job stability which in turn supports psychological health in the workplace.* Without decent work, the union movement is missing its foundation. To promote a decent work agenda in the U.S., here are some additional ideas on policies, programs, and practices that would strengthen these weak links.

Decent Work Policy Reform

As examined by labor historian, Joseph McCartin, the heart of a stable employment system is the 40-hour week and fixed hours of work (McCartin, 1997). Precarious work, often referred to as contingent work, continues to be a challenge for the U.S. employment system. Here we have two examples—one good and one bad of policy dialogue to promote decent work and job security. Let us first take a modest program of decent work led by the New Foundation in the U.S. (Damme, 2021). This 2011 initiative established a series of decent work indicators, but without a context for its usage in policy or political dialogue, it led to little change or impact. Compare this to the Oxfam-University of Warwick program of decent work in Scotland, which proposed decent work measures within the context of the 2016 political election (Pautz et al., 2021). The project conducted research and their findings fed into a national election debate. The main outcome established a decent work agenda for the government. Wellness, work, and wages were the main elements of the new strategy.

Wellness and Decent Work for All

Wellness programs have become the response of large companies to the mental health challenges of the U.S. workforce. Approximately one in five adults suffers from mental health challenges each year, with a high price tag of $200 million lost workdays and $200 billion in lost wages and productivity. A wide array of wellness benefits are now offered by elite corporations, such as children's play areas, food offerings, and exercise and counseling programs. Small businesses have few resources for these luxury benefits so that such benefits are rarely offered to low-wage and uneducated laborers. More importantly, some simple benefits—a compassionate manager, an emotionally available co-worker, a flexible workplace schedule, or mental health education, are glaringly missing in all firms. Focusing on simple wellness benefits that can be applied to all of the workforce would allow us to define decent work and wellness for all (Lieberman, 2019).

Weakest Link of All: Education and Decent Work

At all levels of education, there is little mention of the concept of decent work in the U.S. The national policy promotes career and technical education through the Perkins V Education program. Approximately $1.3 billion annually of U.S. federal funding is available to promote this career education and job mobility. Additionally, the non-profit sector funds similar programs through their education in economics programs. Yet for the majority of the essential workforce, career ladder concepts do not address the needs of workers in low-rung jobs within the system. This is particularly relevant for the low-income and rural labor workforce. Policy reform is urgently needed to address these shortcomings.

Decent work establishes basic standard protections, such as the 40-hour work week, wellness and safety, and basic respect for employees. Decent work also addresses the weakest links of the U.S. labor system, in that it includes every worker, not just those that have representation and secure jobs. The U.S. needs an educational and economic system that recognizes the value of a decent work agenda and reforms key policy priorities. Simply put, we need to strengthen our weakest links of our system, which were revealed during the COVID-19 pandemic.

References

Bauer, L., Broady, K., Edelberg, W., & O'Donnell, J. (2020). *Ten facts about COVID-19 and the U.S. economy*. Brookings Institution. www.brookings.edu/research/ten-facts-about-covid-19-and-the-u-s-economy/.

Blustein, D. L. (2019). *The importance of work in an age of uncertainty: The eroding work experience in America*. Oxford University Press. https://psycnet.apa.org/doi/10.1093/oso/9780190213701.001.0001.

Damme, L. (2021). Decent work indicators. *New America Foundation*. www.newamerica.org/economic-growth/policy-papers/decent-work-indicators/.

International Labor Organization. (2014). *A manual on decent work indicators: Guidelines for producers and users of statistical and legal framework indicators*. www.ilo.org/wcmsp5/

groups/public/—dgreports/—integration/documents/publication/wcms_229374. pdf.

Kovalski, M. A., & Sheiner, L. (2020). *How does unemployment insurance work? And how is it changing during the pandemic?* Brookings Institution. www.brookings.edu/blog/ up-front/2020/07/20/how-does-unemployment-insurance-work-and-how-is-it-changing-during-the-coronavirus-pandemic/.

Lieberman, C. (2019, August 14). What wellness programs don't do for workers. *The Harvard University Business Review: Health and Behavioral Science.* https://hbr.org/2019/08/ what-wellness-programs-dont-do-for-workers.

McCartin, J. A. (1997). *Labor's Great War: The struggle for industrial democracy and the origins of modern American relations, 1912–1921.* University of North Carolina Press.

Oddo, V. M., Zhuang, C. C., Andrea, S. B., Eisenberg-Guyot, J., Peckham, T., Jacoby, D., & Hajat, A. (2021). Changes in precarious employment in the United States: A longitudinal analysis. *Scandinavian Journal of Work, Environmental & Health, 47*(3), 171–180. https://doi.org/10.5271/sjweh.3939.

Pautz, H., Wright, S., & Collins, C. (2021). Decent work in Scotland, an agenda-setting analysis. *Journal of Social Policy, 50*(1), 40–59. https://doi.org/10.1017/ S0047279419000916.

35 Our Purpose is People

Aron Ain

Imagine a company where everyone loves to work, where employees feel not just satisfied but truly cared for, respected, and energized. When you put people first, inspired work follows. I firmly believe that if you provide a great culture that inspires people, they will deliver better products and provide better services leading to a great experience for customers and improved outcomes for any organization.

When we formed UKG through a merger of two of the greatest places to work—Kronos Incorporated and Ultimate Software—we spent months thinking about our purpose. We came up with something that resonated with employees: "Our Purpose is People"—a way to articulate how people are at the heart of our success—of every organization's success!

This essay takes leaders and managers inside UKG's workplace culture and offers some tips that may be helpful in centering the needs of today's workers in their work settings. I will focus on three specific topics: Trust, Welcoming Everyone, and Fair Pay for All.

Trust Them (Again and Again)

Trust is the magic glue that makes personal and professional relationships thrive. When we trust each other, anything is possible.

We have worked incredibly hard to instill trust throughout our organization, starting with me. Until proven otherwise, we assume everyone's competence, judgment, and good intentions. Because we place so much faith in employees, they return the favor, placing a remarkable amount of trust in our leaders and our organization. Their trust in turn leads to far better performance—more innovation, quicker recovery from mistakes, and more energy and enthusiasm at work.

Years ago, we introduced, under the framework of our three core competencies (character, competence, and collaboration), a set of desired behaviors that apply to employees at all levels. We began basing 40% of employees' annual performance ratings on how well they adopted these behaviors. One behavior within the overall construct we emphasized was "establishing trust,"

DOI:10.4324/9781003272397-42

which we defined as: "Gains the confidence and trust of others through principled leadership, sound business ethics, authenticity, and follow-through on commitments. Establishes open, candid, trusting relationships; treats all individuals fairly and with respect; maintains high standards of integrity."

In formulating this definition, we looked to behavioral norms that had already existed to some extent in our organization, but that had never been highlighted formally. By defining trust, we established it as a key element of our culture.

As our newly formed company of UKG, we have since evolved our desired behaviors to be United, Kind, and Growing, with trust still playing a leading role.

Think of how much more inspired your team members would be if you put your faith in them, if you assume they were competent and would do the right thing. Think of how much better your organization would function if trust prevailed, with more fluid communication and quicker identification of problems as they arise.

Trusting others is not easy, especially if your workplace has a history of strained relationships. Also, although the vast majority of employees prove worthy of your trust, a few do not, and on occasion, you might have to deal with the consequences. That's okay—life is not perfect.

If you haven't trusted others easily in the past, now is the time to start. If you have, then rededicate yourself to deepening your trusting relationships. Are you empowering team members by encouraging their creativity and autonomy? Are you communicating openly and honestly? Are your expectations about trust-promoting behavior as clearly defined as possible?

Despite the effort it requires, trusting others still represents a far easier way to manage. Think of what happens when you learn to let go of fear, anxiety, and control. All that effort you expended worrying about how one of your people would perform, all that time and energy you spent monitoring progress, now can go toward other pursuits that truly add value, like spending more time ideating, collaborating, and innovating. Trusting others does not only yield greater engagement by inspiring loyalty and affection and contributing to others' growth and advancement. It supports engagement indirectly by freeing you up to take a variety of other actions that will help your organization move forward and succeed.

Welcome Everyone

Belonging, Diversity, and Equity (BD&E). There is perhaps nothing more important today than providing a sense of belonging to EVERYONE in the workplace and in life in general.

At UKG, we have placed a great emphasis on creating and nurturing many Employee Resource Groups (ERGs) with the purpose of facilitating engagement and belonging among our people, especially those from marginalized groups. These ERGs are orchestrated by employees with support from our BD&E core team.

We have experienced great success with participation in a range of intersectional groups created to address the issues of healthcare concerns; employees who identify as lesbian, gay, bisexual, and gender non-binary; people who identify as Black/African American; people who identify as Hispanic/Latino and as Asian and Pacific Islanders; veterans; women in the workplace; people with disabilities; and so much more.

Our Purpose is People is the UKG brand. This can only be realized when our employees feel respected and safe bringing their whole selves to a workplace where everyone has a voice. A place where unique identities and perspectives are welcomed but also sought out, celebrated, and well-represented. An equitable workplace where everyone has abundant opportunity to grow and reach their full potential. Though we are individually unique, we proudly identify as the U Krew family, where we believe in the same values, and each and every employee belongs. "Uniquely You, Uniquely Valued" sums up how we think about our U Krewers. We have made BD&E a business imperative. It is a "must do" for our organization.

Our BD&E strategies and approach are geared toward a recognition that the best-run organizations meet their clients "where they are" as we believe they want to do business with partners who share these values.

As reflected by the head of BD&E at UKG,

> Our Purpose is People, and the effort we are pouring into our belonging, diversity, and equity strategy aims to ensure that purpose is felt throughout every aspect of our business. Our goal is to prescribe programs and practices that address belonging, diversity, and equity holistically—ensuring that the many intersectionalities of gender, race, ability, orientation, and more are not lost in the process. It is a big goal, but one that we can and must achieve.

Our BD&E leader at UKG believes,

> Together, we have a goal to make UKG the greatest people company in the world. To get there, we must always evolve, keep learning, and live Our Purpose is People every day as UKG transcends the standard for what it means to be a company where all individuals feel welcome, well respected, equally valued, and confident that they belong there.

Creating an environment in which every employee feels welcome and engaged takes work. UKG is not perfect, although I am proud of the progress we are making in this area. I have been open in my welcome for growth and learning regarding belonging, diversity, and equity. I have told members of our ERGs that I will lean on them for education and guidance and help pave the way for the expansion of how we approach being a best place to work for ALL.

If your organization is seeking to become more inclusive, consider networking with BD&E leaders whose companies are focused in this area. Create a diversity initiative that spans beyond what people typically think of diversity and includes belonging and equity. Your employees will thank you.

Fair Pay for All

In addition to thriving ERGs, UKG continues to focus on our approach to how we compensate U Krewers for the work they do—it is one of the fundamental ways we demonstrate that Our Purpose is People. Our philosophy is centered on compensating employees fairly and consistently for the work they do. When we say, "fair and consistent," it means that we are applying consistent governance, a career framework, guidelines, and principles to each U Krewer's compensation package.

"Fair and consistent" does not always mean that two U Krewers in the same role will earn exactly the same. Why? While U Krewers may perform similar work, other factors may influence pay such as the individual's skill set, experience level, job performance, and length of time with UKG—all within our guidelines and our Global Career Framework.

This ties into our beliefs around pay equity. Pay equity means compensating employees similarly when they perform the same or similar job duties accounting for factors such as skill set, job performance, tenure, and experience level, regardless of race, color, religion, gender, gender identity or orientation, national origin, disability, age, or other characteristics. The Global Career Framework and incentive compensation programs that UKG has put in place are two of the foundational components that will help us meet our goals in this area.

UKG also recently announced a marketing initiative: *Close the Gap*. This external initiative is designed to drive awareness and action to address the pay disparity between men, women, and underrepresented groups that continues to significantly impact today's workforce. According to U.S. Bureau of Labor Statistics, for every dollar a man in the U.S. earned in 2020, a woman made $0.82—a gap of 18 cents. The disparity is even greater for Black, transgender, and immigrant women.

Through this campaign, UKG is committing millions of dollars toward creating meaningful and lasting change to address this disparity. This includes a $3 million investment in critical programs and initiatives, philanthropic support, launching a pay equity research study, creating educational resources to increase awareness, and inviting all people to join the Close the Gap Pledge to address inequality in the workplace.

Perhaps some of the programs we are putting in place at UKG will inspire other companies to do the same. If your organization does not already have one, consider exploring the development of a Career Framework to provide a foundation for harmonizing job titles; competitive, consistent, and equitable pay programs; and understanding careers and the availability of opportunities for development.

Conclusion

UKG is certainly not perfect. We have much work to do in the areas covered in this essay. We all have work to do as leaders. We do not focus on BD&E just because it is good for our business. Of course, it is. We also do it because it is the right thing to do. The topics covered here are some of the pressing items we are focused on at UKG. Perhaps you will glean a bit from this essay as you rethink work at your organization.

Note: Some excerpts lifted from WorkInspired: How to Build an Organization Where Everyone Loves to Work, written by Aron Ain, published in 2019.

36 Securing Decent and Dignified School-to-Work Transitions

Jonas Masdonati

Transitioning From School to Work as a Challenging Task

After graduating from high school with difficulty, Anita decides to look for a job in order to quickly become independent. After six months of unsuccessful searches, she finally manages to find a fixed-term, part-time contract as a cooking assistant. Being used to cooking at home, she thought she would be happy with the job. But she was wrong: her supervisor only gives her degrading tasks, the atmosphere in the kitchen is terrible, and she often has to work at night. Moreover, she does not earn enough to leave her parents' home and rent an apartment on her own. When the owner of the restaurant announces a downsizing, she is not too disappointed to be the first to be fired. Except that, she now has to look for a new job and the competition is tough, especially since she only has a high school diploma. How can she manage to quickly find another job and avoid another poor experience? Who can help her face this new challenge and not give up?

Unfortunately, the story of Anita is rather ordinary, and answering her questions is hard. Transitioning from school to work is indeed a major challenge for young adults around the world (International Labour Organization [ILO], 2019). The school-to-work transition (STWT) can take time and often leads people to experience job insecurity before finding satisfying employment—if they ever do (Grosemans et al., 2020). This task is particularly tricky in tense socio-historical circumstances, with young workers being the most impacted by economic crises in terms of risk of unemployment and job insecurity (Akkermans et al., 2021; Schoon & Heckhausen, 2019). Moreover, the STWT process tends to emphasize social inequalities. Young people from low socioeconomic backgrounds and without qualifications, as well as women, are overrepresented among the *not in education, employment, or training* (NEET) category, which is considered the most-at-risk population group (ILO, 2019; Organisation for Economic Co-operation and Development [OECD], 2017). Given the complexity and importance of the transitional task, it is essential to clearly pinpoint what constitutes a

DOI:10.4324/9781003272397-43

successful transition and which factors affect individuals' ability to cope with it, which in turn help in identifying the best avenues for interventions aimed at securing STWTs.

Accessing Decent and Dignified Work

Scholars agree on the fact that succeeding in the STWT is more than simply leaving school and finding a job; it also implies that young people "perform well, achieve person—career fit, and develop in their work and early career, with the aim of securing employment and laying the foundation for a sustainable career" (Akkermans et al., 2021, p. 80). Therefore, the efforts needed to find a job and the characteristics of this job must be considered when studying STWTs (Ling & O'Brien, 2013). Accordingly, we recently suggested conceiving a successful STWT as the first step toward decent, dignified work (Masdonati et al., 2021). First, the jobs young people access should be decent, including guaranteeing physical and interpersonal safety, a just salary, fair working hours, health protections, and work values that align with people's personal values. Second, jobs should sustain newcomers' dignity, meaning that they should be consistent with their expectations of a working life. These expectations vary depending on their particular experiences and contexts and may include engaging in fulfilling activities, providing a social role or purpose in life, or supporting personal development (Cohen-Scali et al., 2022). In contrast, an STWT is to be considered unsuccessful when it results in a job that does not match the purposes individuals ascribe to their worker role. Going back to Anita's vignette, we observe that her first work experience is neither decent nor dignified. Her job as a cooking assistant is not decent because working conditions (e.g., hours, salary, and work climate) are highly unsatisfactory. It is also not dignified because it does not seem to meet what Anita expects from work, namely, being happy with its contents and gaining autonomy.

Research shows that the quality of the STWT and the chance of accessing decent and dignified work result from the interplay of social, institutional, and psychological factors (Akkermans et al., 2021; Ling & O'Brien, 2013; Masdonati et al., 2021; Schoon & Heckhausen, 2019). An adverse family background (e.g., lack of parental support), socioeconomic constraints (e.g., low socioeconomic status), and belonging to marginalized groups (e.g., early school leavers and migrant people) are among the main social threats to a successful transition (OECD, 2017; Schoon & Heckhausen, 2019). A clear sense of vocational and work identity (i.e., making appropriate career choices and being ready to endorse the work role) and some key transitional resources, such as work volition (i.e., feeling able to make choices despite constraints) and career adaptability (i.e., being ready to cope with transitional tasks), are the main psychological factors that impact the STWT process (Grosemans et al., 2020; Medvide et al., 2019). Concerning institutional factors, education systems might attenuate or, inversely, exacerbate the impacts of these contextual and psychosocial factors. Highly selective education systems and those that lead to abrupt passage from education to the labor market tend to aggravate social inequalities and increase the complexity of STWT challenges (Schoon & Heckhausen, 2019). In contrast, the STWT is less discriminating in countries with a comprehensive education system, and it is smoother in countries with strong and socially valued vocational education and training tracks that ensure a progressive and institutionalized integration into the labor market.

Securing School-to-Work Transitions

Given the impacts of STWTs on careers, it is crucial to create conditions that help young people experience secure STWT processes, which in turn could lead to decent and dignified work, foster equal labor market integration opportunities, and, in the long run, promote sustainable careers (Fuertes et al., 2021). This effort involves contextual initiatives to promote transitions to decent jobs as much as psychosocial interventions to foster access to dignified work (Medvide et al., 2019).

Contextual initiatives cover the promotion of education systems that facilitate gradual, smooth, and inclusive passages from school to work as well as labor market policies that prevent young adults' precariousness. Two main lines of development concern education systems. First, education systems should avoid not only early school leaving but also premature allocation of pupils into different school tracks based on their school performance. Inversely, comprehensive and inclusive school systems should be promoted to prevent the reproduction of social inequalities in the improvement of STWTs. The implementation of educational allowances is a promising solution in this sense (Schoon & Heckhausen, 2019). Second, school systems should implement transition programs enabling young adults to smoothly integrate into the labor market—for example, structured internships, inclusive vocational training programs, or transition years that prepare pupils to enter the workforce (Ling & O'Brien, 2013).

From a labor market policy perspective, employers should be made aware of the importance of ensuring the young people they hire benefit from decent working conditions (e.g., just salary, appropriate hours, and secure work settings) and career opportunities (e.g., access to permanent contracts or concrete career perspectives within or outside the organization; Fuertes et al., 2021; Masdonati et al., 2021). More ambitious initiatives also deserve consideration, such as providing a universal basic income for individuals' first working years and conceiving intensive labor market integration programs that allow people in the NEET category to gain qualifications and find decent jobs without experiencing precariousness. Country-level measures that stimulate the creation of training opportunities leading to permanent contracts, such as the "Youth Impulse" and "Youth Guarantee" programs in Portugal (Cueto et al., 2018), are clues as to how these principles can be implemented to promote not only job entry but also sustainable careers.

Psychosocial interventions should focus on providing access to jobs that allow young adults to experience dignity in work. These interventions could make young adults' work expectations explicit and help them identify organizations offering work environments that fit the purposes they ascribe to work in their lives (Fuertes et al., 2021). Moreover, interventions should focus on the construction of a clear sense of vocational and work identity, which implies helping young adults find occupations that fit their interests, values, and personalities and be prepared to switch from student to worker roles. Furthermore, young adults should be prepared to cope with possibly challenging transitions, for example, through the improvement of their career adaptability and volition (Medvide et al., 2019). However, advocacy counseling should be implemented to avoid putting excessive pressure on young people and to share the responsibility of securing transitions. This would require prioritizing interventions that empower people who have insufficient transitional resources, such as marginalized young adults and NEETs, and advocate the creation of conditions that make labor market fluctuations a fruitful exploration period rather than a jeopardizing process (Fuertes et al., 2021; Grosemans et al., 2020).

References

Akkermans, J., Blokker, R., Buers, C., Van der Heijden, B., & De Vos, A. (2021). Ready, set, go! School-to-work transition in the new career. In E. A. Marshall & J. E. Symonds (Eds.), *Young adult development at the school-to-work transition: International pathways and processes* (pp. 77–103). Oxford University Press.

Cohen-Scali, V., Masdonati, J., Disquay-Perrot, S., Ribeiro, M. A., Vilhjálmsdóttir, G., Zein, R., Kaplan-Bucciarelli, J., Moumoula, I., Aisenson, G., & Rossier, J. (2022). Emerging adults' representations of work: A qualitative research in seven countries. *Emerging Adulthood, 10*(1), 54–67. https://doi.org/10.1177/2167696820963598.

Cueto, B., Martín-Román, A., Moral, A., & Moreno Mínguez, A. (2018). Youth employment in the Iberian Countries. In M. Á. Malo & A. Moreno Mínguez (Eds.), *European youth labour markets* (pp. 27–43). Springer. https://doi.org/10.1007/978-3-319-68222-8_3.

Fuertes, V., McQuaid, R., & Robertson, P. J. (2021). Career-first: An approach to sustainable labour market integration. *International Journal for Educational and Vocational Guidance, 21*, 429–446. https://doi.org/10.1007/s10775-020-09451-2.

Grosemans, I., Hannes, K., Neyens, J., & Kyndt, E. (2020). Emerging adults embarking on their careers: Job and identity explorations in the transition to work. *Youth & Society, 52*(5), 795–819. https://doi.org/10.1177/0044118X18772695.

International Labour Organization. (2019). Labour market access—a persistent challenge for youth around the world. *ILOSTAT Spotlights on Work Statistics, 5.* https://ilo.org/wcmsp5/groups/public/—dgreports/—stat/documents/publication/wcms_676196.pdf.

Ling, T. J., & O'Brien, K. M. (2013). Connecting the forgotten half: The school-to-work transition of noncollege-bound youth. *Journal of Career Development, 40*, 347–367. https://doi.org/10.1177/0894845312455506.

Masdonati, J., Massoudi, K., Blustein, D. L., & Duffy, R. D. (2021). Moving toward decent work: Application of the psychology of working theory to the school-to-work transition. *Journal of Career Development, 49*(1), 41–59. https://doi.org/10.1177/0894845321991681.

Medvide, M. B., Kozan, S., Blustein, D. L., Kenny, M. E. (2019). School to work transition of non-college bound youth: An integration of the life design paradigm and the psychology of working theory. In J. G. Maree (Ed.), *Handbook of innovative career counselling* (pp. 157–172). Springer. https://doi.org/10.1007/978-3-030-22799-9_10.

Organisation for Economic Co-operation and Development. (2017). Transition from school to work: How hard is it across different age groups? *Education Indicators in Focus, 54*. https://doi.org/10.1787/1e604198-en.

Schoon, I., & Heckhausen, J. (2019). Conceptualizing individual agency in the transition from school to work: A social-ecological developmental perspective. *Adolescent Research Review, 4*, 135–148. https://doi.org/10.1007/s40894-019-00111-3.

37 Dignity in the Workplace

Donna Hicks

For more than two decades, I facilitated dialogues for warring parties around the globe, trying to help them resolve the political issues that divided them. My organization, *The Program on Conflict Analysis and Resolution*, located at the Weatherhead Center for International Affairs at Harvard University, was often invited to help the parties manage their conflicts, in the hope of finding a way to a peaceful resolution of the issues that divided them. After sitting at countless negotiating tables, helping them in their struggle to come to agreements, it became clear to me that there were more than just the political issues that divided them. As a psychologist, I was always interested in the "human dimension" of conflict; ways in which people reacted to being treated as less than human by the other side. The problem was that this dimension was never talked about at the negotiating tables, yet I saw evidence of it no matter where I was working in the world. People react strongly when they are treated badly. I knew I had to come up with a way to discuss these highly charged emotional events. After several failed attempts, I finally found the right way to open the discussion about these underlying emotional reactions that were wreaking havoc on negotiations. The word I discovered was *Dignity*. What was it about this word that gave the parties permission to discuss what it felt like to being treated as if they didn't matter?

The word has remarkable power. What I found was that the desire to be treated with dignity was a universal human yearning. My simple definition is that dignity is our inborn value and worth, along with our inborn vulnerability to having it injured. We don't hesitate for a second to accept the fact that we humans are all physically vulnerable to injury. But accepting that we all have dignity, and that it can be injured, is not something we all take for granted.

Research in social neuroscience shows that our brains don't know the difference between physical pain and social pain inflicted on our dignity (Lieberman, 2013). Humans react badly when they experience dignity wounds. I felt that I had discovered a missing link in my understanding of conflict. Dignity violations contribute to conflict in invisible ways, but their impact is as serious as a physical injury. I figured out that by asking the

DOI:10.4324/9781003272397-44

parties to discuss times in which they felt their dignity had been assaulted by the conflict, the floodgates opened. People were willing to talk about not only their wounds but also those of their ancestors. It was always a profound experience for the parties. After addressing these previously unspoken injuries, the parties were able to do a much better job negotiating over the political issues. I felt like I had struck gold—gold in the form of the word *Dignity*.

I quickly realized I had to write about the power of dignity for my conflict resolution community. Assaults to dignity were an integral part of intractable conflicts, and we needed a way to talk about them. After a seven-year struggle to operationalize dignity, my first book, *Dignity: Its Essential Role in Resolving Conflict* was published (Hicks, 2011). My target audience was my conflict resolution community, however, to my great surprise, the book touched a nerve in the business world, healthcare, education, faith communities, and organizations of all kinds. I was asked to consult in the corporate world and discovered that the same dignity issues that I saw in the international arena were showing up in the workplace (Hicks, 2018).

I was asked by corporations to address conflicts that they were unable to resolve with traditional means. My *Ten Elements of Dignity* resonated with both management and employees. These elements, once violated, give rise to conflict. The elements are as follows: *Acceptance of identity* (people want their identity accepted no matter their race, religion, ethnicity, sexual orientation, or physical capacity); *Recognition* (people want to be given credit for their efforts); *Acknowledgment* (people want acknowledgment for the suffering they have endured); *Inclusion* (people want to feel a sense of belonging); *Safety* (people want to feel physically safe as well as psychologically safe, safe to speak up and to be their authentic selves); *Fairness* (people want to be treated justly, with equality, and in an evenhanded way); *Independence* (people want to act on their own behalf, so that they feel in control, not micromanaged or constrained); *Understanding* (people want to be understood for who they are, not judged by stereotypes); *Benefit of the Doubt* (people want to be treated as if they have integrity and have a good reason why they feel the way they do); and *Accountability* (people want an apology when someone does them harm).

What is powerful for people once they understand the Ten Elements is that they give them a vocabulary to talk about what happened when they felt that they had been mistreated. So often, people walk away from a bad reaction feeling bad. Naming what gave rise to the bad feeling helps understand the source of the bad feeling. Saying, for example, that "I was excluded from that important meeting, or I was treated unfairly, or I felt I was discriminated against because of my race," helps externalize the problem. I always say, "you may feel bad, but you are not bad. Something bad *happened to you*—you had your dignity violated." It always jump-starts the healing process by placing the cause of the pain outside of the self.

After several forays into the corporate world, I soon came to appreciate the profound role leadership plays in ensuring that the dignity and well-being of its people are intact and that the culture itself protected and promoted dignity. What I observed was that when those in leadership positions became aware of the ways in which they (often unconsciously) violated the dignity of their people, they were shocked. They were good people with good intentions who simply were never exposed to any knowledge related to dignity. After all, it is not something that is regularly taught in business schools. In fact, the ignorance that I discovered by people in leadership positions was vast. Learning about dignity, and the ways in which people react when their dignity is violated and honored, was a profound experience for most leaders. What really helped in getting them to recognize the importance of treating their people with dignity was the neuroscience evidence that I talked about earlier. Once they understood that the brain experiences dignity violations in the same way that it processes a physical injury, it was hard to dismiss them.

The other piece of the Dignity Model that shocks leaders into an awareness of the need to honor dignity is the Ten Temptations to Violate Dignity. When I was researching my first book, I came across the literature in Evolutionary Biology and Evolutionary Psychology (Barkow, 2006). It directly addresses some of the hardwired responses we humans experience when we feel we are being threatened. We all have heard of the flight, fight, and freeze responses—self-preservation instincts that get called up in a moment's notice when we feel we are being harmed. I found that they were not the only instincts we have wired in our brains. There are more. What are the Ten Temptations? First, we *take the bait*, when someone does us harm, our instinct is to get even, return the harm; *we try to save face*, in order to avoid looking bad in the eyes of others, as well as *shirk responsibility* to avoid public embarrassment. We engage in *false dignity*, our instincts tell us our worth comes from how people treat us. We also engage in *false security*, thinking that it's better to stay in a dignity-violating relationship because we need it to feel secure. We are *conflict avoidant*. We'd rather suffer silently than confront the person who harmed us. We *assume we are the innocent victim in a failed relationship*. We *resist feedback*. It feels too much like shaming criticism. We will *shame and blame others to deflect our guilt*. Finally, we will engage in *gossip* to punish people who violate our dignity rather than to confront them.

These Ten Temptations are part of our evolutionary legacy. These automatic, involuntary responses were meant to promote survival, but they are no longer serving us well in the 21st century. The biologists tell us that we first need to recognize that it is one of the hallmarks of being human that we fall prey to these instincts (Barkow, 2006). They are a part of the human struggle that we all face. They also say that we need to know them to control them. Barkow says *biology is not destiny unless we ignore it*. We need to first recognize when we are taken over by these instincts, then push the pause button, and let another part of our brain take over our decision-making.

Fortunately, we are equipped as humans to be able to create a bypass around these instincts. Our neo-cortex is the savior—one of the more recent parts of our brain to evolve.

The reason this knowledge is so important for not only leaders, but everyone in an organization is because the truth is that even though honoring dignity (ten elements of dignity) may sound like common sense, it is, but it's not common knowledge or common practice. We humans are more likely to naturally be dignity violators because we live in a harsh world where our ignorance of these matters dominates our consciousness. We are stuck in a survival mode of being when relationships so often are considered a source of threat rather than a source of well-being. We can shift the survival default setting if we choose. We simply need to recognize the need for dignity education and integrate it into our workplace culture.

While it is critically important for people in leadership positions to be knowledgeable of all matters related to dignity—to treat their people well, gaining interpersonal skills is not enough. They need to make the knowledge system-wide. When I do consultations with leaders, I convince them of the importance of creating opportunities for everyone in the organization to engage in dignity education. It is one thing for leaders to model dignified behavior, but everyone in the organization—management and employees alike, needs to take responsibility for making dignity a way of life within the culture.

Finally, leaders must also be committed to developing system-wide policies that protect and promote dignity. For example, it is important that policies are developed that do not discriminate against any group of employees or systemically violate any of the elements of dignity. Are all policies fair? Do they promote a sense of belonging? Is it part of the explicit norms of the organization to take responsibility for our actions and apologize when we do harm to others?

Becoming "dignity conscious" takes time, effort, and a commitment to learning a new way of being together in the world. It won't happen overnight, but the slow and deliberate choices we make to see the value and worth of every human being we encounter will not only affect our relationships but impacts us as well; because when we honor the dignity of others, we strengthen our own.

References

Barkow, J. (2006). *Missing the revolution: Darwinism for social scientists.* Oxford University Press.

Hicks, D. (2011). *Dignity: Its essential role in resolving conflict.* Yale University Press.

Hicks, D. (2018). *Leading with dignity: How to create a culture that brings out the best in people.* Yale University Press.

Lieberman, M. D. (2013). *Social: Why our brains were wired to connect.* Crown.

38 Bonded Labor

The Student Debt Crisis and Decent Work

Patton O. Garriott, Sandra Bertram
Grant Solis, and Kristen Jiin Park

Student loan debt is the second highest consumer-debt category in the United States reaching over $1.7 trillion (Board of Governors of the Federal Reserve System, 2020). The debt crisis affects 44.7 million people with more than one in four adults living with an average student loan debt of $39,351 (Hanson, 2021). Student loan debt affects short-term financial stability (e.g., meeting basic needs) and long-term financial security, such as retirement savings. Student debt impacts career and life choices; for example, 61% of people defer from starting a business and 22% cannot afford their own rent (Deller & Parr, 2021; Scott & Bloom, 2021). While student loan debt issues are systemic and consequential for individuals, families, and communities, its outcomes and challenges are not borne equally.

Black (90%), Indigenous (76%), and Latina/o/x (72%) students are more likely to take out loans for their education than inherit familial wealth (Espinosa et al., 2019; Shermer, 2021). Racially biased funds (i.e., educational redlining) elicit economic harm; for instance, Black people owe $25,000 more in student debt than White peers, Indigenous people owe the highest monthly payments, and 69% of Latina/o/x borrow $40,000 or more in private loans (Hanson, 2021). Relatedly, low-income borrowers (40%) hold 20% of educational debt, with higher delinquency and default rates, negative credit, and social security offsets (Board of Governors of the Federal Reserve System, 2020; Welbeck, 2020). Systemic inequities, such as the racial wealth gap, drive racial and economic stratification that leaves people of color and lower socioeconomic status struggling to repay debts and unable to accumulate and maintain wealth.

How We Got Here

Over the past 70+ years, the U.S. government has created policies aimed to help students and families pay for higher education. The end of World War II brought the Servicemen's Readjustment Act (GI Bill) to remedy the higher education gap between those who served and their peers who did not. The Higher Education Act of 1965 followed and allocated federal

DOI:10.4324/9781003272397-45

funds directly for higher education institutions to create scholarships and increase need-based support for students. Since then, there have been several additions and reauthorizations of the Higher Education Act to address the increasing cost of higher education and growing need-based support of students, such as the Pell Grant program.

However, there has been a major shift in reliance on loans due to the rise in tuition and decreased scholarship and grant availability. Between 1991 and 2021, average tuition and fees increased yet total federal grant aid decreased by 32% between 2010 and 2021 (College Board, 2021). Furthermore, within the past five years, student loan debt has increased by 32.8% and in the past 20 years, the total federal student loan debt balance has increased by 584% (College Board, 2021).

Legitimizing myths, or beliefs that serve to preserve the status quo, have built and sustained the student debt crisis. For example, a number of legislative proposals to address the student debt crisis treat debt as a product of poor personal choices. This ideology captures economic meritocracy beliefs—the notion that, as rational decision-makers, we reap the financial seeds we sew. In reality, despite genuine efforts to make good choices and do as they are told (i.e., earn a bachelor's degree), students have been exploited by a privatized higher education industry. What was once considered a public good has become a private commodity for the intergenerationally privileged. Thus, the argument that the student debt crisis is an artifact of poor choices fails to capture the most relevant choices—those made by policymakers and institutional leaders seeking to capitalize on a broken, and largely unregulated, system.

The economic meritocracy myth is closely related to a second legitimizing myth—that social welfare programs encourage laziness and deception. Through the lens of this legitimizing myth, humane approaches to college cost, such as significantly reduced or no tuition policies, are viewed as encouraging a sense of entitlement. Thus, government interventions to relieve or cancel student debt are often met with resistance, as their beneficiaries are perceived as undeserving. Government projections show that educational debt, in addition to delinquency and default rates, will continue to rise without significant policy change.

The creation of racial and economic hierarchies via student loan debt burden is also a product of a third legitimizing belief—economic fatalism, or the belief that dominance and subordination are part of the natural order. People are less likely to desire policy change if they believe that an underclass is a necessary condition of economic well-being. Further, people who strongly endorse economic fatalism are more likely to place emphasis on hard work and individual merit to succeed. Legitimizing myths about income inequality are strongly associated with modern expressions of racism, which may help explain the racialization of student debt, its connection to work, and ultimately, the racial wealth gap (Coleman et al., 2021).

Student Loan Indebtedness and Work

Racial and economic disparities in student debt have significant implications for finding and securing *decent work*, which includes: "a) physically and interpersonally safe working conditions, b) hours that allow for free time and adequate rest, c) organizational values that complement family and social values, d) adequate compensation, and e) access to adequate health care" (Duffy et al., 2016, p. 130). Debt-to-income ratios and loan default are two primary circumstances that bond student debt to decent work. Defaulting on one's student loan payments can also negatively impact one's credit score. Although incorporating credit score reports into hiring practices has been outlawed in a number of states, it remains legal in a majority of states and may be used to disqualify a job applicant. This means that some job applicants are subjected to a credit review and this information can be used against hiring applicants with poor credit.

In addition to the challenges of securing work, Black, Indigenous, and Latina/o/x borrowers do not reap the same benefits as their White counterparts when they do find employment. Converging factors such as lower intergenerational wealth, higher debt upon graduation, and employment discrimination reduce the net gains of a salary. As a result, Black and Latina/o/x borrowers report the highest levels of delaying life milestones such as starting a family or purchasing a home, as well as inability to afford basic necessities, such as food, rent, healthcare, a savings account, and child care (Bishop & Davis, 2021; Hanson, 2021). These factors push individuals to work excessive hours and in multiple jobs to meet their basic needs, leaving less time for family and personal wellness.

Pathways to Equity and Justice

In 2007, President George W. Bush signed the College Cost Reduction and Access Act which featured the public service loan forgiveness (PSLF) program. In its original inception, there were strict conditions to qualify for the program, which is reflected in the low rates of applications and the small amount of debt that has been forgiven under this legislation. In 2021, the Biden-Harris Administration issued educational loan forgiveness for people with disabilities to address the student debt crisis, in addition to temporarily pausing student loan repayment, interest, and collections. In hopes to remedy the PSLF gap and the economic instability of COVID-19, on October 6, 2021, the U.S. Department of Education overhauled the program to address its major limitations. Although qualifications for the program were expanded under the limited waiver, this applied to only 1% of borrowers (Lake, 2021).

Additional legislative proposals are also currently under consideration. These proposals can be classified as preventive (e.g., free college tuition and limits on borrowing), forgiveness (e.g., forgiving all student loans), and limited cancellation (e.g., using debt-to-income ratio or amount borrowed to determine forgiveness). Streamlining, simplifying, and expanding qualification for student loan forgiveness will be a critical intervention for addressing the student debt crisis. Clarifying qualifying payment requirements for PSLF programs is also critical to ensure that another generation of borrowers is not left behind. Canceling a flat rate of student debt along with a financial recommitment to higher education would be a clear way to address the racial wealth gap. Penalizing predatory lending, outlawing credit score checks for employment, and expanding the amount of debt an employer is able to pay off are additional tools that can be used to mitigate the deleterious effects of students' loans on decent work.

Student debt is inextricably linked to one's ability to secure and experience the benefits of work. Debt affects college access, educational experiences, and post-graduation options, with disparate impacts on Black, Indigenous, and Latina/o/x students. While it is unclear whether current political and institutional actors will establish the necessary policies to enact meaningful change, it is clear that demands for intervention will continue to strengthen. Addressing the student debt crisis offers a crucial opportunity to right historical wrongs and weaken links of oppression between education and employment.

References

Bishop, J., & Davis, J. (2021, October 20). *Jim Crow debt: How Black borrowers experience student loans.* https://edtrust.org/resource/jim-crow-debt/.

Board of Governors of the Federal Reserve System. (2020). *Survey of Consumer Finances (SCF).* www.federalreserve.gov/econres/scfindex.htm.

Coleman, J., Garriott, P. O., & Kosmiki, M. (2021). Construction and initial validation of the Legitimizing Income Inequality Scale. *The Counseling Psychologist, 50,* 67–95. https://doi.org/10.1177/00110000211049544.

College Board. (2021). *Trends in college pricing and student aid 2021.* Author. https://research.collegeboard.org/trends/college-pricing.

Deller, S., & Parr, J. (2021). Does student loan debt hinder community well-being? *International Journal of Community Well-Being,* 1–23.

Duffy, R. D., Blustein, D. L., Diemer, M. A., & Autin, K. L. (2016). The psychology of working theory. *Journal of Counseling Psychology, 63,* 127–148. https://doi.org/10.1037/cou0000140.

Espinosa, L. L., Turk, J. M., Taylor, M., & Chessman, H. M. (2019). *Race and ethnicity in higher education: A status report.* American Council on Education. https://1xfsu31b52d33idlp13twtos-wpengine.netdna-ssl.com/wp-content/uploads/2019/02/Race-and-Ethnicity-in-Higher-Education.pdf.

Hanson, M. (2021). Student loan debt by race. *Education Data Initiative.* https://educationdata.org/student-loan-debt-by-race.

Lake, S. (2021, August 26). *Four things to know about Biden's recent student loan forgiveness announcements.* https://fortune.com/education/business/articles/2021/08/27/4-things-to-know-about-bidens-recent-student-loan-forgiveness-announcements/.

Scott, III, R. H., & Bloom, S. (2021). Student loan debt and first-time home buying in USA. *International Journal of Housing Markets and Analysis, 15*, 80–93. https://doi.org/10.1108/IJHMA-09-2020-0118.

Shermer, E. T. (2021). Why massive forgiveness won't solve the student-debt crisis. *New Labor Forum, 30*, 88–98. https://doi.org/10.1177/10957960211036039.

Welbeck, K. (2020, October 16). *Race: Examining legal remedies for disparate student debt outcomes*. Consumer Finance Law Quarterly Report, Student Borrower Protection Center Research Paper. https://ssrn.com/abstract=3712516.

39 Not Just One Employee's Problem

Improving Workers' Well-Being Through Consultation, Education, and Advocacy

Brandon L. Velez

For the last eight years, I have regularly taught a graduate course on career counseling, which uses theory and research on career development to promote students' reflection on their own work-related attitudes and experiences, as well as their comfort with helping future clients resolve common concerns related to work, such as choosing a career, dealing with conflicts between oneself and one's coworkers, balancing work with other areas of life (e.g., family), or coping with job loss. Teaching the class has been a highlight of my experience as a faculty member. Each semester, students—who are mostly mental health or school counseling master's students or counseling psychology doctoral students—seem to genuinely enjoy exploring topics like the messages they received from their parents and peers about which careers are worth pursuing, how access (or lack of access) to resources expanded or narrowed their perception of which careers were attainable, or which careers would fit them best based on their personality, interests, abilities, or values. I enjoy witnessing the students arriving at these insights—which I hope will remain helpful to them long after the semester has ended.

Over time, however, I have developed this nagging feeling that my class is not addressing the root cause of most people's work-related concerns. It is no secret that most theories of career development covered in my class (and all classes like it) emphasize what we call "individual-level" interventions—actions that individuals can take to change their specific attitudes or behavior. This likely reflects the fact that the discipline of career development was developed by socially privileged theorists drawing inferences from socially privileged research samples—and intended to be used (at least implicitly) to improve the work lives of other socially privileged people. If the foundation of an academic discipline takes for granted the resources and power that comes with white, middle-to-upper class, male, and heterosexual privilege, it should come as no surprise that the discipline emphasizes individuals' ability to make autonomous choices that are not limited by their circumstances. A more parsimonious explanation for why the career development literature focuses on individual-level interventions is that the alternative—trying to change the societies in which people work—is significantly more complex and daunting.

DOI:10.4324/9781003272397-46

To be clear, I think trying to identify ways that people can improve their work lives through their personal agency is a worthwhile goal. Nevertheless, I don't think it can continue to be the exclusive goal of career development professionals—or anyone else invested in the world of work. Students in my class are increasingly voicing frustration with the world of work in which they find themselves—a national context in which 21 states have a minimum wage at or below the federal minimum wage of $7.25 per hour (National Conference of State Legislatures, 2021); only six states and D.C. have laws that guarantee workers paid family leave (ShelterPoint, 2021); more than half of Americans depend on their employers for their health insurance (Keisler-Starkey & Bunch, 2022); and 27% of people in the United States in 2020 earned some of their income through the gig economy (Board of Governors of the Federal Reserve System, 2021), which is characterized by fewer benefits and stability than other sectors of the workforce. The tenuousness of employment was brought into sharp relief by the COVID-19 pandemic: in the first year alone, approximately 9.6 million people in the United States lost their jobs (Pew Research Center, 2021). Furthermore, socially marginalized groups like Latina women, immigrants, and people with less education were disproportionately likely to lose their jobs during this time (Pew Research Center, 2020). Framed by these policies, laws, and socioeconomic trends, I don't blame my students for feeling daunted about facilitating change in the work lives of their future clients—or, for that matter, in their own lives.

But what can be done about these issues? I assuage some of my anxiety regarding my students' training by reminding myself that they also complete a course on organizational consultation. Based on the assumption that aspects of an organization (e.g., community agency, school, or workplace) may be dysfunctional and thus negatively impact the individuals that operate within the organization, students learn how to implement interventions that focus on changing the organization. The ability of consultation to help address some career issues should be clear. Consultants may draw from research to demonstrate to employers that workplace policies pertaining to issues like the provision of paid sick leave or family leave or increasing employees' wages are directly connected to employees' well-being and indirectly connected to the organization's bottom line. Similarly, employers who are invested in enhancing diversity, equity, and inclusion within the workplace may be encouraged to reframe the provision of decent wages from being a human resource issue to a way of communicating to the public the organization's commitment to social justice.

Organizational consultation—whether conducted by mental health professionals or any other professional invested in career issues—certainly has the potential to improve the working lives of many people. Encouraging or requiring career development professionals to complete coursework or continuing education training in organizational consultation may promote more systemic change. Nonetheless, organizations often have to seek out consultants, which requires them (1) to already know or suspect the existence of organizational problems; (2) to be open to making a change to organizational policies or practices; and (3) to know where to seek out consultants with relevant training. Moreover, though organizational change efforts have the potential to affect many more people than individual-level interventions like career counseling or coaching, they nevertheless affect one organization at a time. Thus, workplace issues that are endemic to a society continue to be addressed in a piecemeal fashion.

What else can people invested in improving workers' well-being do? One option is to better educate the public about labor policies or laws that shape their work lives. In recent years, because of the influence of progressive political candidates, the public appears more familiar and invested in federal legislation on topics like the minimum wage. However, the average citizen may be less familiar with state or city legislation on the same topic, trends in workplace policies in the private sector, or research documenting the associations of labor policies or laws with workers' psychological, physical, or economic well-being. Education can certainly take place in classes like mine, but it can also occur through presentations delivered at primary or secondary schools, places of worship, nonprofit organizations, or community centers. Larger audiences may be reached by penning op-eds for local or national publications that argue for the importance of policies or laws that would improve the workplace experiences and functioning of employees. Through such strategies, we may begin the arduous (but worthwhile) work of changing public opinion and, eventually, voting behavior.

Another strategy to consider is direct engagement with legislators. Experts on labor policies or laws may leverage their knowledge by delivering brief speeches at local townhall meetings. By working with or through professional organizations (e.g., the American Psychological Association and the National Career Development Association), they may craft an organization's stance on important labor policies or laws—perspectives that may be considered by lawmakers when drafting or voting on relevant legislation. Professional organizations may also issue amicus briefs that convey their stance to state or federal courts that must make decisions with implications for labor law.

As an educator, I still struggle with determining how to adequately cover individual career counseling, organizational consultation, and public outreach or social justice advocacy in one semester. Exhaustively covering any of these topics may be beyond the scope of just one course—or, for that matter, one type of graduate program or field of study. However, it is my hope that discussions of work increasingly frame work issues as not merely personal matters requiring individual behavioral change but also organizational or societal concerns that may necessitate more comprehensive reform.

References

Board of Governors of the Federal Reserve System. (2021). *Economic well-being of U.S. households in 2020*. www.federalreserve.gov/publications/files/2020-report-economic-well-being-us-households-202105.pdf.

Keisler-Starkey, K., & Bunch, L. N. (2022). *U.S. Census Bureau, current population reports, P60-278, health insurance coverage in the United States: 2021*. https://www.census.gov/content/dam/Census/library/publications/2022/demo/p60-278.pdf.

National Conference of State Legislatures. (2021). *Increasing the minimum wage*. www.ncsl.org/research/labor-and-employment/increasing-the-minimum-wage.aspx.

Pew Research Center. (2020). *Hispanic women, immigrants, young adults, those with less education hit hardest by COVID-19 job losses*. www.pewresearch.org/fact-tank/2020/06/09/hispanic-women-immigrants-young-adults-those-with-less-education-hit-hardest-by-covid-19-job-losses/.

Pew Research Center. (2021). *Fewer jobs have been lost in the EU than in the U.S. during the COVID-19 downturn*. www.pewresearch.org/fact-tank/2021/04/15/fewer-jobs-have-been-lost-in-the-eu-than-in-the-u-s-during-the-covid-19-downturn/.

ShelterPoint. (2021). *Paid family leave across the nation*. https://info.shelterpoint.com/blog/paid-family-leave-national-landscape-2021.

U.S. Census Bureau. (2020). *Health insurance coverage in the United States: 2019*. https://www.census.gov/library/publications/2020/demo/p60-271.html.

40 A Degree Isn't What It Used to Be

Supporting College Students and Non-Completers Amid the Student Debt Crisis

Gloria G. McGillen

Completing a college degree continues to hold tremendous power in the U.S. cultural imagination. Crowds of new graduates flinging their mortar boards into the air are a well-recognized symbol of accomplishment and the expected transition to a life of security relative to those who have not obtained a college degree. But over the last decade, new scenes have started to emerge from college graduations. Mortar boards doubling as billboards, bearing messages like, "Who's hiring?," and "$70K," illustrate the anxieties of millions of millennial and Gen Z college graduates caught amid the student debt crisis.

These moments are the outcome of several decades of neoliberal policymaking that have reshaped U.S. higher education. Today, about 70% of college students hold student debt (Despard et al., 2016), reflecting a shift to a primarily debt-financed higher education system. The racist and classist underpinnings of this trend have resulted in a crisis within a crisis for underrepresented college students and non-completers of color (i.e., those who do not obtain a college degree), and those from class-marginalized backgrounds, many of whom are also first-generation college students.

The complex picture of these students' academic and career trajectories reflects trade-offs extending over many years. It also illustrates U.S. activists', policymakers', and higher education professionals' attempts to strengthen the reality of the ideal of college as a pathway to opportunity and social equity in recent decades, by introducing supportive campus services and charting new policy visions. A number of these efforts are highlighted, and suggestions for their extension are introduced.

Economic and Policy Foundations

The 1980s were pivotal in establishing the policies that have led to the student debt crisis and the dilemmas it entails for debt-burdened college graduates and non-completers. U.S. higher education received substantial public funding after World War II, with an intention to build national

DOI:10.4324/9781003272397-47

economic power (Newfield, 2016). Neoliberal economic policy, defined by an emphasis on privatization, initiated a shift away from this model to an expectation that individual students and families would finance most college costs. This trend created a lucrative lending environment for financial institutions offering private and government-backed student loans. By 2020, average public, in-state college tuition reached $11,260 and private tuition $41,426 (Boyington et al., 2021), while average student debt climbed to $37,693 (Hanson, 2021).

Despite these stark figures, college enrollment rates have increased most years in recent decades (BLS, 2021). Widespread optimism about the "college premium," the average income advantage expected from a college degree, helps maintain this trend. While the premium continues, it has been found to reflect declining real wages among high school-educated workers rather than regular income benefits to college graduates (Morgan & Steinbaum, 2018). College costs and student debt have increased simultaneously, leading to widespread financial strain for college-educated workers (Britt et al., 2017; Elliott & Lewis, 2015).

Subsets of indebted graduates and non-completers face pronounced hardships (Despard et al., 2016). These include exceptionally high student loan burdens of roughly $61,000 or more in the upper 20% of borrowers (Looney & Yannelis, 2018), as well as class and racial discrimination impacting many within this group (Morgan & Steinbaum, 2018). Student experiences within many for-profit universities are emblematic of these concerns (Cottom & Angulo, 2017). Across for-profit institutions, and more broadly, underrepresented students of color, those from class-marginalized backgrounds, and first-generation college students are the likeliest to accrue high levels of student debt (Furquim et al., 2017), disenroll without completing a degree (Holzer & Baum, 2017), and experience a range of challenging post-college outcomes, including default on a student loan, individual bankruptcy, and general financial hardship (e.g., food insecurity, eviction; Despard et al., 2016).

College and Post-Enrollment Impacts

The myriad effects of student debt follow individuals throughout their studies and into post-college life (Despard et al., 2016; Looney & Yannelis, 2018). Several trends in the college and post-graduate experiences of individuals with student debt stand out for their implications for long-term career development and financial well-being.

During college, holding student debt shapes academic performance. It is associated with higher stress and reduced well-being (Britt et al., 2017). This contributes to lower academic achievement, with evidence suggesting that holding student debt leads to reduced cognitive functioning under stress (Destin & Svoboda, 2018). Given these conditions, and higher perceived constraints among indebted students on their ability to afford their educations, these students are likelier to disenroll (Britt et al., 2017).

Anticipation of entering student loan repayment also influences the selection of a college major. Indebted students are less likely to select majors tied to careers that offer medium incomes, such as K-12 education and nonprofits, and to pursue their first-choice occupation (de Gayardon et al., 2018). These trade-offs suggest financial pragmatism; however, longer term, individuals with student debt report lower job satisfaction (de Gayardon et al., 2018), which is associated with a range of negative career outcomes. Early pragmatism may therefore not yield career stability or financial rewards when individuals feel compelled to work in occupations they do not enjoy.

Overall, indebted students frequently enter the post-college job market in less competitive positions due to factors ranging from early disenrollment, to reduced academic performance, to selection of career paths that lead to lower job satisfaction. These conditions create barriers to successful career development that they must navigate alongside student loan repayment. A substantial minority, more than 20% (Looney & Yannelis, 2018), also experience profound financial hardships associated with their debt, including insolvency. These deepened burdens predominantly fall along well-established racial and class lines (Cottom & Angulo, 2017).

Adaptations and Advocacy: Suggested Directions

Student debt is a part of the generational experience for a majority of millennials and members of Gen Z. It has a substantial influence on their educations, financial lives, and careers. Although outcomes are diverse, deflated "college premiums," financial stress, and navigation of complex, long-term financial and career trade-offs are now the norm. This reality diverges from the national ideal of higher education as a broadly shared pathway to opportunity and social equity, with its costs realized most heavily among underrepresented students of color and class-marginalized students.

At the institutional level, higher education professionals have responded to these conditions by enriching campuses' academic advising, career counseling, and financial literacy services. Universities today also offer a broad array of pre-professional programs in fields such as healthcare, business, engineering, and technology that often yield stable incomes without additional education (Holzer & Baum, 2017).

Nationally, consumer advocates have established income-driven repayment programs, which allow borrowers to adjust their repayments to their incomes and discharge remaining student debt after 20–25 years (Looney & Yannelis, 2018). These programs have received criticism from some activists and consumer advocates for not addressing the roots of the student debt crisis that lie in neoliberal funding models. In response, national political figures, including U.S. Senators Elizabeth Warren and Bernie Sanders, and President Joe Biden, have put forward proposals to eliminate public higher education tuition, with some focusing on four-year universities and others on community colleges (Murakami, 2020).

In both its broad impact on the U.S. economy and its effects on individual academic, career, and financial life, the student debt crisis presents complex dilemmas. Impacted students and families, and professionals, advocates, and policymakers serving them, may benefit from the following guidance:

1. **Keep in mind the history of debt-financed higher education and structural constraints facing borrowers.** The history of debt-financed higher education is relatively brief. Models of public financing existed before the neoliberal shift of the 1980s (Newfield, 2016) and appear to be gaining renewed traction that may lead to a free public higher education system. This context is important. Debt is frequently treated as a moral issue. Within current markets, however, few families can afford higher education debt-free. Having a highly educated populace is a public good, essential for a strong economy. Neoliberal funding practices, unfortunately, displace the risk of this collective benefit onto individuals.

2. **Take action to learn about concepts of "good" and "bad" debt.** The consequences of holding student debt are complex. The "college premium" continues to hold, benefitting the average college graduate over a high school graduate; however, student loan investments vary widely in quality and risk, depending on the type of institution a student attends, and their college readiness, career goals, and exposure to discrimination. "Good debt" describes debt that leads to long-term benefits (Seamster & Charron-Chénier, 2017). While not all student debt is "good debt," academic and career counseling can provide insight into prudent choices and help minimize severe pitfalls.

3. **Consider higher education affordability as a racial and economic justice issue.** The risks and negative impacts of our debt-financed higher education system are not distributed equally and predominantly fall on underrepresented students of color, class-marginalized students, and their families. Public narratives that broadly promote higher education as a pathway to opportunity and equity place these students and families at risk of hardship without concurrent education on the types of academic investments that hold up as "good debt," as well as the reality of predatory practices within some areas of higher education financing and academic services (Seamster & Charron-Chénier, 2017)

Many student borrowers and their families can be spared degrees of anxiety and regret regarding their college financing decisions with additional information on systemic and historical forces that have given rise to the student debt crisis, and prudent guidance on avoiding the greatest risks of today's debt-financed higher education system. However, these resources are no replacement for continued advocacy to reform to the neoliberal policy architecture that undergirds the crisis. Obtaining a college education can be a career-enhancing and personally transformative experience that opens doors to opportunity and a good life regardless of background. While that ideal is in jeopardy today, its fuller realization is possible through continued momentum toward equitable reform.

References

Boyington, B., Kerr, E., & Wood, S. (2021, September 17). 20 years of tuition growth at national universities [Web article]. *U.S. News & World Report.* www.usnews.com/education/best-colleges/paying-for-college/articles/2017-09-20/see-20-years-of-tuition-growth-at-national-universities.

Britt, S. L., Ammerman, D. A., Barrett, S. F., & Jones, S. (2017). Student loans, financial stress, and college student retention. *Journal of Student Financial Aid, 47*(1), 25–37. https://eric.ed.gov/?id=EJ1141137.

Bureau of Labor Statistics. (2021, April 27). *College enrollment and work activity of recent high school and college graduates* [Press release]. www.bls.gov/news.release/pdf/hsgec.pdf.

Cottom, T. M., & Angulo, A. (2017). A radical education platform for the 21st century. *Harvard Journal of African American Public Policy, 31*–35. www.proquest.com/scholarly-journals/radical-education-platform-21st-century/docview/2187897045/se-2?accountid=146930.

de Gayardon, A., Callender, C., Deane, K., & DesJardins, S. L. (2018). *Graduate indebtedness: Its perceived effects on behaviour and life choices—A literature review* (CGHE Working Paper No. 38). Centre for Global Higher Education. https://discovery.ucl.ac.uk/id/eprint/10074778/.

Despard, M. R., Perantie, D., Taylor, S., Grinstein-Weiss, M., Friedline, T., & Raghavan, R. (2016). Student debt and hardship: Evidence from a large sample of low-and moderate-income households. *Children and Youth Services Review, 70,* 8–18. https://doi.org/10.1016/j.childyouth.2016.09.001.

Destin, M., & Svoboda, R. C. (2018). Costs on the mind: The influence of the financial burden of college on academic performance and cognitive functioning. *Research in Higher Education, 59*(3), 302–324. https://doi.org/10.1007/s11162-017-9469-8.

Elliott, W., & Lewis, M. (2015). Student debt effects on financial well-being: Research and policy implications. *Journal of Economic Surveys, 29*(4), 614–636. https://doi.org/10.1111/joes.12124.

Furquim, F., Glasener, K. M., Oster, M., McCall, B. P., & DesJardins, S.L. (2017). Navigating the financial aid process: Borrowing outcomes among first-generation and non-first-generation students. *Annals of the American Academy of Political and Social Science, 671*(1), 69–91. https://doi.org/10.1177/0002716217698119.

Hanson, M. (2021, July 10). Average student loan debt [Blog post]. *EducationData.org.* https://educationdata.org/average-student-loan-debt.

Holzer, H. J., & Baum, S. (2017). *Making college work: Pathways to success for disadvantaged students.* Brookings Institution Press.

Looney, A., & Yannelis, C. (2018). *Borrowers with large balances: Rising student debt and falling repayment rates.* The Brookings Institution. www.brookings.edu/wp-content/uploads/2018/02/es_20180216_looneylargebalances.pdf.

Morgan, J. M., & Steinbaum, M. (2018). *The student debt crisis, labor market credentialization, and racial inequality: How the current student debt debate gets the economics wrong.* Roosevelt Institute. https://rooseveltinstitute.org/wp-content/uploads/2020/07/RI-Student-Debt-Crisis-Labor-Market-Credentialization-201810.pdf.

Murakami, K. (2020, March 9). Big differences in Biden and Sanders's plans [Article]. *Inside Higher Ed*. www.insidehighered.com/news/2020/03/09/higher-ed-plans-biden-and-sanders-differ-scope-specificity.

Newfield, C. (2016). *The great mistake: How we wrecked public universities and how we can fix them*. Johns Hopkins University Press.

Seamster, L., & Charron-Chénier, R. (2017). Predatory inclusion and education debt: Rethinking the racial wealth gap. *Social Currents*, *4*(3), 199–207. https://doi.org/10.1177/2329496516686620.

Technology and Work

41 The Future of Work–Family Relations

Hopes for Beneficial Flexibility

Rachel Gali Cinamon

Introduction

Managing work and family roles simultaneously has been and continues to be a challenge due to the importance of these two spheres to individuals and societies and due to time and energy restrictions. The influx of women to the paid labor market has stimulated researchers to investigate and explore the boundaries between these roles, known as the work–family interface. Investigating boundaries is extremely important since boundaries between social roles help us to define who we are, what we do, and with whom we interact. Women's participation in paid work outside of the home sphere disrupts the traditional gender division of labor and stimulates rethinking of and critical thinking about the roles of work and family and the boundaries between them. I argue that the recent technologies that enable remote working and remote learning call for another wave of discourse and research about the social and psychological boundaries as they are reflected in the work and family interface.

The early periods of research on the work–family interface focused on conflictual relations between work and family. Work–family conflict was defined as a form of inter-role conflict in which the role pressures from the work and family domains are mutually incompatible in some respects (Greenhaus & Beutell, 1985). Three types of conflicts were identified: time, strain, and behavior. The majority of studies focused on time conflict between the domains, meaning that the time allocated to one role reduced or limited the available time that could be invested in the other role. Conflict relations were seen as bidirectional—work can interfere with investing time in family duties and plans, and family can interfere with finishing work duties and goals.

The accumulative studies indicate the adverse results of conflicts between work and family on a variety of outcomes in the work domain (e.g., job performance and job satisfaction), in the family domain (e.g., family satisfaction and parental behavior), and on physical and psychological health (e.g., blood pressure, well-being, and life satisfaction) (for a review, see Whiston & Cinamon, 2015). These results reinforce calls to promote family-friendly

DOI:10.4324/9781003272397-49

policies in organizations and consideration of this subject in career counseling and career education (Cinamon, et al., 2022).

At the same time, the boundaries between the roles can be permeable to positive emotions, knowledge, and skills in one role (work or family) that facilitate accomplishments in the other role (work or family). This type of interface between the roles is known as work–family facilitation or enrichment. Cumulative studies in this area indicate the positive outcomes of enrichment relations on various aspects of the work/family domains and on psychological health outcomes. It should be noted that enrichment relations are receiving less empirical attention than conflict relations.

New technologies now enable remote work and remote learning. These technologies have increased in popularity, use, and adaptation during the early 2020s due to the COVID-19 pandemic. A recent report from the National Bureau of Economic Research (https://www.nber.org/system/files/working_papers/w28731/w28731.pdf) suggests that about half of the workforce in the United States is now working from home, which may result in permanent shifts that last beyond the pandemic. At the same time, distance education and learning (from elementary schools through higher education) were quickly implemented in many countries around the globe during the pandemic to get educational institutions back on track. These technology implementations in work and in education need further investigation, but I propose that they hold a great potential impact on the boundaries and interface between work and family.

The immediate assumption that has been explored is that a boundaryless interface will reduce work–family conflict. A recent study among Canadian workers who worked at home found work–family conflict decreased among workers with no children or workers with children older than 12 years (Schieman et al., 2021). At the same time, working at home may increase work demands like the need to prepare meals three times a day for the family, assist children in connecting with their online distance learning, and spend more time with family. As a result, employees may experience greater family–work conflict. It is clear that further studies are needed (Galanti et al., 2021).

The ability or the need to work and learn from home, the status of borderless interface, creates a new form of conflict relations—space conflict. While a regular apartment includes family spaces like a kitchen, bedrooms, and sleeping rooms, the need to work from home requires unique or shared working spaces. Since big apartments (especially in large Western cities with high populations) are expensive and also rare, this need for working space is in conflict with other family needs. In large families with children in education systems that are participating in distance learning and distance education, this subject of space conflict can become extremely challenging, since they also need learning space. Family members will need to navigate space resource demands and learn to share. This new type of conflict also challenges architects and home designers to rethink how to design a space that captures the new work–family dynamic. At the same time, employers may need to think about paying employees for the use of their home space for work-related activities. Sending prepared meals for the family, offering laundry services, and even coupons for all family members to use community working spaces can be other ways employers can support their workers and their families. Furthermore, legislation regarding the need for building community working and learning buildings or spaces becomes extremely important in times of working and learning from home.

Another new aspect of the work–family boundaryless interface is related to time. When work and family are in different physical locations, time plays a major role as an expensive resource, some of which is spent in traffic. Additionally, investing time getting from one role to another role allows individuals to reflect upon and process the work experiences before returning home and vice versa. When both roles are occurring in the same space, less time is being lost on commuting, but the ability to process experiences while driving is reduced. Furthermore, the ability to decide what to share and when may also be compromised, because other family members are exposed to vicarious work and learning experiences. This situation of vicarious work and educational experiences by family members emphasizes the need to create new boundaries of privacy to structure if, what, and when family members can discuss what happens during their day. Working and learning with headphones (supplied by employers and by the education system) can help as well, along with an agreed schedule of privacy time and space for each family member. Training in short self-care activities like mindfulness and stretching between family tasks and work tasks can enable pause and reflection.

To enjoy and maximize the positive potential of a boundaryless work–family interface, the resources of social support and embedding personal meaning to social roles that reduce conflict and increase the facilitation of relationships should be considered in career counseling and career education. The ability to rethink and discuss gender and age divisions of labor at home becomes extremely important, including the ability to ask for and give help. Furthermore, the ability to reflect upon the personal hierarchy of importance of work and family roles and on personal meanings of work roles and family roles should be discussed to create internal boundaries of individual identities. For example, if someone perceived the worker role as the most important role in their life at this stage, what does it mean to them to be a good worker? Does it mean to be available 24/7 for job demands? To always be an excellent worker? To always prioritize work? Discussing questions like these with an emphasis on diverse examples of good worker/family relationships may enable people to find more flexible and authentic ways to blend life roles effectively.

Gender, culture, and SES have profoundly shaped the work–family interface. These variables may continue to impact this process of navigating a boundaryless work–family interface. Workers from low SES backgrounds who do not have sufficient access to adequate education and training may find it difficult and even impossible to work from home. People who live in very small apartments or do not have access to effective Wi-Fi may find it extremely challenging to work from home. Legislation is needed to encourage companies to find solutions for these people, such as creating some working space for employees who cannot work from home; in addition, municipal investments in public buildings with mutual working areas with computers and high-speed Internet are needed. Members of more traditional cultures may find it challenging to reexamine gendered divisions of labor. Since research has demonstrated gender inequalities during the pandemic (e.g., Qian & Fuller, 2020), career education in schools and universities and career interventions in organizations and communities that address the challenge of work–family interface are an extremely important priority in rethinking work (Cinamon, 2015). We can assume that continued advocacy for equality in work and in family will be needed.

References

Cinamon, R. G. (2015). The Synergy Project: A group career counseling intervention to enhance work-family management. In P. J. Hartung, M. L. Savickas, & W. B. Walsh (Eds.), *APA handbook of career intervention, Volume 2: Applications* (pp. 413–425). American Psychological Association. https://doi.org/10.1037/14439-030.

Cinamon, R. G., Ran, G., Vahaba, C., Yeshaya, M., Segev, E., & Librovsky, I. (2022). The transition from school to work among Female STEM students. Paper presented at the American Psychology Association Conference, Miniapolise.

Galanti, T., Guidetti, G., Mazzei, E., Zappalà, S., & Toscano, F. (2021). Work from home during the COVID-19 outbreak: The impact on employees' remote work productivity, engagement, and stress. *Journal of Occupational and Environmental Medicine, 63*(7), e426–e432.

Greenhaus, J. H., & Beutell, N. J. (1985). Sources and conflict between work and family roles. *The Academy of Management Review, 10*(1), 76–88. https://doi.org/10.2307/258214.

Qian, Y., & Fuller, S. (2020). COVID-19 and the gender employment gap among parents of young children. *Canadian Public Policy, 46*(S2), S89–S101.

Schieman, S., Badawy, P. J., Milkie, M. A., & Bierman, A. (2021). Work-life conflict during the COVID-19 pandemic. *Socius: Sociological Research for a Dynamic World, 7*, 1–19. https://journals.sagepub.com/doi/pdf/10.1177/2378023120982856.

Whiston, S. C., & Cinamon, R. G. (2015). The work-family interface: Integrating research and career counseling practice. *The Career Development Quarterly, 63*(1), 44–56.

42 Workplace Surveillance Shapes Worker Experiences

Jerod C. White and Tara S. Behrend

Most workers from across a wide range of fields experience technological monitoring by their employers in the course of doing their jobs. The ubiquity of monitoring technologies may lead one to presume that employers get some benefit from doing so. Yet, many workers feel intense discontent and injustice regarding the practice. It is not clear that either of these perspectives is correct. We argue that the effects of technological monitoring are complex; monitoring can have positive or negative effects, depending on how the tools are implemented. The technological tools used for monitoring are, in a vacuum, neutral; we must look beyond the tools themselves and consider their *uses* to understand their effects.

We thus argue for the value of a psychological, as opposed to solely technological, lens to understand monitoring tools and their potential harms and benefits. We view technology as a stimulus whose psychological effects can be organized according to several dimensions. For example, we can describe a given monitoring tool not by its hardware but by its purpose (e.g., used to punish versus develop workers) and its transparency (e.g., clearly communicated to workers versus ambiguously implemented). To demonstrate, consider the following three examples:

First, one delivery company has recently adopted artificially intelligent (AI) cameras to encourage safe behind-the-wheel behavior for van drivers (Gurley, 2021). The AI cameras were designed to record drivers when a dangerous event (e.g., distracted driving) is detected. During these events, verbal feedback is given to drivers, and footage is sent to the company. Drivers then receive safety scores, which are used to determine bonuses and prizes. From a technological perspective, the AI cameras themselves tell us little about whether they help or hinder drivers. To understand such effects, we must adopt a psychological perspective.

The psychological effects that AI cameras have on drivers are complex. For example, cameras allow for timely feedback that can help drivers quickly adjust their behavior to become safer drivers. However, the same feedback has been described by some drivers as distracting because it is *too* frequent. Further, the monitoring practice lacks transparency in that the company communicated to employees that it would benefit their well-being (a safety

DOI:10.4324/9781003272397-50

purpose), yet they used the monitoring data to compare employees for reward allocations (an evaluation purpose). Ideally, monitoring data about driver safety would directly relate to monitoring data about driver performance, but this has not been the case. Many skilled drivers have noted that their performance reviews worsened after cameras were adopted, arguing that cameras wrongfully flagged safe driving events as unsafe (e.g., bringing the van to an abrupt halt when other cars suddenly enter their lane). The transparency of the monitoring systems is even lower when noting that drivers have had few opportunities to review the camera's evaluations with managers. As a result, many delivery drivers have expressed dissatisfaction with the monitoring practice despite its high synchronicity and its intended safety purpose.

Second, other companies have begun using AI–enabled audio tools to provide customer service representatives with feedback to develop their interpersonal skills (IBM, 2020). These companies have been using AI models trained on thousands of emotional speech data samples to extract meaning from real-time conversations. For each representative's interaction with a customer, the AI model measures tone of voice to not only detect customer satisfaction but also coach representatives on ways to improve the interaction. For example, the tool may detect that a customer is feeling frustrated, thus prompting the representative to slow their speech and speak in a reassuring tone.

Emotion AI (i.e., AI that detects and interprets human emotions) has had varied effects on representatives. Many representatives have reported that the tool helped them develop their interpersonal skills. Through repeated feedback, some representatives identified their own weaknesses and addressed them in subsequent customer interactions. Still, many representatives also reported that such tools are too invasive because they collect data on some emotions that they would otherwise prefer to conceal and restrict their autonomy to freely interact with customers. Given the tool's early promise in developing interpersonal skills, a growing number of organizations are adopting emotion AI. Still, researchers have much to understand about the tool and its appropriate uses before organizations can confidently use it for employee development.

As a third example, many police officers are now required to wear body cameras that continually record their behavior and surroundings to promote effective job performance (Ovide, 2020). Because the cameras can record the most unexpected police–civilian interactions, they presumably encourage police officers to remain alert and perform optimally while on the job. A central component of police officer performance is to protect citizens, so the cameras also serve the purpose of promoting civilian safety. As a result, many police departments, especially those with histories of police brutality, implement body cameras as a means of promoting optimal police officer performance and safety.

In practice, body cameras have mixed effects on police officers. Contrary to their intended purpose, body cameras often have no (or even negative) effects on officers' safety and performance. One explanation is that cameras may not actually deter officers from engaging in dangerous behaviors. Rather, some officers (e.g., those who fear being punished for behaving unsafely) have learned to modify their camera recordings (e.g., covering up the microphone). Another explanation is that officers occasionally report feeling burnt out after having their behavior recorded for prolonged periods of time, thus making them less diligent on the job. Still, the use of body cameras is not inherently negative. Other officers have reported more favorable views of the cameras, noting that their department encourages them to get together with each other to review one another's footage. Some officers have found this to be a worthwhile developmental exercise, ultimately preparing them for dangerous situations. As is the case with any monitoring tool, it is the implementation, not the tool itself, that determines when body cameras will have desired effects on officers.

With these examples and many others in mind, we recently conducted a meta-analysis based on a formal framework of psychological elements to understand the effects of technological monitoring (Ravid et al., 2022). We first found that the mere presence or absence of technological monitoring is a poor predictor of worker attitudes and perceptions, with the exception that workers generally feel stressed when monitored. For most outcomes (e.g., performance and job attitudes), the effects depend on specific characteristics of monitoring. Most notably, we found that organizations that monitor less invasively and more transparently can expect more positive attitudes from workers. We also found that monitoring without an explicit purpose was not associated with any increases in performance. These results suggest that while it is tempting to monitor based on new technological capabilities, organizations should instead focus on the psychological effects of monitoring tools.

An important question remains regarding whether our findings will hold over time, particularly in light of the recent COVID-19 pandemic. The pandemic has led to a drastic change in the kinds of monitoring practices that organizations adopt, with a new interest in physiological monitoring (e.g., temperature checks and viral and antibody tests). As a result of these changes, we explored whether the increased exposure to such forms of monitoring (and others) during the pandemic has shaped employee perceptions of the acceptability of these work practices. Using data we collected prior to and during the pandemic, we found that workers have become more accepting of physiological monitoring practices. This finding suggests that attitudes toward technological monitoring are malleable and sensitive to societal contexts. In this case, physiological monitoring affects employees in a more direct and positive manner than it has in the past. Still, many questions remain regarding the temporal characteristics of monitoring reactions, especially concerning whether they will hold once the pandemic has run its course.

Our hope is to encourage policy and scientific dialogue as well as future scientific collaboration between social scientists and technologists. Modern monitoring practices involve algorithms and AI that can help organizations make personnel decisions, yet researchers, policymakers, and the general public are increasingly wary that these tools are unfair or biased. Such concerns are well-warranted, given that monitoring poses threats to policies aimed at preventing and remedying unlawful discrimination in organizations (e.g., the U.S. Equal Employment Opportunity Commission and the American AI Initiative). Despite widespread concerns, scholars across academic disciplines struggle to collaboratively address issues of fairness and bias due to fundamental mismatches in terminology, values, and goals. We argue that effective collaboration of social scientists and technologists first requires each group to learn about the other's ways of thinking about and studying AI models (see Landers & Behrend, 2021) followed by interdisciplinary communication, research, and dissemination (see White et al., 2022 for opportunities). Social scientists should not wait for technologists to create monitoring tools, nor should technologists create tools without considering their social and psychological implications. Technological monitoring is a complex and multifaceted process; scholars must cross disciplinary boundaries to account for this complexity and conduct meaningful, policy-relevant research.

We also urge scientists and employers to think critically about the ethics of monitoring. Many workers globally lack legal protections regarding the information their employers can digitally collect about them. The constantly evolving nature of monitoring further complicates ethical considerations, as the capabilities of monitoring have increased dramatically in invasiveness. We argue that the ethicality of monitoring depends in part on whether the benefits outweigh the costs. The benefits of an invasive form of health monitoring, for example, may outweigh the risks in some contexts (e.g., virologists in a lab), but not others (e.g., remote workers at home). Importantly, employers must be transparent and honest about their monitoring practices in order for workers to determine whether the benefits outweigh the costs in their own jobs.

Another key ethical consideration is whether monitoring practices promote fairness and equity at work. Many monitoring practices, particularly those that are implemented to support organizational goals at the expense of worker goals, pose serious threats to fairness and equity. Inequities are likely when employers monitor workers differentially; technological monitoring increases inequalities when employers monitor workers in precarious jobs more invasively than those in higher-status jobs. Our research suggests that workers of lower status experience more unacceptable forms of monitoring than those of higher status. Creating a more positive experience for these workers requires employers to design monitoring practices with the well-being of workers in mind and implement the practices fairly across workers.

Technological advancements and broad societal changes spurred by the COVID-19 pandemic have created a work environment where organizations can monitor employees in many ways and with great intensity. We argue, however, that although organizations *can* adopt new monitoring practices, it does not mean they should. Technological monitoring does *not* automatically result in worker performance improvements. Rather, it is a complex process (with effects depending on the psychological characteristics of the practice) and dynamic (with effects varying over time and societal contexts). To account for these complexities, we urge employers, social scientists, and technologists to think critically about monitoring. Though surveillance is not inherently positive, it is also not inherently negative; worker well-being can be preserved when organizations build technological monitoring practices on sound psychological principles.

References

Gurley, L. K. (2021, September 20). Amazon's AI cameras are punishing drivers for mistakes they didn't make. *Vice*. www.vice.com/en/article/88npjv/amazons-ai-cameras-are-punishing-drivers-for-mistakes-they-didnt-make.

IBM. (2020, June 25). How AI is revamping the call center. *Forbes*. www.forbes.com/sites/insights-ibmai/2020/06/25/how-ai-is-revamping-the-call-center/?sh=15be39534b2b.

Landers, R. N., & Behrend, T. S. (2021). Auditing the AI auditors: A framework for evaluating fairness and bias in high stakes AI predictive models. *American Psychologist*. Advance online publication. http://dx.doi.org/10.1037/amp0000972.

Ovide, S. (2020, December 7). Can body cameras improve policing? *The New York Times*. www.nytimes.com/2020/12/07/technology/body-cameras-police.html.

Ravid, D. M., White, J. C., Tomczak, D. L., Miles, A. F., & Behrend, T. S. (2022). A meta-analysis of the effects of electronic performance monitoring on work outcomes. Advance online publication. *Personnel Psychology*.

White, J. C., Ravid, D. M., Siderits, I. O., & Behrend, T. S. (2022). An urgent call for I-O psychologists to produce timelier technology research. *Industrial and Organizational Psychology: Perspectives on Science and Practice*, *15*(3), 441–459. https://doi.org/10.31234/osf.io/785xf.

43 On Embracing Automation and Loving Work

Or Why We Should Not Be Afraid of Our Washing Machines

Tristram Hooley

Introduction

I never seem to have enough time. My life is full of work, both paid and unpaid. An amazing amount of my time is spent collecting clothes from my children and myself, putting them in the washing machine, then the dryer, folding them, taking them back upstairs, and putting them away. I'm sure that my partner would roll her eyes and say that it is she who does the lion's share of this task. Yet regardless of who (certainly not either of the teenagers in the house) does the washing, within days, the clothes have been worn and reappeared on the teenagers' floors. Surely, this kind of repetitive, low-skilled activity is ripe for automation?

The process of washing clothes by hand has long been recognized as one of the most backbreaking forms of toil, rubbing women's hands raw and leaving them with little time to do anything else. As far back as the 15th century, Jacob de Strada invented a contraption with "heavy wooden beaters, operated by a large hand wheel, which agitate the wash load in the trough" (Maxwell, 2003, p. 8). But it was not until the 1860s that washing machines became big business, and not until the 20th century that domestic washing machines appeared (Green, 2016).

By the 1950s, the automatic washing machine was starting to revolution-ize the lives of women in the United States and elsewhere in the Global North. The development of such "labour saving devices" in the 1950s and 1960s was viewed as emancipatory. Machines were offering us more time, autonomy, and control over our lives and technology seemed to promise that this process would continue. More machines would equal more free time and a better society. The truth was somewhat different, particularly because of the gendered nature of domestic work. While some domestic technologies did free up women's time, it often freed it up to be reallocated to other domestic tasks (Wajcman, 2010). Furthermore, it allowed women to move more fully into the labor market without requiring any redistribu-tion of domestic tasks from women to men and leaving women with what Hochschild and Machung (2012) call "the second shift" of domestic work after paid work is complete.

DOI:10.4324/9781003272397-51

In 1930, the economist John Maynard Keynes observed the trajectory of the automation of work and predicted that we would move to a 15-hour working week. People would have more time to choose what to do with their lives. Perhaps even more excitingly, Keynes (1930, p. 7) wrote these changes would make us better, more considerate human beings, leaving us with the problem of "how to live wisely and agreeably and well."

Yet, if we run the film forward into the 21st century, when Keynes and others might have expected that their predictions would have come to pass, we can see that, like me, people still feel that time is short and that they spend many of their days in various forms of drudgery. Despite the increase in digital technologies and automation, the Brookings Institution found that 44% of people in the U.S. still work long hours to earn low wages in precarious conditions with little opportunity to access training or career development (Escobari, 2019).

Some have argued that Keynes was a ridiculous utopian and that his predictions of a declining working week were absurd, but the data suggest that he observed a real phenomenon. In 1929, the year before Keynes wrote his essay, the average U.S. worker worked 2,316 hours (equivalent to a 46-hour working week, assuming 50 weeks of work per year) in paid employment; 50 years later, it was a 36-hour week with a particularly steep decline during the period in which the washing machine and other labor saving devices were being introduced (Giattino & Ortiz-Ospina, 2021). But, by 2017, the decline had slowed and the average worker was putting in a 35-hour week.

And yet, in recent years, we have regularly heard the panicky cry "the robots are coming, the robots are coming." In his much-discussed book, Martin Ford (2015) argues that we are experiencing the "rise of the robots" and a corresponding death of work. The response to this possibility has mostly been one of horror and fear. If we are replaced by robots, how will we be able to put food on the table? Where will we find meaning and purpose in our lives? And what will prevent the wealthy, robot-owning class from taking all of the goodies of life?

What is it that has transformed automation from a utopia into a dystopia? Why have workers yet to see many benefits from the rising robot age? Why are we all so busy, if our automation is so imminent? I can ask Alexia to help me to schedule yet another work meeting, but she still will not gather the clothes from my teenagers' floor and put them into the washing machine. If robots are taking over, we might legitimately ask them to get a move on, "I've got other things to do with my time," as I often say to my teenage children. But, many of the promises of automation are overblown, and as with the automation of washing, such leaps forward, typically make more, newer kinds of work, frequently distributing and compensating for this work unequally, and rarely lead to the disappearance of work altogether.

Indeed, my ongoing frustration about the clothes on my teenagers' floor forces me to reflect on what "work" actually is and ask whether it is really disappearing at all. Ford's argument is essentially an economist's one. In his mind work is what is paid for, with all other forms of activity occupying another category. So, writing this essay (which I rather enjoy doing) is *work*, because the universities that employ me recognize it as such and categorize it as a legitimate use of my (paid) time, while picking up clothes from teenagers' floors (which frustrates and annoys me) is *not work* because no one would pay me to do it.

So, when people like Martin Ford worry about automation making human beings redundant, they are not actually talking about an end to work at all. Rather, they are discussing the fact that our already flawed economic system is likely to become more flawed still if automation encroaches further on forms of work that traditionally attracted wages. If we automated washing teenagers' clothes, no one would lose out because that is work that is not currently paid for. But, if we automate car manufacture, the driving of trucks or worst of all (for me at least) the writing of academic essays, business owners would get to keep more of their profits (assuming that robots ultimately prove to be cheaper than human beings). In such a world, work and wages no longer serve as a mechanism to redistribute wealth, leading to increased consolidation of wealth by 1%, growing inequality, and ultimately social and political unrest.

Various policy solutions have been advanced in response to these systemic economic problems. Some of which, like the idea of *universal basic income*, seek to break the link between paid work and a decent standard of living. In a world in which people do not need wages to live, perhaps because robots are doing some of the work, the question is what will they do with their time. Will they as Keynes argues, devote their time to the betterment of others, will they spend more time with their families and contribute more to their communities, paint their masterpieces or learn to play the tuba? Alternatively, will they sit around watching game shows or endless scrolling through Tiktok?

Nobody knows. But, there is a strong philosophical tradition encompassing figures as diverse as Benjamin Franklin, Karl Marx, and Hannah Arendt which views humanity's engagement in work as fundamental. Human beings are, *homo faber*, man the maker and are compelled to transform the world around them. Such a desire to transform the world does not begin when we are paid to work; rather, it is innate to who we are. The anthropologist David Graeber (2019, p. 83) notes that

> children come to understand that they exist, that they are discrete entities, separate from the world around them, largely by coming to understand that "they" are the thing which just caused something to happen-the proof of which is the fact that they can make it happen again.

So, we do not work because we must or because people pay us; rather, we work because we are compelled to interact with other people and the world around us, we work, because we love it. At least we love it when it is typified by the opportunity to express ourselves, to collaborate with others, to transform our environment, and to do something that is needed and socially valuable and when we can rely on having enough food to eat, clothes to wear, and a roof over our head. Often work is not like this, it is oppressive, pointless, and exploitative, but even in such cases, our bosses still use our sense that work should be valuable and enjoyable to extract more value (Jaffe, 2021).

Therefore, the people who worry about robots taking our jobs have got it dangerously confused. They have pitted the robots against humanity when the reality is that humanity is using robots against itself. As the political economist Harry Braverman noted when studying the wave of automation that was transforming U.S. working life in the mid-20th century, "machinery comes into the world not as the servant of 'humanity', but as the instrument of those to whom the accumulation of capital gives the ownership of the machines" (Braverman, 1998, p. 133). So, we cannot blame robots, but we can ask questions about who owns those robots and what use they put them too. If an employer chooses to use automation to cut jobs, break unions, and reduce wages, we need to make sure that blame is directed where it belongs.

More fundamentally, we need to recognize that a society in which wages were no longer the sole guarantee of access to the good life would be a step forward. That without wages, work would not stop, but rather human beings would be likely to find new, more creative ways to work. If automation can take us in this direction, then it is nothing to be feared. Political economists Srnicek and Williams (2015) argue that this requires a political transformation through which we embrace automation and use it to reduce the length of the working week while ensuring that what work is available is equally distributed. We then provide people with a universal basic income and encourage people to reconceptualize work as something that is positive and creative and not solely linked to the payment of wages.

There is no doubt that automation has the power to reorder and remake work for all of us. Alarmist accounts of automation typically overemphasize the speed of this change, narrow the definition of work to what is possible within our current economic system, and misdirect blame away from those who benefit from the status quo toward assemblages of steel and plastic or lines of code.

But, despite such accounts of the future, we are not, and cannot be, in a war with the robots any more than we are in a war with the washing machines. New technologies pose new challenges for our societies, and our responses to these challenges can either exacerbate inequalities or address them. The alignment of work with what can be paid for has a distorting effect on our lives. It downgrades the status of much that is valuable, even though such work still needs to be done, and celebrates forms of work that attract high salaries, even where such work is destructive or pointless. Given this, embracing automation is part of a wider political project to free human beings to work on what matters.

In such a world, if I could not buy a robot butler, I could at least spend more time teaching my teenagers how to work the washing machine themselves, but that, perhaps, is just science fiction.

References

Braverman, H. (1998). *Labor and monopoly capital: The degradation of work in the twentieth century*. Monthly Review Press.

Escobari, E. (2019). *The economy is growing and leaving low-wage workers behind*. www.brookings.edu/blog/education-plus-development/2019/12/19/the-economy-is-growing-and-leaving-low-wage-workers-behind/.

Ford, M. (2015). *Rise of the robots: Technology and the threat of a jobless future*. Basic Books.

Giattino, C., & Ortiz-Ospina, E. (2021). *Are we working more than ever?* https://ourworldindata.org/working-more-than-ever.

Graeber, D. (2019). *Bullshit jobs*. Penguin.

Green, C. (2016). Agitated to clean: How the washing machine changed life for the American Woman. *McNair Scholars Research Journal*, *12*(1), 10. https://scholarworks.boisestate.edu/mcnair_journal/vol12/iss1/10.

Hochschild, A., & Machung, A. (2012). *The second shift: Working families and the revolution at home*. Penguin.

Jaffe, S. (2021). *Work won't love you back*. Hurst.

Keynes, J. M. (1930). *Economic possibilities for our grandchildren*. www.econ.yale.edu/smith/econ116a/keynes1.pdf.

Maxwell, L. M. (2003). *Save womens' lives. History of washing machines*. Oldewash.

Srnicek, N., & Williams, A. (2015). *Inventing the future: Postcapitalism and a world without work*. Verso.

Wajcman, J. (2010). Domestic technology: Labour-saving or enslaving? In C. Hanks (Ed.), *Technology and values: Essential readings* (pp. 272–288). Blackwell Publishing.

44 Preparing for a 60-Year Career

Stephanie Malia Krauss

Science has made it possible for people to live longer than ever. With the right resources and opportunities, young people could live to see 100, at least (Gratton & Scott, 2019). Soon enough, a 100-year life will be the expectation rather than the exception. The prospect of a longer life demands that we take a different approach to preparing young people for the future of work. Living longer means working longer. Today's young people—tomorrow's workers—could work for 60 years or more. This means working through adulthood and well into old age.

The conditions of a longer working life differ depending on the environments and experiences that shape someone's childhood and adult life. The link between living and learning will intensify. Adults will work while parenting, grandparenting, and even great-grandparenting; healthy, sick, or caretaking; loving or grieving; exploring and enduring; transitioning and transforming. There will be periods of not working, or working too much. A "lifetime" of work will include many jobs and multiple careers. There will be likely returns to school to upgrade knowledge and skills or to learn something totally new.

Making a long life a good life requires ample resources and opportunities—exceptional cases, excluded. This is because living and longevity depend on good health and fitness, supportive relationships, and economic and environmental stability (Levitin, 2020).

As lives lengthen, the purpose of education and preparation will need to shift from a focus on college and career readiness to a focus on long and livable lives. Instead of asking, "what do you want to be when you grow up?" we will need to ask, "what type of working life will enable you to thrive over the long-haul?"

Tomorrow's workforce will be different from today's. These are young people growing up in a time defined by crisis and catastrophe. Their working lives will be similar. For them, life comes with constant change, unprecedented challenge, and new opportunities.

DOI:10.4324/9781003272397-52

Who Is Tomorrow's Workforce?

Today's Kids Are Tomorrow's Workers, and They Are Digital Natives

Young people have grown up online and are able to go in and out of analog and virtual worlds. They are used to ever-changing technology. They are hyperconnected and know how to connect to and engage in the issues and causes they care about. This tech-savviness will serve them well in future work.

Tomorrow's Workers Are Disruption Natives

Young people are growing up during historic and unprecedented global events, with intense personal impacts. These young people have feared for their lives, afraid of violence at school, illness or death in a pandemic, and loss or displacement from extreme weather. They worry about complex issues because they are proximate to many societal and environmental problems. They will be the first generation of workers to be majority people of color and will bring firsthand experience of the harms of systemic racism and structural injustice (Krauss, 2021).

When asked what they want for their futures, the message from tomorrow's workers is clear. They want safety and stability. A good life for themselves and their families. A working life that doesn't require giving up people, culture, and community to get ahead. Jobs that are meaningful and pay the bills. They want assurance that things will be okay and predictable. These are young people who dream of personal accomplishments that don't overlap with global pandemics, recessions, war, or worse.

Tomorrow's workers find it hard to imagine a long life because they worry about what's happening right now. Pandemics, divided politics, deepening disparities, racial violence, extreme weather, and economic crises have defined their lives, and the stability they yearn for will be unlikely in the future. The impact of these events while they're working will range from disruptive to devastating. Whenever work is lost, so are wages, daily structure, meaningful relationships, a sense of purpose, and aspects of identity (Blustein, 2019).

Uncertainty will be a hallmark feature of the future of work. This means tomorrow's workers need to have creative ways to experience financial, social, and emotional security beyond their jobs. They will need to work during times of adversity. They will need benefits that aren't exclusive to a single employer, perhaps extending to include community, friends, and family (Shell, 2018). As for financial security, tomorrow's workers will continue to count on jobs for the cash they need. That is, unless we have a universal basic income. Moving forward, tomorrow's workers will need policies that expand and flex unemployment benefits or provide direct cash assistance during periods of not working or making less than they need to get by. In a long working life, young people will need to know where to go and what to do when they are in financial and employment trouble (Morduch & Schneider, 2017).

Tomorrow's Workers Will Be Powerful Changemakers

Living through turbulent times means global problems are personal ones. As today's young people enter the workforce, they will bring their passion, purpose, and pain with them. Because of their lived experience, they are best-suited to solve our most complex problems and create the solutions we need.

What Is Tomorrow's Working World?

Thriving across 60 or more years of work will have to do with the jobs available, and even more to do with a worker's journey overall.

It took the COVID-19 pandemic for us to acknowledge and accept how interdependent our work and well-being are. When life or health issues arise, it's hard to keep working or to do our work well. When things get too hard, work might stop or be lost entirely. When things are hard to begin with, it's difficult to find work in the first place (Carnevale et al., 2021).

Work demands a great deal of energy and time. In the United States, workers spend more time on the job than anywhere else (Shell, 2018). Workers who don't make enough from one job must take on side gigs and second jobs. This kind of work life in combination with life stressors is overwhelming and exhausting (Lipsky, 2018). It can create toxic, chronic stress. Working conditions, including being overworked and underpaid, are something we have to fix. Otherwise, tomorrow's workers might burnout before they make it even midway through their working lives.

Tomorrow's Working World Will Be Defined by Rapid Change

The workforce is always evolving, expanding, contracting, and changing. Although projections differ from year to year, most researchers and employers agree that young people will compete for never-before-seen jobs. Acceleration and innovation change the job market and economy as much as disruption. In a technologically advancing society, robots will take many jobs and create many more (Daugherty & Wilson, 2018).

Tomorrow's Working World Will Be Volatile

Transition and change will be the norm. Things will be hardest for those who are marginalized, including people of color, those who are poor, and those with disabilities. For young workers, it may be easiest to get gig jobs and contract work, but they are temporary, lack benefits, and are rarely the work people want or need.

Tomorrow's workers will have to take on daunting challenges related to climate, politics, justice, and society. These issues will impact their livelihoods and families, likely defining and deciding their working lives. As long as the job market depends on the global economy, it will continue to sway precariously with the weight of these challenges.

Tomorrow's Working World Has Plenty to Be Discovered

For all of the predictions we can make, there are many aspects of the future yet to be discovered. This is because tomorrow's workers will shape it. Our future workers are still growing up and being formed by their upbringings, experiences, and environments. They will go on to invent and innovate in ways that are informed by their own lived experience. They will harness the power of technology in ways we never could. This will be a workforce full of healers, helpers, builders, and creators. While this time in history seems bleak, we can draw hope from the power of tomorrow's workers, who will bring with them their unmatched strength, resilience, and ingenuity.

What Types of Jobs Must Tomorrow's Workers Prepare for?

We cannot stop living in challenging times. However, we can change how we think about work readiness and how we prepare young people for their working lives. When we shift the focus of workforce readiness from individual jobs to the working life, we allow ourselves to think more broadly and holistically about the types of work young people will benefit from and need across many decades.

The future of work will favor those who obtain work that is durable, transferable, lovable, and livable.

- *Durable Work.* Durable work includes jobs and careers that will be resilient to future shocks, including technology and large global events. Durable work can be in high-growth industries, as well as those that are high value. These tend to be in areas that require human skills and talents, such as education and counseling, entrepreneurship, the humanities, and healthcare. While these types of work may be durable, employers need to modernize policies and practices to ensure they are endurable, addressing the conditions that make many of these fields places with high turnover and employee burnout. This includes offering competitive pay and generous benefits, including sufficient paid time-off and incentives such as sabbaticals.
- *Transferable Work.* Transferable work can be at the level of job or skill. With the job market changing so much and quickly, workers will need

to be ready to shift into new jobs, roles, and responsibilities—with their employer, on their own, or with a new employer. With transition as the norm, young people must be able to move seamlessly into new jobs and roles. This requires better policies around credit for prior learning and licensure reciprocity to ensure that education and training transfer too. Longer working lives will include many transitions and young people will need to be ready to shift and shape what they know and can do into new and different opportunities.

- *Lovable Work.* Life is challenging and turbulent. Tomorrow's workers should have work that makes them happy and offers meaning and purpose; work and colleagues they enjoy. Long-life work readiness is about helping young people discover the problems they want to solve, the questions they want to ask, the inventions they want to create, and the ideas they want to interrogate. From there it's figuring out which career paths to pursue, and what supports will be needed along the way. Young people will have richer, more vibrant work lives if they enter adulthood with a sense of direction, purpose, and passion.

- *Livable Work.* Above all else, young people must be able to get jobs that offer a living wage and benefits. Too often, young people are steered toward jobs that don't pay enough to get by. Longer working lives should be livable. This means having work that pays well, and jobs where workers earn more over time. Policies should be in place that require all employers to pay workers a living wage with employer benefits and protections. It should also be easy for workers to find benefits and protect themselves when working independently or for the gig economy. Young people should know how to find work that offers them the wages and well-being they need and deserve.

Ideally, tomorrow's workers will find work opportunities that are durable, transferable, lovable, and livable. When that's not possible, opportunities should be at least one or two of the four. We can educate and equip tomorrow's workers in ways that give them the greatest chance of securing these types of work opportunities, immediately and over the long-haul.

Making Preparations

Today's young people will live and work longer than all of us. For these digital and disruption natives, their working lives will look a lot like their younger years: constantly changing, volatile, and open for discovery. In adulthood, they will face uncertainty and loss, and also opportunities to challenge and solve persistent and perilous problems. Without incredible policy and societal change, they will work in a world that continues to be unjust and unfair, limiting opportunities for workers of color, as well as for those who are disabled, systems-involved, and poor.

With the prospect of a working life spanning six to seven decades, young people will need the practical and personal resources to keep going. To thrive, they will need us to do everything possible to help them be ready and able for whatever is ahead.

References

Blustein, D. (2019). *The importance of work in an age of uncertainty*. Oxford University Press.

Carnevale, A. P., Gulish, A., & Campbell, K. P. (2021). *Youth policy: How can we smooth the rocky pathway to adulthood?* (p. 38). Georgetown University Center on Education and the Workforce.

Daugherty, P. R., & Wilson, H. J. (2018). *Human + machine: Reimagining work in the age of AI*. Harvard Business Review Press.

Gratton, L., & Scott, A. (2019). *The 100-year-life: Living and working in an age of longevity* (4th ed.). Bloomsbury.

Krauss, S. M. (2021). *Making it: What today's kids need for tomorrow's world*. Jossey-Bass/ Wiley.

Levitin, D. J. (2020). *Successful aging: A neuroscientist explore the power and potential of our lives*. Dutton.

Lipsky, L. V. D. (2018). *The age of overwhelm: Strategies for the Long Haul*. Berrett-Koehler Publishers, Inc.

Morduch, J., & Schneider, R. (2017). *The financial diaries: How American families cope in a world of uncertainty*. Princeton Press.

Shell, E. R. (2018). *The job: Work and its future in a time of radical change*. Currency Books.

Conclusion

45 Concluding Thoughts and Future Directions for Building a Better Workplace

Lisa Y. Flores and David L. Blustein

The confluence of events at this particular period of time—the ongoing COVID-19 global pandemic, racial oppression in the United States, declining economic growth, and wars—have all impacted the labor market and workers across every industry and international context. These events have magnified the disparities in the world of work and highlighted the precarious nature of work that many experience (Blustein et al., 2022). The opportunity for meaningful transformations in the workplace and labor markets in response to these events is now, to prevent further entrenchment in social divides and to ameliorate existing inequities. We embarked on this book with a focus on workers and with the hope that solutions to the challenges that workers are encountering in the workforce can be found among workers, organizational leaders, and those who research work.

The authors of these essays were invited to think big and to be creative in presenting new ideas for long-standing problems in the institution of work. We believe that the authors met this call, and we hope that industry leaders, lawmakers, labor unions, and workers themselves are as inspired by these essays and recommendations as we were. We hope that readers feel empowered to take action to initiate changes in the world of work that increase the availability of decent jobs, elevate and enhance the work experiences for all, and provide opportunities for all to engage in work activities with dignity. Collectively, the set of essays in this book increases consciousness and understanding of the world of work and the interconnection between work and life and provides varied experiences of people's relationship with work at different life stages.

In this concluding chapter, we summarize the key messages of the essays within each theme. As a reminder, these themes include function of work; changing nature of work; race and culture; inequality; systematic and policy perspectives; precarity, unemployment, and underemployment; and technology. We note areas of debate, important recommendations, and potential barriers to workplace transformation and policy change. We conclude this chapter with a summary of the major implications of the set of essays, with a focus on public policy, individual and psychological well-being, and community impacts.

DOI:10.4324/9781003272397-54

The Function of Work in People's Lives

Five essays addressed the major functions of work in today's society. The tensions between work and career modes of engaging with employment activities were highlighted by both McMahon (this issue) and Arulmani and Kumari (this issue). Career perspectives assume that individuals can exert some level of agency in choosing vocational pathways and focus primarily on the career development of the most privileged members of society. On the other hand, work perspectives expand the lens and focus on the vocational experiences and pathways of all members of society, with an emphasis on those that are marginalized and with limited access to decent work options (Blustein, 2001, 2006). McMahon cautions readers to avoid further privileging the most advantaged workers in discussions of labor reform and suggests the use of co-design, a strategy for developing solutions for building better work structures alongside those that are most impacted. Arulmani and Kumari speculate that how people are making meaning of work is shifting from a careerist approach to a livelihood approach and that these shifts in the role of work in one's life are contributing to the trend of people voluntarily leaving their positions in search of other work opportunities.

Changing perspectives on how work functions in one's life were addressed by several authors. Based on discussions with a diverse group of people in her network, Davis (this issue) identified a taxonomy of why people work and what they received from work that included survival, purpose, thriving, and accomplishment. Schwartz (this issue) emphasizes that work is more than making money and that many people work for meaning, respect, and to make a difference in their communities or the world. How younger generations of workers, including Millennials and Generation Zers, are approaching work was the focus of the essays by both Krauss (this issue) and Liang, Lincoln, and Lai (this issue). Krauss emphasizes that future jobs will need to change to appeal to younger generations to be durable, transferable, lovable, and livable. Liang and colleagues provide counter-evidence to the stereotypical descriptions of today's youth and argue that this generation is seeking employment that aligns with their values of purpose and meaning. The opportunity to transform the functions of work is critical for marginalized and less privileged workers as well as workers from younger generations. Reform efforts must engage these workers and reflect their needs and wants or we will risk further marginalizing significant segments of the labor force.

Changing Nature of Work

Six essays focused on significant ways in which the world of work has changed or will change and in turn, how these changes can alter available work and how work is performed (i.e., remote work, gig work). Allan (this issue) offers a new conceptual paradigm for envisioning the conditions in which workers can flourish. His model provides a roadmap for how workers can flourish, comprised of decent work, human rights and dignity, social justice and equity, strong social safety net, well-being and mental health, fulfilling work, and worker voice and protections.

Cinamon (this issue) discusses how technological advances have altered the work–family dynamic by allowing people to work and learn from home, creating space conflict, and blurring the lines between work and family. These remote work opportunities invite discussions on the value of space, time, and domestic work. Krauss (this issue) highlights that the future of work should account for the possibility that longer life-span expectations may translate into longer work lives. Rochat and Rossier (this issue) address that the future of work needs to change in consideration of the environment and the planet. Together, these essays consider the changing boundaries between work and both life and environmental sustainability.

Both Leung (this issue) and Tien (this issue) address the changing nature of work in Hong Kong and Taiwan, respectively. In Hong Kong, the pandemic expanded existing social challenges such as the economic gap, the availability of decent jobs, and mental health difficulties. In Taiwan, learning remotely and mental health concerns were compounded by new barriers to the job search among students. Tien identifies coping strategies that students utilized in dealing with these challenges and highlights ways in which higher educational institutions can adapt to support students in their transition to work. The future of work must adapt to the changing life and contextual landscapes and attend to the psychological well-being of workers and the preservation of the planet.

Seven essays cover the role of race and culture and the role of work among culturally diverse workers (i.e., race, gender, social class, and their intersections). Culturally diverse workers are faced with explicit and hidden biases in the job search and in the workplace. Jackson and Guarino (this issue) address the importance of diversity, equity, and inclusion training in the workplace to reduce discrimination and improve interpersonal relationships at work.

Ervin (this issue) provides a historical and contemporary account of the abuses experienced by Black and Brown workers in the poultry processing industry in the United States. Cha-Jua and Neville (this issue) provide a historical analysis of how Black workers in the United States have been exploited. Their highly compelling essay provides a critical perspective of how racial inequalities are reproduced in work institutions and call for a radical transformation of work as we have known it to recreate a system where Black people can succeed and thrive. Wilkins-Yell and Farra (this issue) provide data from interviews of 107 Black women about the sources of marginalization and racism that they encounter in the workplace and share recommendations for making work more equitable for Black women. Fouad and Burrows (this issue) highlight consistent inequalities in workforce participation and engagement among women and diverse racial/ethnic

groups in the United States that continue to sustain occupational segregation. These authors summarize both internal and external barriers to these
groups' participation in sectors of the labor force in which they have long
been underrepresented.

Finally, the essays from Hoffman (this issue), Garriott, Grant Solis, and
Park (this issue), and McGillen (this issue) address the empowerment of
students from marginalized groups. Hoffman focuses on critical aspects of
working that jobseekers, particularly those from marginalized groups, should
know. These include understanding working conditions, benefits, the value
of networks, and the influence of sociocultural identities on future careers.
Both Garriott, Grant Solis, and Park and McGillen's essays discuss the rising
amount of student loan debt and how this has caused deeper divides in racial
and socioeconomic inequities. The authors explain the association between
student loan debt and both life and career opportunities and decisions and
discuss ways to enhance access to college among marginalized youth without the significant debt load we are seeing today.

Inequality and Work

Inequities, which have long persisted in the workplace, received significant
attention among the essays. These essays address inequalities across occupations as well as inequalities in the treatment, experiences, and opportunities of people based on gender, social class, sexuality, nationality, and
other groups. Sultana (this issue) eloquently describes two cases of workers
to magnify the disparities in work experiences. He passionately appeals to
readers to care for decent work opportunities for all who work.

Occupational inequalities are reflected in the societal bias of favoring professional work (and those employed in these positions) and in the benefits
offered to workers in professional positions. Essays call for universal benefits
in the form of paid time off from work for all workers, regardless of their
position (Ali & Bywater, this issue), and for recognizing the value of international students and workers (Arthur, this issue), Black workers (Cha-Jua &
Neville, this issue; Ervin, this issue), and immigrants (Cadenas & Carlos
Chavez, this issue; Ervin, this issue) on a country's economy. Autin and
Ezema (this issue) argue for the value of nonprofessional employment and
the important role that many nonprofessional workers played during the
global pandemic. These authors indicate the need to shift societal perspectives of occupational stratification and the differential value placed on professional work sectors. Woods and Millner (this issue) raise awareness of the
work experiences of individuals with serious mental health issues, and Davis
highlights SES and generational differences in how people relate to work.
Finally, Garriott and colleagues (this issue) and McGillen (this issue) remind
us of the occupational inequities experienced by young adults carrying significant student loan debt, and the disproportionate number of them who
come from marginalized groups based on race, social class, and ability status.

Training and workplace advocates can address inequalities at work. In some cases, vocational training programs and postsecondary educational programs can play a role in diminishing the effect of oppression in the workplace by enhancing representation in the workplace and in occupational fields. Varghese (this issue) advocates for educational and job training programs in prisons and job seeking support after release from prison to prevent recidivism and returning to prison among individuals who have been incarcerated. Glosenberg (this issue) proposes a critical entrepreneurial mindset training to increase entrepreneurs from marginalized groups who in turn, can work toward environmental sustainability and social justice. These work inequalities can also be supported, in part, by the limited training offered to mental health professionals. Duffy (this issue) notes that vocational psychology largely relies on individually-focused models that ignore systemic issues that harm marginalized individuals and workers. Thus, mental health professionals who work with marginalized workers may not be equipped with the tools to help clients frame issues of systemic oppression in the workplace and may reinforce oppression and invalidate their experiences. Finally, McWhirter (this issue) uses the term nepantleras, adopted from Gloria Anzaldua's writings, to identify the type of people who disrupt the comfort of inequitable systems. She advises readers on how to identify these individuals within systems and involve them in building better, more inclusive workplaces.

Systematic and Policy Perspectives on Work

Essays within this theme reviewed organizational, institutional, and public policies that can support and protect workers and strengthen work as an institution. Almost every essay addresses efforts to shift organizational, professional, or societal attitudes or processes that contribute to work inequities. Systems change can be a long and slow process, but changes start with individuals who use their voices to bring inequities to light. McWhirter's essay is dedicated to those who resist from within and the pushback that they endure for their activism.

Allan's framework on worker flourishing is grounded in social justice and activism, and each component of the model identifies avenues for developing work policies (i.e., mental health) to support workers. The authors of essays challenge readers to reflect on definitions of job quality (Rubin, this issue) as well as differential values ascribed to various jobs (Autin & Ezema; McWha-Herman). Rubin notes the important role of workforce development organizations in helping both employers and employees to improve their competitiveness in the eyes of the other. Rubin suggests that workforce development organizations can help by expanding traditional definitions of "job quality," prioritizing employers that offer quality work, changing how job training programs operate by connecting employers with future employees at the start of training and training workers from marginalized groups, and creating policies with employers to recruit and retain employees and provide opportunities for advancement. Autin and Ezema note the importance of a cultural shift in how jobs are stratified, whereas McWha-Herman discusses cultural influences on definitions of fairness and provides strategies that organizations can employ to achieve fair pay practices.

Ali and Bywater (this issue) argue that paid time off should be a benefit to all who work, not just salaried, professional workers in white-collar jobs, and that this benefit is critical to worker well-being. Arthur (this issue) advocates for changes in work visa policies for international students that account for the contributions that these students make to diversifying learning and work environments and enhancing labor markets. Given the challenges that individuals who have experienced incarceration face in entering the job market after their release from prison, Varghese promotes state and federal policies that provide incentives for employers who hire these individuals. Finally, Cadenas and Carlos Chavez (this issue) address immigration policy reform for enhancing pathways to citizenship for immigrant workers that are so essential to the U.S. national economy.

Both educational and work systems contribute to work inequities. Ervin (this issue) and Cha-Jua and Neville (this issue) very eloquently analyzed historical and structural factors that have shaped work for Black and Brown laborers in the U.S. Ervin provides recommendations for policy changes to rid the meat packing industry of the abuse of its workers, most of whom are Black and immigrant workers, and Cha-Jua and Neville provide five recommendations for initiating a cultural and societal change and reconceptualizing the institution of work for Black people. The role of social institutions in contributing to inequities was further highlighted by Garriott and colleagues and McGillen when they outlined the high costs of higher education, and the long-term disadvantages to working that individuals from historically marginalized can face in accessing higher education. Mann (this issue) notes the diverse ways in which school guidance programs are effective in preparing youth for their work and life futures. It is important that educational policies invest in these programs and ensure that all youth have access to these programs to facilitate effective transitions between school and work. Woods and Millner remind readers that work contexts can and do inhibit the work and career development of people living with serious mental health illnesses and call for systemic changes to lessen the barriers these workers face in their career development.

At the professional level, the first-hand accounts of experiences in the classroom by two of the authors (Duffy and Velez) speak to professional, program, and curricular changes that are needed to broaden the training of psychologists and other mental health providers who provide clinical services to people dealing with work challenges. Systemic changes in training that are needed include developing models and theories that inform systemic interventions and focusing on institutional and structural barriers that maintain social and economic inequities (Duffy and Velez). Further, Velez suggests that training on organizational consultation and advocacy can equip mental health professionals to intervene more effectively in addressing work oppression and inequities.

Sultana notes the successes that resulted from workers' rights movements from the past and how some of these "rights" are being challenged or eroded today. Ain outlines the strategies that one company has implemented to create a workplace setting that draws and keeps workers and continuously strives to be a great place for workers. Ain addresses what his company does to develop trust, welcome and celebrate diversity among workers, and offer fair pay. Finally, Leung (this issue) offers recommendations for systemic interventions to rebuild hopefulness among workers in Hong Kong by addressing social inequities, improving work–life balance, and attending to the mental health of workers.

Precarious Work, Unemployment, and Underemployment

A significant number of our authors addressed topics such as the rise of precarious work, unemployment, and underemployment. Essays in this theme cover temporary work in the gig economy or work that provides low pay and benefits and little security and protection to workers. Essays within this theme also focus on ways to lessen unemployment and underemployment.

To counteract the rise in precarious work, unemployment, and underemployment, significant efforts are needed to shift societal attitudes about nonprofessional work and marginalized workers (Ali & Bywater; Autin & Ezema; Cadenas & Carlos Chavez; McMahon; McWha-Hermann; Varghese) and to create new conceptual tools that help us better understand the work conditions that contribute to workers' well-being and flourishing (Allan) and decent workplace cultures (Hicks, this issue). Hicks makes a strong case for considering dignity consciousness at work as a means of improving how people are treated and underscores the responsibility of organizations in increasing consciousness of how workers are treated. Fawcett (this issue) defines key characteristics of quality, decent work, including wages, benefits, psychological wellness, and stability, and she argues that we need to create more opportunities for decent work. Carr (this issue) addresses the moral and ethical mandate for Decent Work as proposed by the International Labour Organization and suggests that one pathway for decent work is focusing on creating sustainable livelihood jobs, which provide living wages and jobs that care for the environment.

Interventions can help people access decent and dignified work. Lent suggests two approaches, large-scale systemic interventions and supplementing individual career development interventions, to limit the impact of a precarious, unstable occupational future, whereas Masdonati and Tien focus on interventions during the school-to-work transition to promote a successful transition and access to decent work, particularly for young adults.

Rochat and Rossier highlight that career counseling interventions can play an important role in promoting environmentally sustainable practices at both the worker and employer levels. Sharone (this issue) provides a model for managing the stigma associated with unemployment. Drawing on interviews of long-term unemployed white-collar workers, Sharone found that workers who dealt with the stigma directly reported improved well-being and resilience in searching for a job. Finally, Rubin presents an illustration of a community-based workforce development organization enacting social change to improve the workplace by empowering jobseekers.

Technology and Work

Technology affects all aspects of work and the work environment today. Technology has improved working conditions and increased productivity, but it has also replaced workers, eliminated jobs and introduced considerable challenges in the workplace. A set of essays addresses how technology will reshape the world of work, including work itself and interactions within work environments.

Cinamon discusses the significant shifts in work–life balance as a result of technological advancements that allow people to work remotely. Remote work was increasing prior to the pandemic, but since the majority of workers experienced remote work during the pandemic, more workers are now seeking opportunities to continue working from home. With these changing trends in the workplace, employers need to develop strategies for supporting workers to manage roles and relationships both at work and home.

Behrend and White (this issue) focus on the use of technology to monitor employees and raise questions about the potential of further power concentrated in the hands of employers who use surveillance in the workplace. Hooley offers an alternative perspective to the dominant view that technology and automation are a threat to workers. Instead, Hooley provides a firsthand account of how technology is a positive force that can enhance positive work experiences by providing time to be more creative in the work that we do and in doing work that matters. He also extends the impact of technology on personal lives and in freeing people to engage in other leisure activities to pursue other work activities.

Important Messages Across Essays

In the following paragraphs, we identify seven key takeaways from the essays. These important messages can help to guide future directions on improving the institution of work and removing structural barriers that limit all workers from accessing dignified work.

First, we need to take the time to reflect and imagine how work will look in the future. The world has changed in significant ways in recent years, and it will continue to do so as we move forward. We need to adjust the institution of work in ways that reflect societal and technological shifts as well as the changing values of society and future generations of workers. We must embrace the changes that are occurring around us and not be afraid to take bold steps to redefine and transform how we think of work, our relationship with work, and workplace structures. We need to center the experiences of the most vulnerable, marginalized workers in our society and involve individuals from these groups in transforming work for the future.

Second, we need new ideas, new models, and new tools that creatively and effectively address problems in the development and maintenance of equitable workplace structures. Persistent problems call for creative and innovative solutions. We need innovations in the form of theories, models, and strategies to implement and sustain the workplace transformations that are discussed in the essays. Several advancements are introduced in this text, such as Allan's worker well-being model and Arulmani and Kumar's livelihood model. Other authors provide new strategies for improving the workplace or workers' experiences, including Hicks' dignity model and Sharone's stigma model for unemployed workers. These novel ideas are critical to advancing visions for work and should be shared broadly so that they can be applied and assessed in the world of work.

Third, we need to think systemically and move beyond change at the individual level. Supervisors and employers can make a difference in the work experiences of a worker, but the biggest impact of workplace transformation will come from large-scale organizational changes and marco-level policies that can affect multiple workers across an organization and in society. Systematic changes are needed in how we train vocational psychologists (Duffy; Velez) and school guidance counselors (Mann; Masdonati), as well as business managers and leaders. We need to consider how interventions are designed and implemented, and expand interventions beyond individual, one-on-one approaches to large-scale programs implemented in educational settings (Lent; Mann; Masdonatti) and job training programs (Rubin). Organizational policies and local, state, and federal legislation are critical avenues for increasing access to decent work for all workers and increasing access to occupational fields and opportunities for advancement that workers from marginalized groups have been prevented from pursuing because of structural barriers. Policies can transform work and societal beliefs about the role and functions of work in our lives.

Fourth, we need to embrace workers that have been marginalized in the past and reflect on the value of people and all forms of employment. Several authors wrote passionately about the need to acknowledge how work as an institution has harmed, taken advantage of, and undervalued the labor of large segments of society. This text includes outstanding essays about the importance of undocumented immigrants (Cadenas & Carlos Chavez), women and people of color (Fouad & Burrows), Black workers (Cha-Jua & Neville; Wilkins-Yel & Farra), individuals from low-income backgrounds (Garriott et al.; McGillen), individuals who were incarcerated (Varghese), international workers (Arthur), community college students (Hoffman), and essential workers (Autin & Ezema; Ervin). Further, we need to reflect on the language that we use when we speak about work and workers and embrace language and models that are inclusive of all workers and place value on all lines of work.

Fifth, we need to counter efforts to reduce workers' rights and advocate for effective policies that affirm the lives and welfare of workers and their families. During the past few decades, neoliberal policies, which have centered the needs of employers and investors over the needs of workers and their families, have been widely adopted, resulting in a significant diminishment of workers' rights. As a means of resisting the hegemony of neoliberal ideas, several essays have provided clear models for a renewed effort to create worker-centric policies. Sultana's evocative essay comparing the lives of workers in dramatically different fields and circumstances provides a poignant reminder of how workers' rights have changed the lives of so many people. As means of building on the successes of past generations (which have been challenged in this neoliberal era), Ali and Mitchell advocated for paid time off for all workers while Fawcett argued for a more intentional adoption of the International Labor Organization Decent Work Agenda. The essays, when considered collectively, created a strong case that governments and institutions need to prioritize workers and combat the commodification of working people. In effect, discussions about work in public policy, academia, economics, legal studies, and psychology need to be politicized in order to ensure that working people are centered in relevant discourses and policy recommendations.

Sixth, we need to acknowledge the tension between work for survival and work for self-determination and address the privileges of those who have the power to change the institution of work. A key theme that emerged in many of the essays is that work entails vastly different sorts of activities and outcomes depending on access to opportunity, social class, economic constraints, marginalizing social identities, and other aspects of the context, writ large. The essays provided a map of the broad continuum of work that ranges from a focus on survival to self-determination. The essays from Sultana, McMahon, Arulmani, and Kumari, in particular, conveyed the broad expanse of working experiences and conditions that so powerfully shape people's lives. Like many of the essayists, we believe that research, practices, policies, and advocacy are needed to embrace the dream of a working life of meaning, purpose, dignity, and decency for all who work and who want to work.

Finally, we need to develop new pathways for communication and increase cross-fertilization between countries, disciplines, researchers, employers, employees, organizers, and work organizations. There are a lot of different groups who are dealing with different issues and who offer different perspectives about work. Some of these groups overlap in their focus or efforts, and some do not. However, the likelihood of success is strengthened only when we are sharing and learning from one another. Future efforts can capitalize on the ideas shared in this text by developing sustainable mechanisms for bringing these different groups together to tackle work issues and to develop plans for transforming work institutions.

References

Blustein, D. L. (2001). Extending the reach of vocational psychology: Toward an inclusive and integrative psychology of working. *Journal of Vocational Behavior, 59*, 171–182. https://doi.org/10.1006/jvbe.2001.1823.

Blustein, D. L. (2006). *The psychology of working: A new perspective for career development, counseling, and public policy.* Routledge.

Blustein, D. L., Smith, C. M., Wu, X., Guarino, P. A., Joyner, E., Milo, L., & Bilodeau, D. C. (2022). "Like a tsunami coming in fast": A critical qualitative study of precarity and resistance during the pandemic. *Journal of Counseling Psychology, 69*(5), 565–577. http://dx.doi.org/10.1037/cou0000615.

Index

Printed in the United States
by Baker & Taylor Publisher Services